CW09647244

HICKMAN'S FARRIERY

A Complete Illustrated Guide

'A Craftsman'

'A proper mode of shoeing is certainly of more importance than the treatment of any disease, or perhaps of all the diseases incident to horses. The foot is a part that we are particularly required to preserve in health; and if this art be judiciously employed, the foot will not be more liable to disease than any other region.' – Professor E. Coleman, 1765–1839.

HICKMAN'S FARRIERY

A Complete Illustrated Guide

SECOND EDITION

JOHN HICKMAN
MA, FRCVS, Hon. FWCF
and
MARTIN HUMPHREY
BVMS, MRCVS, Dip.WCF

J. A. ALLEN
London

First edition published in Great Britain 1977 under the title *Farriery*

Second edition 1988

ISBN 978-0-85131-451-8

J.A. Allen
Clerkenwell House
Clerkenwell Green
London EC1R 0HT

J.A. Allen is an imprint of Robert Hale Limited

www.allenbooks.co.uk

10 9 8 7 6

A catalogue record for this book is available from the British Library

Edited by Lesley Gowers
Designed by Dick Vine

Printed and bound in China by 1010 Printing International Ltd

CONTENTS

FOREWORD

by

HRH The Princess Royal, GCVO

Master of the Worshipful Company of Farriers
1984–1985
and member of the Company's Court of Assistants

Good, regular attention to the feet and shoeing is a vital element in the correct management of the horse. Today's farriers are better trained than ever before, and the first edition of *Farriery* has played an important part in this achievement. With the horse population growing and diversifying the new edition catches up with the advances and shows the range of skills and services that the farrier has to offer.

Unfortunately, many in the horse world today are not sure what a healthy, well-shod foot should look like. Novice owners, especially if competition minded, may not be sufficiently sensitive to the horse's long-term needs and the farrier's role in the welfare of the horse is not always appreciated.

Good communications are the key to progress. This book is particularly welcome as it can be shared by farriers, veterinary surgeons and horse owners, offering a common understanding which can only benefit the most important customer of all, the horse.

ACKNOWLEDGEMENTS

We wish to record our indebtedness to Her Royal Highness The Princess Royal for so graciously agreeing to write the foreword.

Our utmost appreciation is due to John Christiansen of Fen Drayton, Cambridgeshire, for the care and precision with which he has drawn the anatomical illustrations, the horseshoes and diagrams featuring in Figs 1.8–1.13, 1.15–1.17, 1.19, 1.28, 2.7, 2.10–2.19, 2.21–2.25, 2.33–2.35, 2.38, 2.40, 2.41, 2.45, 2.47, 3.1–3.23, 3.25–3.28, 3.31–3.34, 4.1, 4.4–4.8, 4.10, 4.11, 5.15–5.19, 5.21, 5.22, 5.24–5.30, 7.1–7.15, 7.17, 7.19–7.22, 7.49–7.52, 7.80, 7.81, 7.83, 8.2, 8.4–8.6, 10.1, 10.3, 10.5, 10.7, 10.9, 11.1–11.10, 11.12–11.14, 11.16–11.18, 11.21–11.27, 11.30, 11.33, 11.42, 11.43, 11.45, 11.48, 11.50.

We are indeed grateful to Mr T. Ryan FWCF of Willington, Bedfordshire for demonstrating the procedures in Figs 6.32–6.176, 11.15, 11.19, 11.20, 11.29 and also Mr N. Chalmers Dip. WCF of Willington for Figs 6.1–6.10, 6.23–6.31 and for drawing Figs 7.16 and 7.23.

Many thanks to Farrier Sergeant Major D. Symons FWCF (Hons) for demonstrating and arranging the subjects for Figs 7.24–7.48, 7.50–7.53, 7.60–7.79, 7.82, 9.8–9.15, 11.34–11.40; the photographs of which are due to the skill of Mr P. Lancaster, and to Mr H. D. Williamson for Figs 7.59–7.65.

We wish to thank Mr G. Owen for photographing the material for Figs 1.18, 1.20, 1.21, 1.24–1.26, 11.11; Mrs J. Patten for Figs 2.22, 2.23, and 2.27; and Mr P. Price for Figs 9.2, 9.3 and 9.5, Miss Janet Butler of the Animal Health Trust for her skill in drawing the illustrations for Figs 2.1, 2.6, 2.26 and 11.41; and Mr C. Bond for preparing the histological sections in Figs 2.39, 2.42 and 2.43.

We have drawn freely on the generosity of colleagues for a number of illustrations and wish to thank Drs P. C. Mishra and D. H. Leach of the University of Saskatchewan for Figs 2.27, 2.28, 2.30 and 2.31, Dr P. Ryder-Davies MB, BS, BVSC, MRCVS and Mr R. Clark FWCF (Hons) for Fig. 4.9, Mr J. Moor for Fig 4.12, Mr D. R. Ellis, BVet. Med., FRCVS of Newmarket for Fig. 8.7, Farrier Sergeant Major C. J. L. Williams AWCF of the RAVC School of Farriery and Mr T. Stern FWCF of Yalding for making the shoes illustrated in Fig. 4.14 and Figs 6.177, 6.178 respectively.

For other illustrations our thanks are due to the Curator, Museum of Archaeology and Ethnology, University of Cambridge for Fig. 1.1, Mr A. Clark of the Museum of London for Fig. 1.13, Dr S. Ward, University of Reading, Institute of Agricultural History and Museum of English Rural Life, for Figs 1.4, 1.6 and 1.8, and the Editor of the *Veterinary Record* for permission to reproduce Figs 2.36 and 2.37 from *In Practice* Vol. 3, no. 4, 1981 drawn by Mr D. H. Steven, MA, VetMB, FRCVS.

The following firms have kindly provided photographs or items of equipment for illustrations and we wish to record our thanks to A. J. Pledger and Co. (Metals) Ltd for Fig. 3.9; Kerckhaert *BV* Holland for Figs 3.30 and 4.5, Unit Equipment Company for Fig. 4.3, Flamefast Technology Ltd for Figs 5.34 (a) and 5.35, A. Cottam and Co. (Horseshoes) Ltd for Fig. 5.34(b), Parweld Ltd for Figs 9.16–9.21, Mordax for Figs 9.1, 9.4, 9.6 and 9.7, Adtec Welding Alloys Ltd for Fig. 3.24 and Vaughans (Hope Works) Ltd for Fig. 5.35.

We are most grateful to Mr P. G. G. Jackson FRCVS, MA, BVM&S and Miss A. Schwabe BSc of the Department of Clinical Veterinary Medicine, University of Cambridge for their advice, assistance and supplying the photographs, without which Appendix 2 illustrating the hoof care of cattle, sheep and goats would not have been possible.

Finally, we must express our gratitude to the publishers J. A. Allen and Co. Ltd of London and especially to Lesley Gowers who has afforded us the most helpful cooperation and encouragement at all times.

JOHN HICKMAN

MARTIN HUMPHREY

Cambridge
November, 1988

PREFACE

Primarily this book is written for farriers and apprentice farriers, but it is hoped it will serve as a useful book of reference for veterinary surgeons and veterinary students, and for all who are interested in the horse and its welfare.

This second edition is based on the first edition and only the methods of shoeing as practised in the United Kingdom have been included. The subject matter is presented in a concise and logical manner and maintains a balance between theory and practice. Practices and horseshoes no longer in vogue have been relegated to the historical section. To assist apprentice farriers, basic blacksmithing exercises have been introduced which contain all the techniques required for making a horseshoe. To assist farriers presenting themselves for the AWCF and FWCF examinations, details are given of the forging of special shoes. In addition, since farriers are sometimes requested to trim the hooves of house cows, pet goats or sheep a section on the hoof care of these animals has been included in an appendix.

The anatomy and function of the foot has been dealt with in detail as a basic understanding of these sciences is essential if the horse's foot is to be protected and preserved and a rational approach to shoeing adopted. The anatomical terminology of the *Nomina Anatomica Veterinaria* has been adopted generally as this terminology is more readily understood by the present generation. A glossary has been included to explain some of the more technical words and to relate them to words in common usage.

Although the care of the feet and the practice of shoeing to preserve normal feet have been emphasised the corrective dressing of the foot and the use of special shoes has not been neglected. Shoes required for defective feet, to prevent injuries due to abnormalities of gait or to assist in the treatment of disease or injury have been described and explained in relation to the condition.

The best way of learning a craft is to assist or watch an expert. Hence special attention has been given to illustrating the text with line drawings and photographs, which, it is hoped, will greatly assist an understanding and appreciation of the subject matter.

To provide the material for this book many authors on farriery have been consulted and the information collated; inevitably in a book of this type some of the illustrations are similar to some previously published. The works consulted by the authors are set out in the bibliography.

Following the introduction of the Farriers (Registration) Act 1975 and the Farriers (Registration) (Amendment) Act 1977, the expansion of the School of Farriery at Hereford and the establishment of the Scottish Farriery Training Centre in Edinburgh, an increasing number of young men have been attracted to the trade and established farriers have been stimulated to seek higher qualifications. It is hoped that the information contained in this book will in some measure assist them in attaining their aims and aspirations and thereby play its part in promoting the welfare of the horse.

CHAPTER 1

INTRODUCTION AND HISTORY OF HORSESHOEING

1.1 Introduction

When the horse was living in its natural environment its hooves provided adequate protection for the underlying sensitive structures of the foot. The wear and growth of the hoof remained balanced. But as soon as man used the horse to carry loads and pull vehicles, the hooves wore away more quickly than they were renewed, exposing the sensitive structures, which resulted in pain and lameness.

With the passage of time the idea of protecting the bearing surface of the hoof with a rim of iron, nailed to the hoof, was developed and it was soon recognised that a shoe could be modified to secure a firm foothold and to alleviate some types of lameness.

For a horse to perform the work expected of it, its feet must be kept in a healthy state and to be an economical proposition it must remain 100% sound. This is attained by the farrier making and shaping a shoe to fit the foot and securing it with nails without causing any injury or damage. But it must not be overlooked that the foot is a living and growing structure and when shod normal wear does not take place and so at each shoeing the hoof must be reduced to its normal proportions.

Horseshoeing is both an art and a science. An art because farriers must be expert craftsmen. They have to be skilled in working with metals to make shoes, and shape them to the foot which has been correctly balanced. It is a science because without a sound knowledge of the anatomy and function of the foot, the art cannot be practised to preserve a healthy foot.

1.2 History

The period covered by the early history of horseshoeing is quite arbitrary, but it is convenient to consider that it extends from about 400 BC when the Gauls and the Celts first nailed a rim of iron to the hooves of their horses, until the fall of the Roman Empire.

Many factors have to be taken into account to determine when man first adopted measures to protect the feet of horses which eventually led to the introduction of horseshoes.

Before the Iron Age the main migration of horses was from Turkistan, over the Caucasian Mountains to Asia, and by 2000 BC they were established in the Middle East.

The Assyrians (2000 BC) are credited with having been the first blacksmiths, and by 1400 BC iron was being used by the Hittites. As a result of wars with their neighbours this knowledge, and their craftsmen, spread to Mesopotamia and thence to Egypt, the Aegean, and then along the Bronze Age trade routes to Italy, reaching central Europe by 700 BC and Britain not earlier than 400 BC.

Account has also to be taken of which race or tribe first recognised the strength, speed, endurance and adaptability of the horse and domesticated it for civil and military purposes. Even so, the environment must have played an important role. The heat and dryness of the Middle East countries are conducive to hard hooves which are capable of withstanding severe wear, whereas the cold and damp of northern Europe results in soft hooves which rapidly wear away when the horse is put to work.

Therefore horseshoeing, as we understand it, could not have commenced before the domestication of the horse combined with a knowledge of working in iron and suitable climatic conditions.

The Ancient Greeks

It is generally assumed that the Ancient Greeks shod their horses, but a study of their sculptures and writings tends to disprove this supposition. Some of the passages from Homer (*c.* 1200–850 BC) have led to the belief that he was familiar with metallic foot defences. He describes the horses that drew Neptune's car as 'brazen-footed' or 'brass-hoofed'. Although brass was in common use in the days of Homer, surely he used the word metaphorically to indicate strength. The poet Tryphidorus states that iron was put on the hooves of the Trojan horse to make its resemblance more complete, but it should not be lost sight of that he lived in the fifth and sixth century AD when horseshoeing was an established practice.

Xenophon (430–354 BC), the Greek general and author, wrote extensive treatises on cavalry training. When selecting horses he emphasised the importance of examining the feet and stated 'If he has not good feet there is no profit in him as a war horse'. He described a good foot as being 'thick not thin, high and with hollow hooves and hard to be fit for service'.

Presumably horses with flat feet were not unknown to him, and because he had experience of their propensity for becoming footsore he emphasised the importance of the concavity or vaulting of the sole which he considered must be preserved. He recognised that damp stable floors were injurious to sound hooves and recommended the floors should be sloped to keep them dry; and to preserve the concavity of the sole he advised that when horses were groomed outside the stable they should stand on a prepared bed of round stones, each weighing about one pound, and surrounded by an iron rim to keep them in place. Undoubtedly if horseshoes had been in use, Xenophon would not have found it necessary to emphasise and describe these methods of preserving the hooves in such detail.

It is interesting to note that the army of Alexander the Great (356–323 BC) on its march through Asia was often impeded because the horses wore down their hooves, became lame and had to be abandoned.

The Greeks portrayed detail with great accuracy and true representation in their sculptures. In the frieze of the Parthenon (447–438 BC) 110 horses are depicted and not one has shoes. Indeed, the perfect shape of their feet indicates that none had ever been shod.

In view of these observations, coupled with the fact that the dry climate of Greece is conducive to hard and durable hooves and that no Greek author writing on military science, animals or agriculture has mentioned shoeing, it is reasonable to conclude that fixing a rim of iron with nails to the feet of horses was not known or practised by the Ancient Greeks.

The Romans

The Romans were not an equestrian nation and their armies, until a later date, depended on their infantry. Indeed, the Ancient Greeks surpassed the Romans in their use and management of horses and much in the Roman literature concerning them appears to have been borrowed from the Greeks.

The Roman authors Varro (116–25 BC) and Virgil (70–19 BC), like their Greek counterparts, stressed the importance of selecting horses with hard hooves. Columella (40 AD) in his works on veterinary medicine not only advised selecting horses for purchase with hard, upright and hollow hooves, but also recommended that when foals were weaned they should be pastured on mountains and other inhospitable places to harden their hooves so as to resist wear and enable them to undertake long journeys. Also it was recommended that the undersurface of the feet of draught animals should be smeared with pitch to make them more resistant.

Suetonius (70–140 AD) writing on the extravagances of the Emperor Nero (37–68 AD) states that he never travelled with fewer than 100 four-wheeled chariots, drawn by mules shod with silver. Poppaea, his wife, not to be outdone, ordered her favourite mules to be shod with gold. This story is often used to support a case for the Romans shoeing their horses, but it cannot be accepted on its face value. Silver and gold, apart from other considerations, are soft metals and would be most unsuitable for horseshoes. The most probable explanation is that the hooves were silvered or gilded or the mules' fetlocks were adorned with silver or gold trappings.

To control inflation, the Emperor Diocletian (245–318 AD) issued an edict fixing maximum wages and included those to be paid to the *mulomedicus*, the sick animal attendant, for clipping, grooming and trimming the hooves of horses and mules. If shoeing was in vogue it would certainly have been included. This view is supported by the writings of Vegitus Renatus Flavius (*c.* 375 AD) who in a military treatise enumerates everything pertaining to an army forge but makes no mention of staff to shoe horses or of any farriery tools. This is further supported by the works of Vegitus Renatus Publius (450–510 AD) on veterinary medicine. He gives detailed instructions for keeping horses' hooves hard and for trimming them, but makes no mention of shoeing or accidents associated with it.

The Romans, especially their sculptors, were very exacting in everything relating to the horse, and so it is not without significance that Trajans Column (*c.* 130 AD) depicts no shod horses and none of the equestrian statues from Pompeii has shoes.

Although the Roman authors consistently draw attention to the necessity for hard hooves and methods to conserve them, they make no mention of actually shoeing horses. But it is obvious from their writings that various forms of hoof protection, when necessary, were provided. The word *soleae* is used in association with footwear for horses and was probably a temporary contrivance such as a leather boot. *Soleae sparteae* were, in all probability, boots made from plaited rope-like materials or woven twigs as used for basket making. It is assumed they were used, because of their temporary nature, only in emergencies for foot-sore horses on the line of march or for retaining dressings. But it is not without interest that in Japan, up until the nineteenth century, shoes for horses were made from plaited rice straw, and on long journeys a supply was carried or was purchased in the villages en route.

Soleae ferreae is generally translated as indicating an iron shoe. Towards the end of the Roman Empire this may well have been true as the art of protecting horses' feet with iron shoes was practised. But before the Romans made contact with the Gauls and Celts the term probably indicated a leather type of boot with metal-studded soles similar to the Roman sandal. Such boots could easily be carried and either used for footsore horses or put on as a

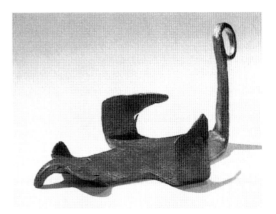

Fig. *1.1* A typical hipposandal, found at Arrington, near Cambridge.

true protective measure when the terrain warranted it.

Hipposandals. There are numerous varieties of hipposandals but basically they comprise an oval metal plate with raised side pieces (Fig. 1.1) and are provided with hooks, rings, and eyes through which cords or leather straps are passed to secure them to the foot. They are made of good-quality iron, are of first-class workmanship and have the ground surface grooved, presumably to prevent slipping.

There is no evidence of hipposandals before Roman times, and they have been found wherever the Romans settled throughout Europe. Horse skeletons have been unearthed and found with hipposandals in actual contact with the bones of the hoof. In spite of this it has been suggested they were used for a variety of purposes, other than as a protection for the horse's hoof, such as stirrups, skid-pans, and even for holding wax candles.

Hipposandals could not have been a very practical form of horseshoe as they would be difficult to secure and it would not have been easy for a horse to travel any distance in them, or at speed, and they would be too small to use as snow shoes or for horses working on marshy ground.

The most commonly accepted theory is that hipposandals were the forerunner of the nailed-on shoe. It has been suggested they were used to keep foot dressings in place, but they could have been used equally well as a temporary measure to protect horses' feet when going over rough and rocky ground, or when excessively worn to prevent them becoming footsore or even for slow draught or pack work.

Roman-Gallic and Romano-British period

The custom of burying the horse with its master is a very ancient one, and horseshoes found in ancient graves have provided evidence to show that the Celts were probably the first people to protect their horses' feet with nailed-on shoes and the practice gradually extended through Gaul, Germany and to Britain.

The dating of horseshoes is not easy because iron rapidly rusts and soon disintegrates. But sufficient horseshoes and horseshoe nails have been found in securely stratified and dated deposits, and in Celtic barrows throughout northern Europe, to indicate that they were in use in Britain, most probably before the Roman invasion and certainly during the occupation. These Iron Age people had arrived in Britain by 450 BC. They were advanced workers in iron, making ploughs and weapons, and used horses extensively for riding and for drawing their chariots. The wet and damp climate was conducive to soft hooves and these people soon would have appreciated the advantages to be gained by nailing a rim of iron to their horses' hooves to prevent them from becoming footsore.

Celtic horseshoes are small and thin, weighing 3–3½oz (about 100 g), not more than 4½ ins (11.5 cm) wide. Where the nail holes are punched the metal bulges which results in the branches of the shoe having a characteristic wavy outline (Fig. 1.2). There are several types of shoe: some are plain whereas others have a slightly convex ground surface, and all have the nail holes reverse punched. Many are fullered, and others have thickened heels or the ends of the branches are turned down to form calkins, and some even had toe pieces. Shoes had four to eight nail holes and were retained with nails which had short and round shanks with 'violin-key' shaped heads. Shoes and nails of this type have been found in Gaul and in Britain on sites occupied between 50 BC and 50 AD. On first sight they appear rather crude, but on a closer

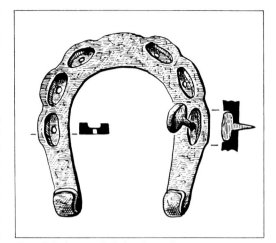

*Fig. **1.2** A typical Celtic horseshoe.*

examination they really are most sophisticated. The shoe protects the bearing surface of the foot, howbeit not perfectly due to the wavy outline, and permits normal function of the sole and frog. The 'violin-key' headed nails are let into slots to give them stability and preserve their usefulness.

Shoes of the classic Celtic variety for both horses and mules with the 'violin-key' headed nails in position have been found on Roman sites in London. It is not possible to say whether these shoes were made by Roman or British craftsmen, but it is interesting to reflect on how long it was before the defects of a shoe with a wavy outline and retained by nails with round shanks were overcome. At a later date shoes had square nail holes and the nails were short, four-sided with tapering shanks, and a head resembling that of a Roman T. The nails were not cut or clenched but the points were simply turned over and flattened against the hoof wall. A plain horseshoe with square nail holes has been found in the Roman gravel layers of the Thames foreshore, which is a securely stratified and dated deposit of the first and second centuries (Fig. 1.3).

Taking everything into consideration, it is reasonable to assume that the most ancient people to nail iron shoes to their horses' feet were the Gauls and Celts, and that the Romans were not acquainted with this art until they assimilated their culture. By the time the Roman legions left Britain, Roman ingenuity

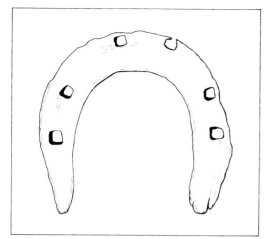

Fig. 1.3 A plain Roman horseshoe with square nail holes found in the Roman gravel layers of the Thames foreshore.

combined with British craftsmanship had overcome the defects of the Celtic shoe retained by 'violin-key' nails which had been replaced by plain shoes retained by square nails.

A number of authors consider that in Eastern Europe and Asia horses' hooves were protected by iron shoes before the foundation of Rome. The shoes fitted resembled a bar shoe which was retained with three clips and not nailed to the hoof. The Arabian shoe is probably a modification of this shoe which protected practically the whole of the sole and the frog and was secured with nails.

The Middle Ages (fifth to fifteenth century)

Following the departure of the Romans from the shores of Britain and until the arrival of the Normans, there appears to have been little change in the pattern of horseshoes. If anything they tend to have been a little heavier and broader than those of the Romano-British period.

The Norman knights brought many horses to England and without doubt attached great importance to shoeing as they were accompanied by their farriers. This influx of farriers must have had considerable influence on the art in Britain. William the Conqueror fully recognised the importance of farriery as instanced by his appointment of Henry de

Farrariis to be in control of his farriers and by his giving, to Simon St Liz, the town of Northampton and the whole hundred of Falkley, to provide shoes for his horses.

It would appear that during the thirteenth and fourteenth centuries it was not the general practice to shoe horses and they were only shod during frosty weather to prevent slipping and when their feet were exposed to excessive wear, such as on a long journey. However, examination of farm accounts of this period reveals that many farm horses were shod, and by calculating the number of shoes made from a given weight of iron it is indicated that they were shod with little more than tips.

But as more and better roads were developed and the heavier type of horse imported from the continent, so the necessity for shoeing increased. During the fourteenth and fifteenth centuries, two main patterns of shoe were in vogue: the so-called Dove shoe (Fig. 1.4) was secured with four to six nails and the heavier Guildhall shoe (Fig. 1.5), which was wide webbed at the toe, with long branches, often with calkins, was secured with six or seven nails and presumably used for draught horses.

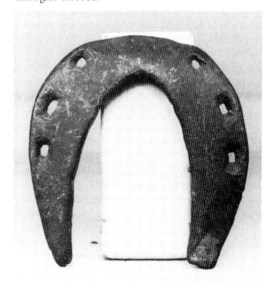

Fig. 1.4 A Dove shoe, a light shoe with square nail holes. (Reproduced by permission of the University of Reading, Institute of Agricultural History and Museum of English Rural Life)

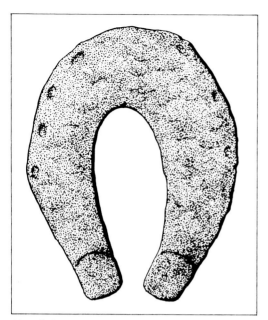

Fig. 1.5 An example of the Guildhall shoe, wide at the toe and with long branches.

When Edward II took his army to France in 1359, forges for making horseshoes were included in the equipment; probably the first field forges to be taken by a British Army on active service. During the fifteenth century quantities of horseshoes were imported into Scotland from Flanders and it is of interest that they were large and fullered.

Although during the Middle Ages there were no notable advances in the art of farriery, its importance did not pass unrecognised. Indeed, it can be said that the establishment of the trade in England was instituted in 1356 by the Mayor of the City of London. In that year he summoned the farriers because 'many offences and dangers' were being committed by people who kept forges in the city and resulted in the loss of many horses. This was followed by the establishment of the Fellow-ships of 'Marshalls of the City of London' and the appointment of wardens with powers to govern the trade.

Sixteenth and seventeenth centuries

During these centuries written works on horse-shoeing appeared in Italy and France. The most important was a complete treatise by

Caesar Fiaschi comprising thirty-five chapters. It was a very remarkable and advanced work for the period which soon was translated into French and published in Paris in 1564. The author described some thirty varieties of shoes. These included shoes with calkins, three-quarter shoes, tips, shoes with clips and toe pieces, bar and bevelled shoes, a shoe with an extended toe piece, a nail-less shoe and a shoe with the branches hinged at the toe. This work obviously had a marked influence on the thinking and practice of horseshoeing throughout Europe.

Towards the end of the sixteenth century Carlo Ruini, a senator of Bologna, published an extensive work on the anatomy and diseases of the horse. He drew attention to the evils of paring the sole, opening up the heels and shoeing with high calkins. He recommended that contracted feet should be treated by fitting a shoe with thin heels to allow the posterior part of the hoof to come into contact with the ground. But the most important contribution to the art of farriery during this period was the publication in 1664 of *Le Parfait Marechal* by the Frenchman Jacques Labessie de Solleysel, which was translated into English and published in London in 1706. The author attempted to put the art on a scientific basis. He pointed out that the shoe should fit the foot and the sole should not be pared or the heels opened up. He advised the use of thin small nails and recognised that nails obtain a better hold at the toe than at the heels because of the thicker wall. He condemned high calkins and recommended the shoe should be as light as possible.

In England at this time the only work of note on farriery was by Thomas Blundevil but there is little doubt his views were greatly influenced by the Italian and French authors. Unfortunately he did not accept much of the sound advice to be found in these publications and made the error of recommending excessive paring and rasping of the feet. On the other hand, Andrew Snape, farrier to Charles II, rendered the art a great service by drawing particular attention to the structure of the foot in his *Anatomy of the Horse*.

There can be little doubt that during the sixteenth and seventeenth centuries the

*Fig. **1.6** A typical keyhole shoe of the seventeenth century. (Reproduced by permission of the University of Reading, Institute of Agricultural History and Museum of English Rural Life)*

*Fig. **1.7** A tongue shoe of the eighteenth century, unfullered, with twelve nail holes. (Reproduced by permission of the University of Reading, Institute of Agrigultural History and Museum of English Rural Life)*

methods of farriery practised and the standards attained, varied considerably throughout the country and any advances made were in no small measure due to Italian and French influence. During this period a shoe with a keyhole-shaped inner edge, a concave bearing and convex ground surface with chamfered heels was in common use (Fig. 1.6). But the importance of farriery was gaining official recognition and a further stage in the establishment of farriery as an approved trade was taken by the City of London. The Fellowship, established in 1356, was incorporated by a Charter of Charles II and in 1692 the Farriers Company was established by the court of aldermen as a livery company.

Establishment of the veterinary schools (eighteenth and nineteenth centuries)

With the establishment of the veterinary schools it was to be expected that enlightened knowledge of the anatomy and function of the horse's foot would be acquired and applied to the problems of shoeing. Towards the end of the eighteenth century and during the first half of the nineteenth century the tongue shoe, which had a 'U'-shaped inner edge, retained with eight to ten nails and frequently fullered to permit the nail heads to be slightly counter-sunk (Fig. 1.7) was popular. Many treatises were published on farriery but attention will be drawn only to those publications which had an important influence, for good or bad, on the art. This was an era of experimentation and also of dogmatism which often led to the perpetration of harmful practices based on drawing incorrect conclusions. In consequence, many years were to pass before the practice of farriery based on sound scientific, anatomical and physiological principles was accepted.

In France, the views of Etienne Guillaume Lafosse contributed greatly to establishing farriery as a science. He based his opinions on a study of the anatomy and function of the foot which he related to its natural wear. He pointed out that only the wall is worn away and as the function of the frog is to prevent slipping, it, together with the sole, should not be pared. As a result of his observations he was able to show that many of the methods of shoeing in vogue were harmful in that they did not conserve the foot but contributed to injury, and in consequence he suggested alternative rational methods. He recommended a shoe

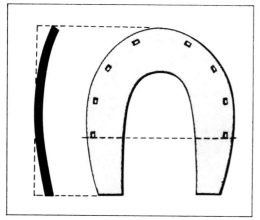

Fig. 1.8 Bougelet's horseshoe. The shoe has a flat foot and ground surface. The toe is turned up equal to the thickness of the shoe and the heels to half the thickness of the shoe.

with flat foot and ground surfaces, with heels reduced in thickness, secured with eight nails equally distributed and considered calkins should only be fitted to prevent slipping. Although his publication contained much good and sound advice, this was slow to be accepted.

The person who had the most profound and lasting influence on shoeing in France during this period was the renowned veterinary surgeon Claude Bougelet. He considered the foot should be maintained as found in nature and recommended a shoe based on his observations of the mechanics of the limb. The shoe he recommended was slightly curved in length, wider in web at the toe than at the heels and with regularly placed nail holes (Fig. 1.8). This shoe has remained in general use in France, with few modifications, well into the twentieth century.

Although the French deserved much credit, especially Lafosse and Bougelet, for improving the standard of horseshoeing in Europe, the contributions made by English veterinary surgeons at the end of the eighteenth century and beginning of the nineteenth century contributed more than is generally recognised. In England at this time three notable works were published on the anatomy of the horse's foot and shoeing. Jeremiah Bridges condemned heavy shoes and excessive paring of the foot. Also he had some novel ideas to

counter contracted feet, which included shoes with sloping clips on the inside of the heels to force them outwards. His practice of making five cuts or scissures on the outside of the hoof down to the quick is, presumably, the forerunner of what is today known as 'grooving the heels'. William Osmer's contribution was based on the teachings of Lafosse. He emphasised the undesirable practices of paring the sole and frog and of opening up the heels and pointed out that shoes with short heels, if left on for too long, would press on the sole and result in corns. Without doubt, of the three, James Clark, Farrier to His Majesty for Scotland, deserves the most credit. He had an enlightened approach to shoeing and developed the theory of expansion of the posterior portion of the hoof during progression, with sinking of the frog and flattening of the sole, and advised turning horses out unshod to promote expansion of the hoof. He recommended a concave fullered shoe with a flat foot surface slightly seated out to take pressure off the sole (Fig. 1.9). It was broad in the web at the toe, with narrower heels to allow the frog freedom and was retained with only eight to ten nails instead of the popular ten to twelve.

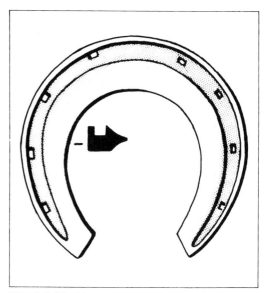

Fig. 1.9 Clark's horseshoe. A concave fullered shoe, seated out and with a wider web at the toe than at the heels.

When the Veterinary College was founded in London in 1791, the era of scientific investigations was just beginning. In consequence, one would have thought the existing knowledge of the anatomy of the horse's foot, coupled with practical and scientifically orientated investigations into its precise function, would soon have led to the art of farriery being established as a science based on sound principles. This was not to be. The horse-owning public and the farriers must have been not only confused but exasperated by the diverse views expressed and so ardently held by many eminent veterinary surgeons. Professor Edward Coleman, Principal of the London Veterinary College, and his pupil Bracy Clark were no exceptions.

Coleman was a medical man. He failed to appreciate the significance of the anatomy of the horse's foot in relation to function and in consequence made a number of incorrect deductions. He held an exaggerated idea of the importance of the elasticity and expansion of the foot and of frog and heel pressure. To this end he recommended the sole be scooped out until it responded to thumb pressure and to ensure frog pressure he introduced numerous artificial pads.

Bracy Clark adopted the views of Coleman but was obsessed with the descent of the sole and lateral distension of the foot. He tried to prove that shoes were unnecessary and when it became obvious they would have to be used to protect horses' feet he introduced several nail-less shoes which, needless to say, met with no practical success. In his view the unyielding rim of iron attached to the horse's hoof was responsible for most diseases of the foot, and to overcome this he turned his attention to developing a hinged shoe (Fig. 1.10) not dissimilar to the one illustrated by Caesar Fiaschi in 1564. This, likewise, met with no success as he failed to appreciate that the branches of the shoe were nailed to the non-expanding toe of the foot. He agreed with Coleman that the sole should not come into contact with the ground and held similar views on the frog.

There is little doubt that the incorrect deductions of these two men concerning the part played by the expansion of the foot and the

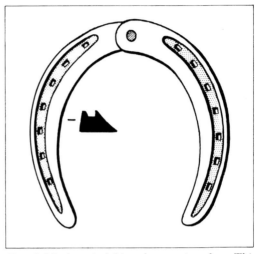

Fig. 1.10 A typical hinged expansion shoe. This type of shoe fails to allow expansion of the foot because its branches are nailed to the non-expanding toe and quarters.

descent of the sole in the normal functioning of the foot, and the practices they advocated to assist these functions, had an unfortunate influence on the practice of farriery which contributed to the all-too-common 'contracted foot' syndrome.

The military authorities adopted a practical approach to shoeing and by 1778 a regimental pattern of shoe had been introduced into the cavalry and any farrier found guilty of making one of another pattern was liable to receive corporal punishment. This shoe was introduced by the tenth Earl of Pembroke and was based on the shoe recommended by James Clark of Edinburgh, from whom he had received instruction. The *Rules and Regulations for the Cavalry*, laid down in 1795, included instructions for shoeing horses. A standard pattern of shoe with flat foot and ground surfaces was introduced and the sole, frog and bars were not to be pared. Also, instructions were given regarding the care of the feet when horses were turned out to grass, which stated that the toes were to be kept short and the edge of the wall rasped round.

By the end of the eighteenth century, due to the interest taken in the function of the horse's foot, considerable progress had been made not only in the making and fitting of shoes but in the preparation of the foot. The necessity for a level bearing surface of the foot and a level foot surface of the shoe, with branches of sufficient length to protect the bearing surface at the heels, were understood and appreciated. Indeed Lafosse in 1754 had related anatomical and physiological principles to the function of the horse's foot and enumerated the defects of excessive paring of the frog and sole, of rasping the wall and fitting shoes which were too heavy.

In 1820 Joseph Goodwin, veterinary surgeon to George IV, published details of a new type of shoe which had a concave ground surface to secure a good foothold and a foot surface that sloped outwards to encourage expansion of the foot and thereby prevent contraction (Fig. 1.11). This shoe only met with limited approval and proved difficult to make and fit. He is credited with being the first to recommend securing a shoe with seven instead of the customary eight nails, four on the outside and three on the inside.

William Youatt, writing in the middle of the nineteenth century, when hot shoeing is said to have been first introduced into England from France, stated that the frog supported weight and assisted expansion of the foot and that

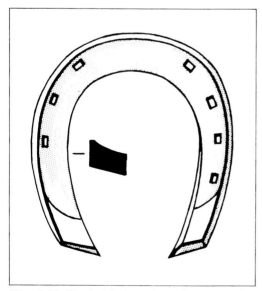

Fig. 1.11 Goodwin's horseshoe. A concave shoe with a sloped foot surface to encourage expansion of the foot.

reducing it in size and raising it off the ground was conducive to contraction of the foot. In spite of this appreciation he considered the frog required only occasional contact and pressure with the ground and, therefore, should be kept trimmed level with the foot surface. He, like many of his colleagues, was obsessed with the descent of the sole and recommended it should be pared down until it yielded under pressure and a seated-out shoe should be fitted to allow its descent.

The cult of the descent of the sole and its mutilation was slow to disappear and some farriers continued to scoop it out well into the twentieth century. But for all practical purposes it can be said that the end of irrational conclusions being drawn from a knowledge of the anatomy and function of the foot and applied to farriery, rapidly came to a close with Sir Frederick Fitzwygram's *Notes on Shoeing Horses*, which was published in 1863. This was an admirable work based on a rational and commonsense approach to preserve the integrity and form of the hoof and to conserve the sole and frog. He recommended a shoe similar to Goodwin's but with a flat foot surface and slightly rolled toe. Although an excellent shoe, based on sound principles, it was not generally accepted and used because it was difficult to make and fit.

In 1865 M. Charlier, a veterinary surgeon practising in Paris, introduced preplantar shoeing, which is generally referred to as the 'Charlier system'. The method comprises embedding a thin rim of iron into the wall to protect the hoof from wear whilst leaving every other part of the hoof entirely to nature. A groove is cut in the wall using a special guarded knife which regulates the width and depth of the groove and enables a perfect fit to be obtained (Fig. 1.12). To prepare a hoof for a Charlier shoe is not easy and fitting and nailing on is not without difficulties. When first introduced the Charlier shoe was fitted the length of the foot but when it became thin due to wear the heels spread, and were easily trodden on by or would injure the opposite leg. In consequence, a short Charlier shoe was adopted (Fig. 1.13), which for all practical purposes only serves the purpose of a tip. The Charlier shoe did not meet the expectations

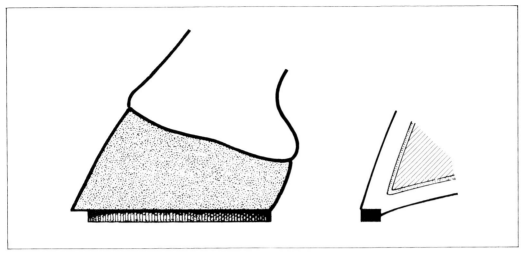

*Fig. **1.12** Charlier system of shoeing. A strip of horn is cut away to form a groove round the wall and into which a thin shoe is embedded.*

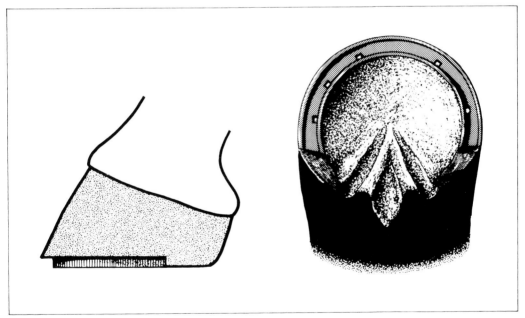

*Fig. **1.13** A short or modified Charlier shoe. It was introduced to overcome the disadvantages of a full-length shoe, but only serves the purpose of a tip.*

and claims made for it, and after extensive trials was rejected.

Towards the end of the nineteenth century farriery had become firmly established based on an appreciation of the anatomy and function of the horse's foot. The introduction of machine-made horseshoes and horseshoe nails was a notable advance, although William Moorcroft had obtained a patent for the former as early as 1796. Horseshoe nails had been made by hand either by the shoeing smith himself or by craftsmen belonging to a special trade of horseshoe nail makers, who were quite separate from the expert workmen of the nail

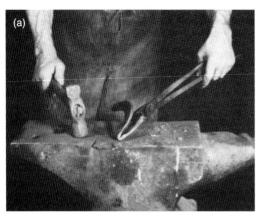 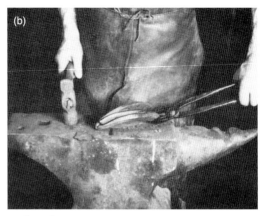

Fig. **1.14** *To obtain a rod of hardened iron for making shoes for horses which wear out their shoes faster than average, it was the practice to weld together old wrought-iron shoes. One and a half old shoes are required to make a new shoe. (a) An old shoe is bent double at the toe. (b) Between the two branches half an old shoe is wedged. The three pieces of metal are brought to a white heat and welded together with blows of the hammer.*

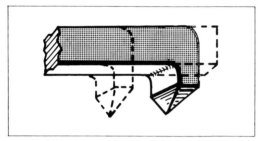

Fig. **1.15** *The heel of a front shoe turned down to form a 'sharp'.*

trade. They did not take apprentices but handed their skills down through families. The hand-made nails supplied had to be finished off by the smith himself by removing the scale, tempering and bevelling the point with a small hammer on a pointing stake (Holmes, Charles, 1949). It was an era when a great variety of ingenious surgical and other shoes were introduced.

Today the solution for horses that wear out their shoes rapidly is to fit either a wide

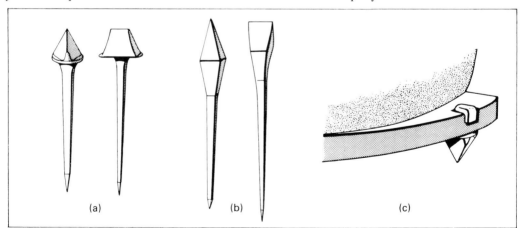

Fig. **1.16** *Frost nails: (a) with flat undersurface of head, used in emergencies by withdrawing the heel nails and driving in a frost nail along the track of the old nail; (b) with a shaped neck to fit a previously prepared nail hole stamped at the heel of the shoe outwards so that the nail does not enter the hoof; (c) method of securing a frost nail.*

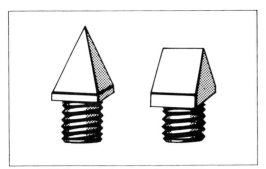

Fig. **1.17** *Frost studs, screw-in types.*

Fig. **1.20** *A rope shoe. This shoe has a groove on the ground surface into which a tarred rope is inserted.*

Fig. **1.18** *An anti-slipping shoe with transverse ridges on its ground surface.*

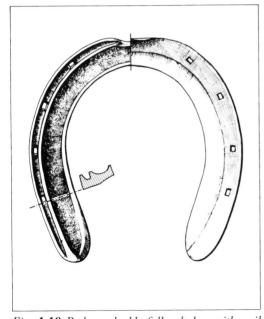

Fig. **1.19** *Rodway double-fullered shoe with nail holes stamped in the outer groove and the foot surface seated.*

webbed or convex shoe made of the customary mild steel and if this does not suffice to harden the surface with tungsten carbide. Heretofore to harden the iron for these special shoes it was the practice to make a rod of iron by welding together old wrought-iron shoes (Fig. 1.14 a-b).

Slipping is a problem, especially during periods of frost and snow, and many methods have been evolved to find a solution, such as drawing out the heels of the shoe to form points, so-called 'sharps' (Fig. 1.15), the use of frost nails (Fig. 1.16 a-c) and frost studs (Fig. 1.17). With the industrial revolution came increased traffic with improved roads which had hard and smooth surfaces conducive to slipping. To counter this problem many ingenious horseshoes were introduced, with various projections: transverse ridges (Fig. 1.18), double fullering (Fig. 1.19) or grooves to take a length of tarred rope (Fig. 1.20) or rubber. They all reduced slipping to some extent until the ridges and rope inserts wore smooth but, in addition, they were difficult to make and to nail on. Also numerous pads were tried including the simple frog pad (Fig. 1.21), bar pad (Fig. 1.22) and Gray's flexible bridge pad (Fig. 1.23), but their disadvantages outweighed any advantages since dirt and grit accumulated beneath them which led to an unhygienic state conducive to thrush, and they deprived the frog of its normal function. Shea-ther's pneumatic pad (Fig. 1.24) was a novel idea with the rubber pad replaced by an air

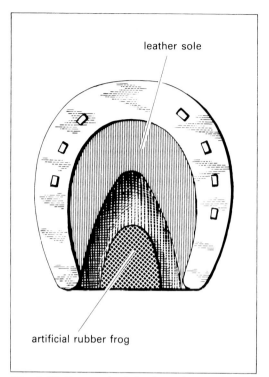

leather sole

artificial rubber frog

Fig. **1.21** *Frog pad. A leather sole to which an artificial rubber frog is attached, and retained in position by the shoe.*

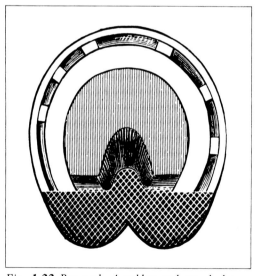

Fig. **1.22** *Bar pad. A rubber pad attached to a sheet of leather or synthetic material which fits across the base of the frog and the heels and is retained in position with a short shoe.*

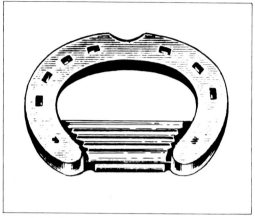

Fig. **1.23** *Gray's flexible bridge bar pad. A rubber pad mounted on a flexible metal base and fixed to the shoe with rivets.*

cushion which covered the whole of the sole and the frog. It served no practical use but it is of interest that the principle has been adopted in the USA for pads to prevent snow banking up in the feet.

George Fleming (1872) had both cavalry and draught horses which were working on smooth and excessively steep roads, shod all round without calkins or toe pieces. He reported he received no complaints of slipping or insecure footing or of horses falling down, and also sprains and injuries associated with calkins were unknown. He concluded that no shoe provided a better grip when working on slippery turf or a smooth road surface than the standard concave fullered shoe, which cannot be bettered in practical terms.

Over the years a great variety of surgical and other shoes have been introduced. Many were devised just for one specific case, whereas others had a more general application, but relatively few have stood the test of time. To name but a few that are no longer fitted, for reasons which require no explanation: the saucer shoe (Fig. 1.25) for chronic laminitis, Smiths' expanding shoe for contracted feet (Fig. 1.26), the 'G' shoe for brushing (Fig. 1.27) and the anchor or 'T' shoe (Fig. 1.28) for corns. The veterinary surgeons and farriers who had the enthusiasm and interest to perceive these shoes in an attempt to alleviate many conditions, are due a debt of gratitude for the enthusiasm they

Fig. **1.24** Sheather's pneumatic pad.

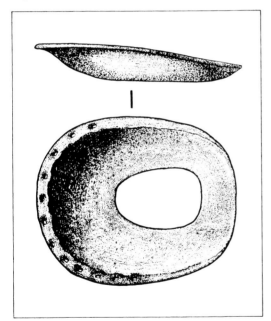

Fig. **1.25** A saucer shoe.

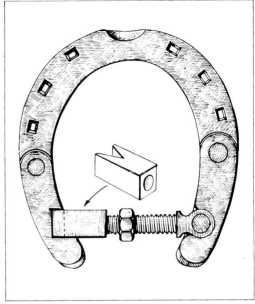

Fig. **1.26** Smith's expanding shoe.

Fig. **1.27** The 'G' shoe – a bar shoe with a calkin on the inside heel and the inside toe finished short with no branch. Used for brushing but has an uneven ground surface, deprives a third of the wall of its bearing surface, and has no practical application.

engendered which has led to a better understanding of how best pain can be relieved and locomotion improved by fitting a shoe based on scientific principles.

In 1889 the Worshipful Company of Farriers resolved to establish an organisation 'for the promotion of skilled farriery and the registration of farriers in London and

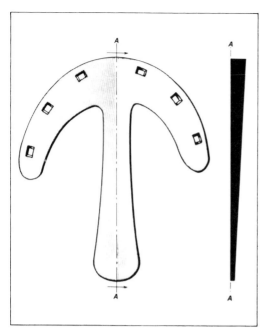

Fig. 1.28 Anchor or 'T' shoe – a tip that is connected to a plate which covers the frog. This shoe was used for the treatment of corns and of contracted feet but does not protect the seat of corn and has no practical application.

1.3 The future

It is often said that the heyday of the horse is past. True, the horse is no longer indispensable to agriculture or the military, and the transport system of the country is no longer dependent on it. But the horse still makes an important contribution to the economy of the country, in particular through the Thoroughbred industry. In addition, the horse continues to play an essential part in sport, entertainment and in a great variety of recreational pursuits. These include hunting, racing, polo, eventing, show jumping and the many activities encouraged by the riding, driving and pony clubs which flourish throughout the country.

After the First World War there was a steady decline in the horse population and it gradually disappeared from our roads and farms. At the end of the Second World War, due to the rapid mechanisation throughout all spheres of life, the number of horses dwindled to such an extent that many feared the days of the horse were over. In consequence, the demand for farriers declined and the future for the trade was indeed black as the majority of farriers still practising were beyond middle age and the prospects were such that it was not being taken up by the younger generation.

Fortunately, the Worshipful Company of Farriers did not take such a gloomy view. They foresaw the country returning to normality and an increasing prosperity which would lead to a resurgence of the horse population. There can be little doubt that during this period, when the trade was in the doldrums, the introduction by the Company of their apprenticeship scheme saved the day as it enabled a small cadre of trained farriers to be maintained.

Farriery is both an art and a science and it is essential that persons practising the trade should learn the art based on sound scientific principles.

The Farriers (Registration) Act 1975 and the Farriers (Registration) (Amendment) Act 1977 were passed to prevent horses suffering from unskilled shoeing, to promote the training of farriers, and to establish the Farriers Registration Council to register farriers.

A four-year apprenticeship with an approved training farrier is the only way to become a

throughout the country'. In 1890–91 they brought into operation a scheme for the examination and registration of shoeing smiths. At first farriers had only to meet the requirements of a short theoretical examination to be enrolled, but this was soon put to rights and the value of the Company's Certificate of Registered Shoeing Smiths, following a practical and oral examination, received the recognition which was its due. The higher qualifications of Associate and Fellow of the Company were introduced in 1907 and 1923 respectively.

In addition, other organisations were interested in encouraging apprenticeships and raising the standard of the trade. The National Master Farriers, Blacksmiths and Agricultural Engineers Association introduced an apprentice scheme; the Berkshire County Council, for example, instituted a travelling farriery school and agricultural societies deserve much credit for making farriery competitions a feature of their shows.

farrier (except through the Royal Army Veterinary Corps). During this time an apprentice will spend a total of six months at the School of Farriery in Hereford. The qualification Dip. WCF (Diploma of the Worshipful Company of Farriers), taken at the end of the apprenticeship, entitles the farrier to registration.

The Worshipful Company of Farriers is a livery company. In the Farriers Registration Act it is given the task of the promotion of farriery which it performs by organising competitions, prizes and examinations.

British farriers do not have a professional association as such but many belong to the National Association of Farriers, Blacksmiths and Agricultural Engineers which publishes a bimonthly journal, *Forge*, formerly the *Farriers Journal*.

Shoeing competitions are a feature of many agricultural shows. They are useful in encouraging forging skills and are a good way for farriers to meet.

Higher examinations are the AWCF (Associate) and the FWCF (Fellowship) which are attained by showing a higher understanding of theory than for the Diploma and an ability to make a variety of surgical shoes.

The Scottish Farriery Training Centre near Edinburgh was opened in 1986 for the further education of farriers and to encourage collaboration between farriers and veterinary surgeons in the area of corrective farriery.

The passing of the Farriers Registration Act will go a long way towards raising the status of the farrier, thereby educating the public in a more enlightened appreciation of his skills. This, it is hoped, will lead to the farrier's advice on shoeing and the care of horses' feet being more readily accepted and result in immense benefit to the horse and its owner.

CHAPTER 2

THE ANATOMY AND PHYSIOLOGY OF THE FRONT AND HIND LEGS

Anatomy is the study of the structure of the body; physiology is the study of function.

2.1 Anatomical terms

1. Positional terms
To describe accurately the parts of the body and their position certain terms are used (Figs. 2.1–2.2):

The *median plane* divides the body into similar halves.

A *sagittal* plane is parallel to the median plane.

A *transverse* plane cuts the body or a leg at right angles to its long axis.

A *frontal* plane is perpendicular to the median and transverse planes.

For the legs below the knee and hock the

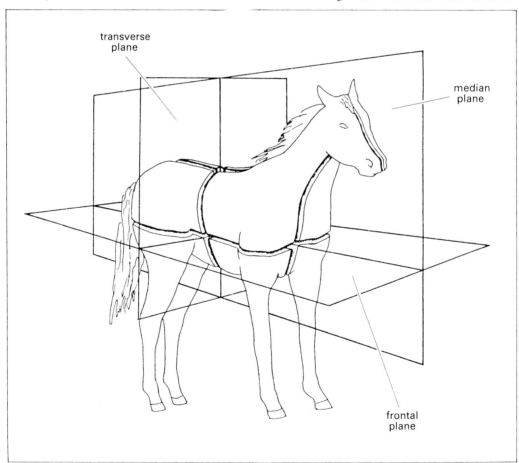

Fig. 2.1 The median, frontal and transverse planes of the body.

18

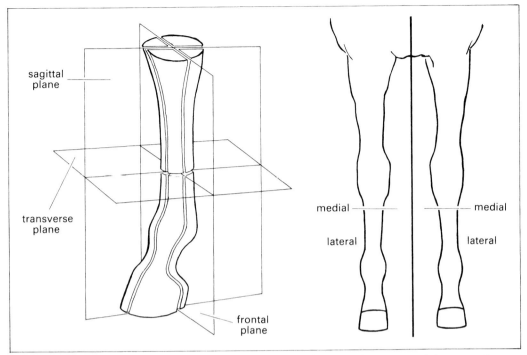

Fig. 2.2 The planes of the lower limb.

Fig. 2.3 Terms of position and direction relative to the median plane.

following terms are used to indicate position and direction (Figs. 2.3–2.4 a-b):

Dorsal refers to the front of the leg.

Palmar refers to the back of the front leg.

Plantar refers to the back of the hind leg.

Medial refers to the inside of the leg (towards the median plane).

Lateral refers to the outside of the leg (away from the median plane).

Axial means towards the long axis of the leg.

Abaxial means away from the long axis of the leg.

Proximal means towards the body.

Distal means away from the body.

2. Descriptive terms

The surfaces of bones have a number of features, some of which are described as follows:

A *process* is a general term for a prominence.

A *tuberosity* is a large non-articular prominence.

A *tubercle* is a small prominence.

A *crest* is a ridge.

A *line* is a small ridge.

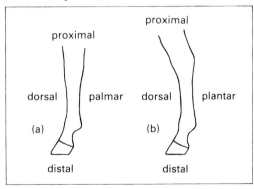

Fig. 2.4 Terms of position and direction in the sagittal plane. (a) Front leg. (b) Hind leg.

A *condyle* is an articular surface that is cylindrical.

An *epicondyle* is a non-articular prominence connected to a condyle.

A *facet* is a small flat articular surface.

A *foramen* is a hole for blood vessels or nerves.

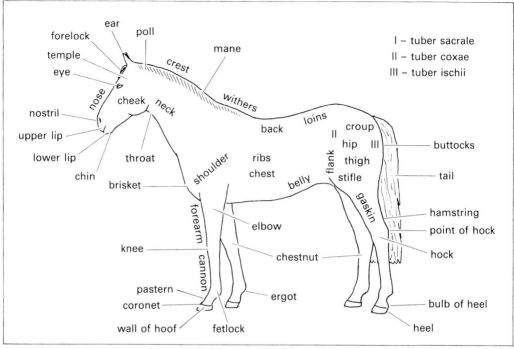

Fig. 2.5 The points of the horse.

2.2 Bones

The study of bones is called osteology. The skeleton is a framework of bones which supports and protects the body (Figs. 2.5–2.6). Without the support of the bones the animal would collapse and without their protection vital organs such as the heart and lungs would be exposed to injury. Bones are complex living structures which serve as supporting columns and as levers concerned with movement. They also act as reservoirs of calcium and phosphorus which are necessary to all living tissues.

Physical and chemical properties of bone
Fresh dead bone is yellowish white in colour, but when exposed in the living body it is tinged bluish pink due to the blood contained in the vessels of the bone. It is very hard and resistant to pressure, having a compressive strength of some 20,000 lbs per square inch.

Composition of bone
Adult equine bone when dried and freed from fat consists of 46% organic (animal) matter,

mainly the protein collagen, which is converted into gelatine by boiling, and 54% inorganic (mineral) constituents being mainly calcium (29%) and phosphorus (13%) with traces of magnesium, sodium and other elements.

If the mineral matter is removed the bone retains its original shape but is rendered soft and pliable. If the organic matter is removed instead the bone becomes brittle and is easily broken. The mineral matter gives bone its hardness. The organic matter provides a degree of elasticity which prevents it from breaking.

Structure of bone
If a bone is cut through with a saw (Fig. 2.7) it will be seen that there is a dense outer layer called cortical bone with porous spongy bone inside called cancellous bone. In many long bones the centre is hollowed out to form the medullary cavity.

Cortical bone varies in thickness to conform with the stresses the bone has to bear. For example the third metacarpal bone is thicker

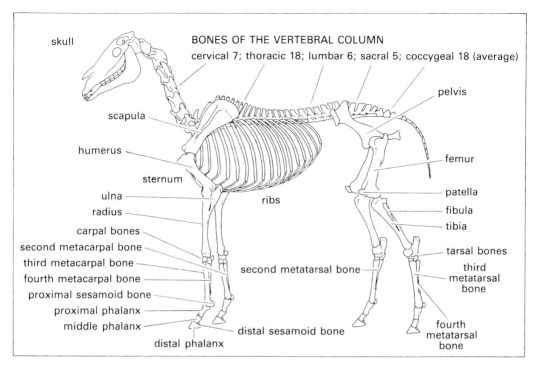

skull

BONES OF THE VERTEBRAL COLUMN
cervical 7; thoracic 18; lumbar 6; sacral 5; coccygeal 18 (average)

scapula

pelvis

humerus

femur

sternum

patella

ulna

fibula

radius

ribs

tibia

carpal bones

tarsal bones

second metacarpal bone

third metacarpal bone

fourth metacarpal bone

second metatarsal bone

third metatarsal bone

proximal sesamoid bone

proximal phalanx

middle phalanx

distal sesamoid bone

fourth metatarsal bone

distal phalanx

Fig. 2.6 Skeleton of the horse. The skeleton comprises 205 bones: vertebral column – 54; ribs – 36; sternum – 1; skull – 34; front limb – 40; hind limb – 40.

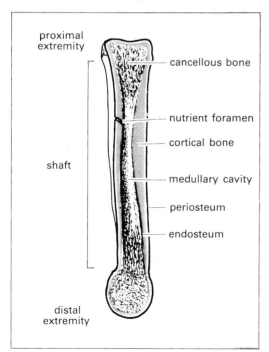

proximal extremity

cancellous bone

nutrient foramen

cortical bone

shaft

medullary cavity

periosteum

endosteum

distal extremity

Fig. 2.7 Third metacarpal bone, sagittal section.

dorsally than palmarly and thicker medially than laterally, which corresponds to the stresses of weight bearing. In long bones cortical bone is generally thicker towards the middle of the shaft and thins out towards the extremities.

Cancellous bone is light and porous. Its structure is arranged so as to resist the stresses of weight bearing. The spaces within it are filled with marrow.

Periosteum is the thin membrane which covers the outer surface of bone, except where it is covered by articular cartilage or where tendons and ligaments are attached. It consists of two layers, an outer protective fibrous layer and an inner cellular layer. In young growing animals the inner layer contains an abundance of cells called osteoblasts, which produce new bone, an activity called osteogenesis which is much reduced in adult life.

Endosteum is a thin fibrous membrane which lines the medullary cavity.

Bone marrow is the soft material which occupies the spaces of cancellous bone and the medullary cavity of long bones. There are two varieties. Red marrow is a blood-forming tissue found in all bones in early life and is gradually replaced by yellow marrow except in a few locations such as the ribs. Yellow marrow is mostly fat.

Blood vessels and nerves of bone

Arteries. Three sets of arteries are recognised – periosteal, nutrient and epiphyseal. The periosteal arteries spread in the periosteum and supply blood mainly to the periosteum itself. In the larger bones the shaft is penetrated by the nutrient foramen through which the nutrient artery passes to divide and ascend and descend the marrow cavity giving off branches which penetrate the shaft of the bone through its endosteal surface. The ends of bones are supplied with many small arteries known as epiphyseal arteries which penetrate through foramina in the cortical bone and divide in the cancellous bone to supply blood to the ends of the bone.

Veins. Three sets of veins correspond to the arteries of bone – periosteal, nutrient and epiphyseal. Periosteal veins drain blood from the periosteum. Near the articular surfaces are found numerous openings which give exit to epiphyseal veins returning blood from the cancellous bone. A nutrient vein accompanies the nutrient artery.

Nerves accompany the blood vessels in the cortical and cancellous bone and in the marrow cavity.

Growth of bone

In the embryo the bones of the limb are composed of cartilage. At birth most of the

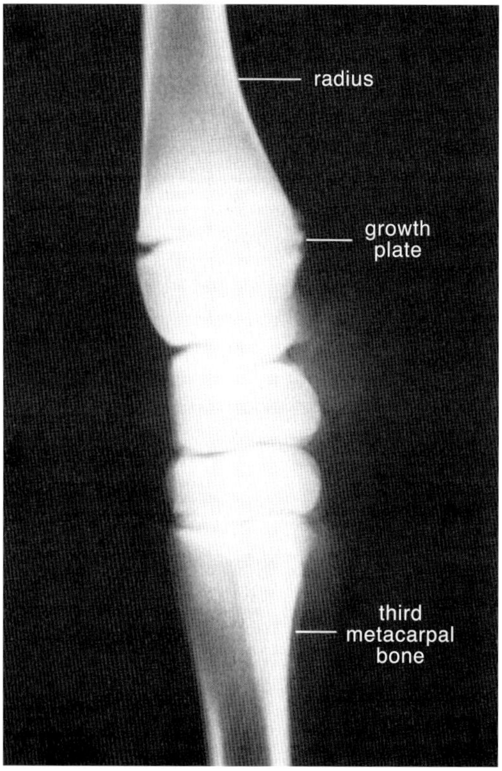

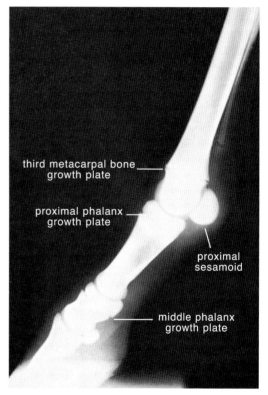

Fig. 2.8 Radiograph of carpus of foal. Note the growth plate of the distal radius which closes at two and a half years of age.

Fig. 2.9 Radiograph of front leg of foal. Note the growth plates of the proximal and middle phalanx which close at six months.

cartilage forming the shaft of these bones has become ossified. After birth the extremities rapidly ossify to form the bony epiphyses. The bony epiphyses are separated from the shaft by a layer of cartilage called the epiphyseal cartilage or the growth plate (Figs. 2.8–2.9). The bone grows in length by the proliferation of the cartilage cells forming the growth plate and their replacement by bone. Uneven growth of the growth plate results in angular deviation of the leg.

When the bone reaches its maximum length proliferation of the cartilage cells stops and the growth plates become completely ossified. The shaft of the bone and the epiphyses are fused and the bone ceases to grow in length. The conformation of the horse is established and cannot be altered.

A long bone grows in overall thickness by the deposition of bone on to the surface from the inner cellular layer of the periosteum. At the same time the marrow cavity is enlarged by the reabsorption of bone.

Closure of the growth plates takes place at definite times in the various bones. The times of closure of the most important growth plates in the lower limb of the horse are as follows:

growth plate	age at closure	rapid growth period
distal radius	2½ years	0–8 months
distal third metacarpal bone	1 year	0–3 months
distal tibia	2 years	0–6 months
distal third metatarsal bone	1 year	0–3 months
proximal proximal phalanx	6 months	
proximal middle phalanx	6 months	

These are average times of closure determined from radiological studies. Books on anatomy tend to quote from bone maceration studies which give later times of closure. Individuals can vary considerably from the average.

Bones of the front leg
Metacarpal bones
In the typical mammalian hand five metacarpal bones are present, one for each digit. In the horse three metacarpal bones are present, the *third metacarpal bone*, which is fully developed and has a digit, and the *second* and *fourth metacarpal bones*.

Third metacarpal bone
The third metacarpal bone is a typical long bone and is vertically orientated between the carpus and the proximal phalanx. It is one of the strongest bones in the skeleton.

The dorsal surface (Fig. 2.10a) is smooth, rounded from side to side and nearly straight in its length.

The palmar surface (Fig. 2.10c) is flat from side to side. On either side of the proximal half is a roughened area for the attachment of the second and fourth metacarpal bones. With the second and fourth metacarpal bones the palmar surface of the third metacarpal bone forms a channel for the suspensory ligament. Towards the junction of the proximal and middle thirds is the nutrient foramen through which passes the nutrient artery.

The proximal extremity has an articular surface for the distal row of carpal bones. On the dorso-medial aspect is a roughened projection, the metacarpal tuberosity, for the insertion of the tendon of the extensor carpi radialis muscle.

The distal extremity articulates with the proximal phalanx and the proximal sesamoid bones. A sagittal ridge divides it into two condyles, the medial being slightly the larger. On either side is a small depression for the attachment of the collateral ligaments of the fetlock joint.

Second and fourth metacarpal bones
The second and fourth metacarpal bones (Fig. 2.10b) are situated one on each side of the palmar surface of the third metacarpal bone.

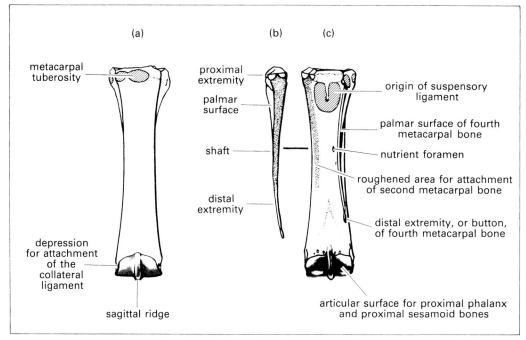

(a) (b) (c)

metacarpal tuberosity

proximal extremity

palmar surface

origin of suspensory ligament

palmar surface of fourth metacarpal bone

shaft

nutrient foramen

roughened area for attachment of second metacarpal bone

distal extremity

distal extremity, or button, of fourth metacarpal bone

depression for attachment of the collateral ligament

sagittal ridge

articular surface for proximal phalanx and proximal sesamoid bones

*Fig. **2.10** Third metacarpal bone (cannon bone) and second and fourth metacarpal bones (splint bones). (a) Third metacarpal bone dorsal surface; (b) second metacarpal bone dorsal surface; (c) third metacarpal bone palmar surface.*

They have a shaft, which has no medullary cavity, and two extremities. They vary in length, thickness and curvature and in most cases the medial bone is the longest.

The shaft is a three-sided slender rod, curved in its length, tapering to its distal extremity. The enlargement of the distal extremity is called the 'button' of the 'splint bone' and is easily palpated in the living horse.

The attached surface is flat and rough except at its distal part. It is attached to the palmar surface of the third metacarpal bone by an interosseous ligament which becomes ossified in older horses.

The dorsal surface is smooth and round.

The palmar surface is smooth and concave.

The proximal extremity is large. The articular surface of the second metacarpal bone has two facets which support the second and third carpal bones. The fourth metacarpal bone has a single facet which supports the fourth carpal bone. Each has two small facets dorsally for articulation with the third metacarpal bone and elsewhere the proximal

extremity is rough for the attachment of tendons and ligaments.

The second and fourth metacarpal bones bear weight from the carpus above and transmit it via the interosseous ligament to the third metacarpal bone.

Proximal sesamoid bones

There are two proximal sesamoid bones in each leg (Figs. 2.11–2.13). They are placed on the palmar surface of the distal extremity of the third metacarpal bone. Their functions are to form a groove for the digital flexor tendons and to give them increased leverage, and to form part of the suspensory apparatus.

Each sesamoid bone has the form of a three-sided pyramid.

The articular surface conforms to the palmar aspect of the distal articular surface of the third metacarpal bone.

The palmar surface is covered by cartilage and with the palmar surface of the opposite sesamoid bone forms a smooth groove for the passage of the digital flexor tendons.

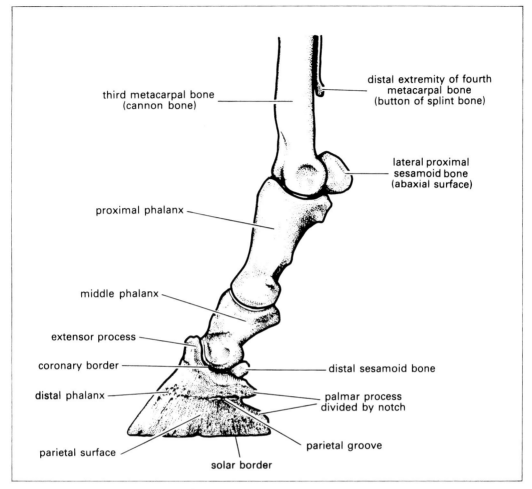

Fig. 2.11 Digit of the horse. Front leg, lateral aspect.

The abaxial surface gives attachment to the collateral sesamoidean ligaments, the collateral ligaments of the fetlock joint and a branch of the suspensory ligament.

The apex is rounded.

The base provides attachment for the distal sesamoidean ligaments.

Proximal phalanx

The proximal phalanx is situated between the third metacarpal bone and the middle phalanx (Figs. 2.11–2.13). It occupies an oblique position being directed downwards and forwards at an angle of about 50° with the horizontal plane. It consists of a shaft and two extremities.

The shaft is wider and thicker proximally than distally. The dorsal surface is smooth and slightly rounded from side to side. The palmar surface is flattened with a rough triangular area for the attachment of the oblique sesamoidean ligament. The medial and lateral surfaces have at their centre a roughened area for the attachment of the palmar ligaments of the proximal interphalangeal joint.

The proximal extremity has a concave articular surface moulded to the distal extremity of the third metacarpal bone. It is divided by a deep groove into two shallow articular cavities. The medial cavity is slightly the larger. The dorsal border has a tuberosity on each side for attachment of ligaments and in the middle is a slight elevation for attachment of the lateral digital extensor tendon.

The distal extremity is smaller, and the articular surface is divided into two condyles by a shallow groove, the medial condyle being slightly the larger. At either side is a depression and a tubercle to both of which the collateral ligament of the proximal interphalangeal joint is attached. Behind the tubercle is the area to which the superficial digital flexor tendon attaches.

Middle phalanx

The middle phalanx is shorter than the proximal phalanx. Its width is greater than its length. It lies between the proximal and distal phalanges and is directed downwards and forwards in line with the proximal phalanx (Figs. 2.11–2.13). It has two extremities and two surfaces.

The proximal extremity articulates with the distal extremity of the proximal phalanx. It is separated into two shallow cavities divided by a low sagittal ridge, the medial cavity being slightly the larger. The middle of the dorsal border is roughened for the attachment of the common digital extensor tendon. The palmar border has a thick overhanging and smooth transverse prominence which is covered with a plate of fibro-cartilage over which the deep

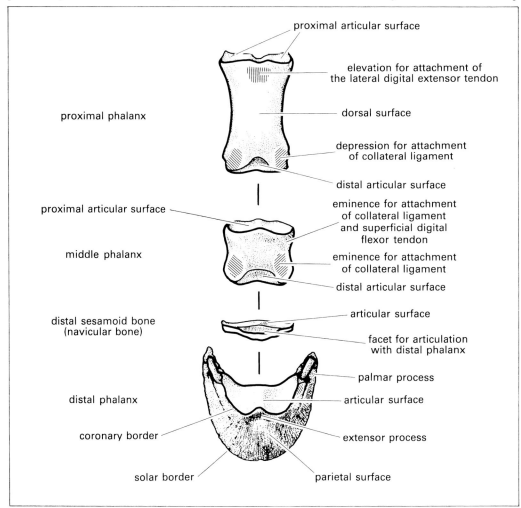

Fig. 2.12 Digit of the horse. Front leg, dorsal aspect.

digital flexor tendon passes. On either side is an eminence for the attachment of the collateral ligament of the proximal interphalangeal joint and the superficial digital flexor tendon.

The distal extremity resembles the lower extremity of the proximal phalanx. It articulates with the distal phalanx and distal sesamoid bone to form the distal interphalangeal joint. On either side is a depression for the attachment of the dorsal collateral ligaments of the distal interphalangeal joint.

The dorsal surface is rough and slightly depressed in the centre.

The palmar surface is smooth and flat.

Distal phalanx

The distal phalanx is enclosed entirely within the hoof, which it resembles in shape (Fig. 2.14). It is composed of cortical bone and is one of the densest bones in the skeleton. It can be described as possessing three surfaces, three borders and three processes.

The parietal surface slopes downwards and forwards at an angle of about 50°. Laterally and medially the height gradually diminishes and the slope becomes steeper. It is rough and perforated by numerous foraminae of various sizes. On either side is a groove, the parietal groove, which runs forward from the palmar process and terminates in one of the large

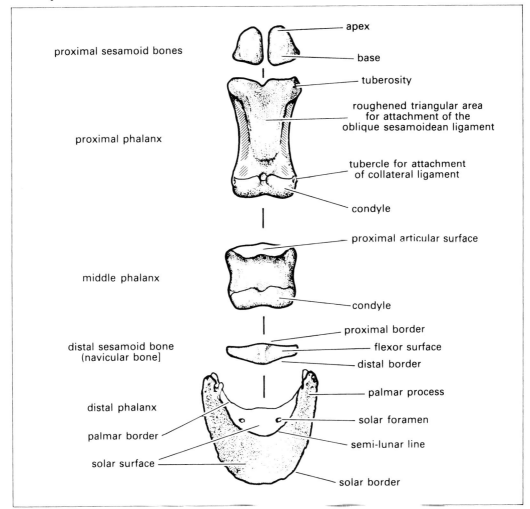

Fig. 2.13 Digit of the horse. Front leg, palmar aspect.

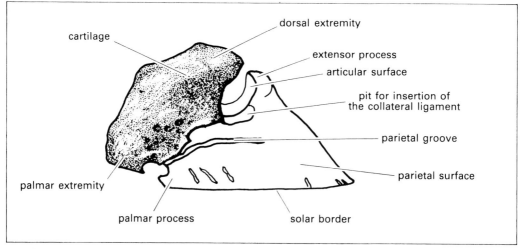

Fig. 2.14 Distal phalanx and cartilage.

foraminae. In life the parietal surface is covered by the laminar corium.

The coronary border which separates the parietal and articular surfaces has a central process, the extensor process, for the insertion of the common digital extensor tendon. On either side is a small pit for the insertion of the collateral ligaments.

The articular surface is moulded on the distal articular surface of the middle phalanx and is divided into two shallow cavities by a low ridge.

Along the palmar border which separates the articular and solar surfaces is a transversely elongated flattened area which forms the articulation with the distal sesamoid bone.

The solar surface is divided into two unequal parts by the semilunar line. The larger area in front of this line is smooth, crescent shaped and slightly vaulted. It corresponds to the sole of the hoof. The smaller area behind the semilunar line has a central rough area for the attachment of the deep digital flexor tendon. On each side is the solar foramen which conducts the medial and lateral digital arteries into the solar canal within the bone.

The solar border is convex, thin and irregular, with often a particularly wide and deep notch in front.

The palmar processes are directed backwards on each side. Each is divided by a notch which leads to the parietal groove. In older horses these processes are often joined by a bridge of bone, converting the notch into a foramen. The proximal borders of the palmar processes are attached to the cartilages of the distal phalanx.

The medial and lateral cartilages of the distal phalanx (Fig. 2.14) are four-sided curved plates attached to the proximal borders of the palmar processes. They are large and extend far enough above the coronet to be palpable. Between them is the digital cushion. In older horses they tend to become converted into bone when they are called 'sidebones'.

Distal sesamoid bone (navicular bone)
The distal sesamoid bone is a small transversely elongated bone, situated behind the articulation of the middle and distal phalanges, and articulates with both bones (Figs. 2.11–2.13).

The articular surface has a central sagittal ridge and articulates with the distal articular surface of the middle phalanx.

The flexor surface is convex and covered by fibrocartilage over which the deep digital flexor tendon glides.

The proximal border is wide and grooved in its middle.

The distal border has dorsally a transversely elongated facet which articulates with the distal phalanx, and below this is a grooved portion perforated by numerous foraminae.

The extremities are rounded.

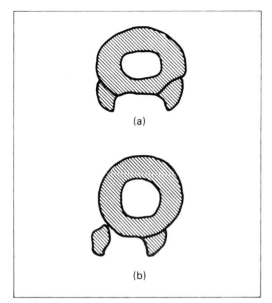

Fig. 2.15 Transverse section of (a) the metacarpal bones and (b) the metatarsal bones. Note that the third metacarpal is oval while the third metatarsal is rounder.

Bones of the hind leg

In the hind leg the term plantar is substituted for palmar to describe structures located towards the back of the leg.

Metatarsal bones
The three metatarsal bones of the hind leg are very similar to the metacarpal bones of the front leg.

Third metatarsal bone
This is slightly longer than the third metacarpal bone, by about 2 ins (5 cm) in the average horse.

The shaft is more cylindrical (Fig. 2.15). On its dorsal and lateral surface is a shallow groove indicating the course of the dorsal metatarsal artery. The medial face shows a similar but fainter groove for the metatarsal vein. On the plantar surface the nutrient foramen, which is sometimes double, is placed relatively higher than that of the metacarpal bone.

The proximal extremity is wider from its dorsal to its plantar aspect than the metacarpal bone (Fig. 2.16). Its articular surface is slightly concave and has a large non-articular depression. On the dorsal surface and slightly to the medial side is a rough ridge for the insertion of the tendon of the peroneus tertius muscle.

The distal extremity differs from the third metacarpal bone only in being larger.

Second and fourth metatarsal bones
The second and fourth metatarsal bones are a little longer than the corresponding metacarpal bones. The proximal extremity of the fourth metatarsal is particularly large.

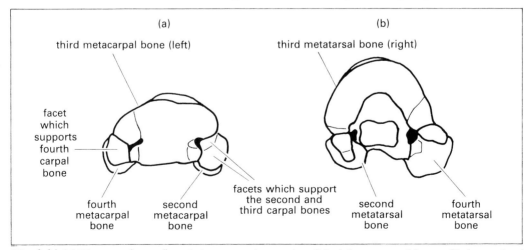

Fig. 2.16 (a) The articular surface of the proximal extremity of the left metacarpal bones; (b) the proximal extremity of the right metatarsal bones.

Proximal sesamoid bones
The proximal sesamoid bones of the hind leg are slightly smaller than those of the front leg.

Proximal phalanx
The proximal phalanx of the hind leg is a little shorter, wider proximally and narrower distally, than that of the front leg.

Middle phalanx
The middle phalanx of the hind leg is narrower and slightly longer than that of the front leg.

Distal phalanx
The distal phalanx of the hind leg is more pointed at the toe and the solar surface is more concave than that of the front leg.

Distal sesamoid bone
The distal sesamoid bone of the hind leg is smaller than that of the front leg.

2.3 Joints

The study of joints is called arthrology. A joint or articulation is formed by the union of two or more bones. All the joints in the leg are synovial joints.

Synovial joints
Synovial joints (Fig. 2.17) have a joint cavity

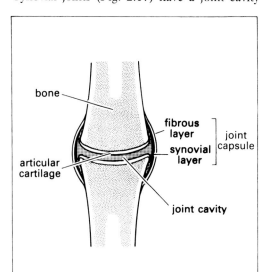

Fig. 2.17 Cross-section of a synovial joint.

and a joint capsule and great freedom of movement. The articular surfaces of the bones vary in form. They are covered with articular cartilage which is very smooth and reduces friction and concussion.

The joint capsule in its simplest form is a tube, the ends of which are attached around the margins of the joint surfaces. It is composed of two layers: the outer fibrous layer and the inner synovial layer. The synovial layer is a thin smooth membrane which secretes synovial fluid, a clear sticky yellow fluid which lubricates the joint.

Ligaments are strong bands of fibrous tissue. Several kinds of ligaments contribute to the stability of synovial joints by connecting the bones together. They are classified according to their position: *periarticular ligaments* form part of or arc near to the fibrous layer of the joint capsule and *collateral ligaments* are periarticular ligaments which are situated at the sides of a joint.

Movements of joints are determined by the shape of the joint surfaces and the arrangement of the ligaments:

Gliding is the sliding of one flat surface on another.

Flexion reduces the angle of the joint.

Extension straightens a joint.

Since the joints of the leg can be hyperextended the terms *dorsal* and *palmar* (or *plantar*) *flexion* are more precise than extension and flexion. Dorsal flexion is a reduction in the dorsal angle of a joint and palmar or plantar flexion is a reduction in the palmar or plantar angle of a joint.

Rotation is a movement of one segment of a joint about the long axis of the other segment.

Abduction is movement of a leg away from the median plane.

Adduction is movement of a leg towards the median plane.

Metacarpophalangeal joint (fetlock joint)
The fetlock joint is formed by the third metacarpal bone, the proximal phalanx and the proximal sesamoid bones. The movements of the joint are flexion and extension but when flexed slight abduction, adduction and rotation are possible. With the horse in the standing position the angle formed by the metacarpal

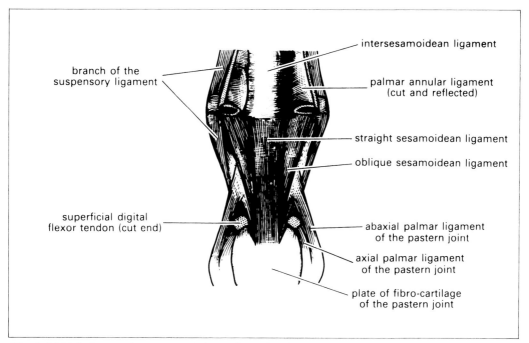

Fig. **2.18** *Fetlock joint (metacarpo-phalangeal joint) palmar aspect, superficial dissection.*

bone and the proximal phalanx in front of the fetlock joint is about 140°.

The two sesamoid bones are united by the *intersesamoidean ligament*. This is a mass of fibro-cartilage which forms a deep groove between them for the passage of the digital flexor tendons.

The *distal sesamoidean ligaments* are three in number (Figs. 2.18–2.19):
(i) The straight sesamoidean ligament is band-like and attached to the base of the sesamoid bones and, distally, to the plate of fibro-cartilage of the middle phalanx.
(ii) The oblique sesamoidean ligament is triangular with thick margins and a thin central portion. It is attached to the base of the sesamoid bones and to the triangular area on the palmar surface of the proximal phalanx.
(iii) The cruciate sesamoidean ligament consists of two layers of fibres which arise from the base of the sesamoid bones, and cross each other to be inserted on to the palmar proximal extremity of the proximal phalanx.

The *collateral sesamoidean ligaments*, lateral and medial, arise on the abaxial surface of each sesamoid bone and divide into two branches

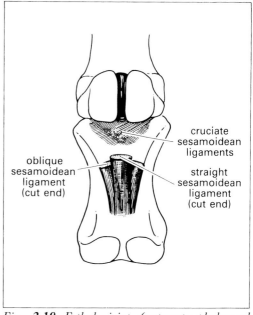

Fig. **2.19** *Fetlock joint (metacarpo-phalangeal joint) palmar aspect, deep dissection. The straight and oblique sesamoidean ligaments have been removed to show the cruciate sesamoidean ligaments.*

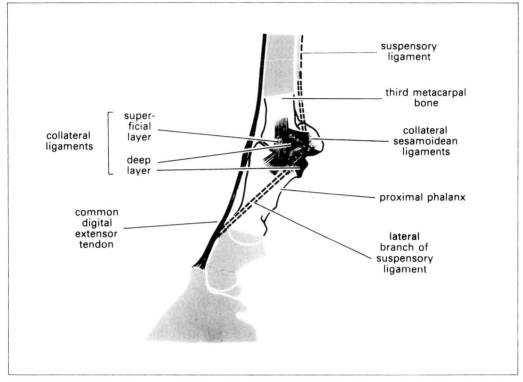

Fig. **2.20** *Fetlock joint (metacarpo-phalangeal articulation) lateral aspect.*

which unite the abaxial surface of each sesamoid bone to the distal extremity of the third metacarpal bone and the proximal extremity of the proximal phalanx (Fig. 2.20).

The *suspensory ligament* (Fig. 2.25) originates from the distal row of carpal bones and the roughened area at the palmar and proximal extremity of the third metacarpal bone. It is more correctly called the middle interosseous muscle. It is largely tendinous and contains a few muscle fibres only in the foal. It has the form of a wide thick band and lies in the groove formed by the three metacarpal bones. Towards the distal extremity of the third metacarpal bone the ligament divides into two branches which diverge towards the abaxial surfaces of the sesamoid bones to which a considerable part of each is attached. The remainder of each branch continues downwards and forwards to the dorsal surface of the proximal phalanx to join the tendon of the common digital extensor tendon. The main function of this ligament is to support the

fetlock joint by controlling excessive dorsal flexion when weight is borne on the leg.

The *collateral ligaments of the fetlock joint* are divided into two layers (Fig. 2.20):
(i) The *superficial layer* which passes vertically from the distal extremity of the third metacarpal bone to the roughened area on the proximal extremity of the proximal phalanx.
(ii) The *deep layer* which originates beneath the superficial layer in the pit at the distal extremity of the third metacarpal bone and passes downwards and backwards to attach to the abaxial surface of the sesamoid bone and to the proximal extremity of the proximal phalanx.

The *joint capsule* of the fetlock joint is attached around the articular margins. It is thickened in front, and here a bursa is located between it and the common digital extensor tendon. Palmarly it forms a pouch which extends upwards between the third metacarpal bone and suspensory ligament. Distension of this pouch is called an articular windgall.

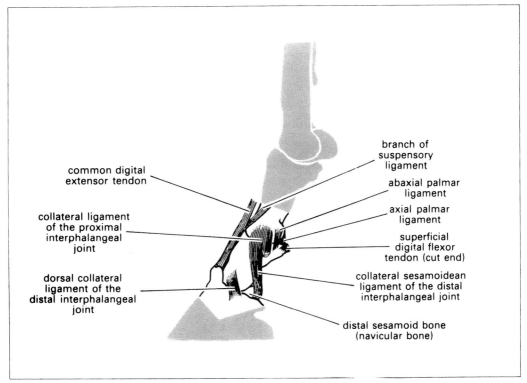

common digital
extensor tendon

collateral ligament
of the proximal
interphalangeal
joint

dorsal collateral
ligament of the
distal interphalangeal
joint

branch of
suspensory
ligament

abaxial palmar
ligament

axial palmar
ligament

superficial
digital flexor
tendon (cut end)

collateral sesamoidean
ligament of the distal
interphalangeal joint

distal sesamoid bone
(navicular bone)

Fig. 2.21 Proximal and distal interphalangeal joints, lateral aspect.

Proximal interphalangeal joint (pastern joint)

The proximal interphalangeal joint is formed between the proximal and middle phalanx (Fig. 2.21). When the horse is in the normal standing position the joint is extended with the proximal and middle phalanges at the same angle. This joint exhibits mainly flexion and extension but when flexed slight adduction, abduction and rotation are possible.

The joint possesses two collateral ligaments and two pairs of palmar ligaments. The palmar articular surface is extended by a plate of fibro-cartilage. Dorsally this supports the joint capsule and palmarly it is part of the dorsal boundary of the digital synovial sheath through which the tendons of the superficial and deep digital flexor pass.

The *collateral ligaments* are short strong bands which are attached proximally to the sides of the distal extremity of the proximal phalanx and distally to the sides of the proximal extremity of the middle phalanx. Some of the

dorsal fibres extend downwards and backwards to form part of the collateral sesamoidean ligament of the distal interphalangeal joint.

The *palmar ligaments* consist of two pairs. The abaxial pair pass from the medial/lateral aspects of the proximal phalanx to the plate of fibro-cartilage, whereas the axial pair, which are shorter, pass from the palmar aspect of the proximal phalanx to the plate of fibro-cartilage.

The *joint capsule* blends dorsally with the common digital extensor tendon and on each side with the collateral ligament. Palmarly it extends proximally to form a small pouch.

Distal interphalangeal joint

The distal interphalangeal joint is formed by the middle and distal phalanges and the distal sesamoid bone (Fig. 2.21). The normal movements of this joint are extension and flexion, but when flexed slight abduction, adduction and some rotation are possible.

The distal articular surface is formed by the combined articular surfaces of the distal phalanx and the distal sesamoid bone. The mobility of the back of the joint helps to reduce concussion.

The *distal impar ligament* is a short ligament that joins the distal border of the distal sesamoid to the adjacent surface of the distal phalanx.

The united distal phalanx and distal sesamoid bone are connected to the proximal and middle phalanx by two pairs of ligaments: the dorsal collateral and the collateral sesamoidean ligaments.

The *dorsal collateral ligaments*, medial and lateral, pass from the side of the middle phalanx to the pit at the side of the extensor process of the distal phalanx.

The *collateral sesamoidean ligaments*, medial and lateral, are in part a continuation of the collateral ligament of the proximal interphalangeal joint. Each originates in and above the depressions on each side of the distal end of the proximal phalanx and passes downwards and backwards to attach to the axial surface of the cartilage. It then continues downwards and axially to terminate on the extremity and proximal border of the distal sesamoid bone and to the palmar process of the distal phalanx. They are somewhat elastic and are also known as the suspensory ligaments of the navicular bone.

The *joint capsule* is supported dorsally by the expanded tendon of the common digital extensor and at the sides by the collateral ligaments. Palmarly it extends proximally forming a considerable pouch, and on each side is a small pouch which lies close to the cartilage.

The *navicular bursa* is a synovial bursa which connects the edges of the flexor surface of the navicular bone to the edges of the opposed surface of the deep digital flexor tendon. It produces synovial fluid which reduces friction between these two structures.

It should be noted that the navicular bursa is lined with synovial membrane except for the cartilage of the flexor surface of the navicular bone and the surface of the deep digital flexor tendon which apposes this cartilage.

Ligaments of the cartilage of the distal phalanx

In addition to the collateral sesamoidean ligaments mentioned above which connect the cartilages to the proximal and distal phalanges and to the navicular bone, there are three ligaments which attach each cartilage to each phalanx in turn (Fig. 2.22):

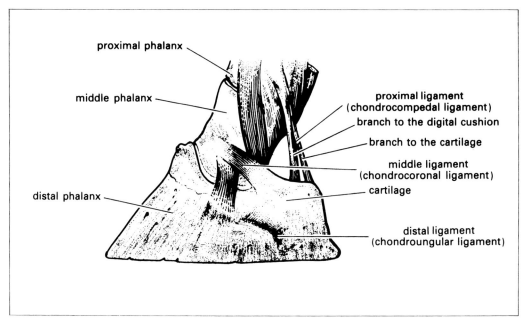

Fig. 2.22 Ligaments of the cartilage of the distal phalanx.

The *chondrocompedal ligament*, medial and lateral, is an ill-defined elastic ligament passing from the middle of each side of the proximal phalanx to the proximal border of the cartilage, detaching a branch to the digital cushion.

The *chondrocoronal ligament*, medial and lateral, is a short strong ligament passing from the eminence on either side of the middle phalanx to the dorsal extremity of the cartilage.

The *chondroungular ligament*, medial and lateral, attaches the lower border of the cartilage to the process of the distal phalanx.

The fetlock joint, suspensory ligament and the interphalangeal joints of a hind leg and of a front leg are very similar.

2.4 Muscles

The study of muscles is called myology. Muscles make up about 40% of the total body weight and have the power of contraction by which movement of the body is produced. There are several types of muscle, but the type which concerns movement of the limbs is called skeletal muscle because it is mainly attached to the skeleton. It is also known as voluntary muscle because it is under the control of the will and as striped or striated muscle because it has this appearance under the microscope.

The fleshy part of a muscle is known as its belly. There is usually a tendon at either end by which the muscle is inserted on to the bone on which it acts. The proximal end is known as the origin and the distal end as the insertion. When the muscle contracts it becomes shorter and thicker, acting on the bones to which it is attached to cause movement of the limb. Muscles are called extensors or flexors according to whether they extend (dorsal flexion) or flex (palmar or plantar flexion) the limb.

Muscles are stimulated to contract by electrical impulses conducted to them by nerves.

There are two kinds of accessory structure associated with muscles: synovial membranes and fascia. Synovial membranes are present in two forms: bursae and tendon sheaths. Synovial membranes are sheets of cells which secrete a little clear yellow sticky fluid called

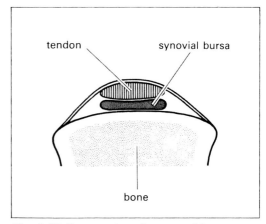

Fig. **2.23** *Cross-section of a synovial bursa.*

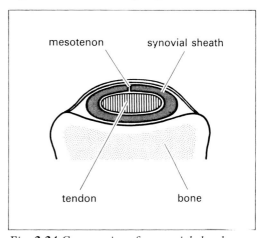

Fig. **2.24** *Cross-section of a synovial sheath.*

synovial fluid. Their function is to reduce friction in areas of movement.

A *synovial bursa* is a closed sac lined with a synovial membrane and containing a little synovial fluid (Fig. 2.23). Synovial bursae are classified as congenital or true bursae to distinguish them from false or acquired bursae.

A false or acquired bursa develops under the skin over bony projections following injury. The fluid swelling fails to be reabsorbed and is surrounded by fibrous tissue with no synovial lining. Typical examples are capped elbows and hocks which follow slight but repeated injury.

A *synovial tendon sheath* is a synovial bursa which is wrapped round a tendon (Fig. 2.24). Like a synovial bursa its function is to reduce friction. Its inner layer adheres to the tendon and its outer layer adheres to the surrounding tissues. The two layers glide easily over each other lubricated by synovial fluid. The inner and outer layers are joined by the mesotenon. Between the two membranes of the mesotenon, blood vessels, nerves and lymphatic vessels pass to and from the tendon.

The *carpal synovial sheath* envelops the tendons of the superficial and deep flexor tendons as they pass behind the carpus. It commences approximately 3 ins (8 cm) above the carpus and extends downward to the middle of the metacarpus. Distension of the carpal sheath is known as a knee thoroughpin.

The *digital synovial sheath* envelops the tendons of the superficial and deep flexor tendons as they pass behind the fetlock. It commences approximately 3 ins (8 cm) above the fetlock joint and extends downward to the middle of the middle phalanx. Distension of the digital synovial sheath is known as a tendinous windgall.

Muscles of the front limb

The front limb is covered by muscles on all but the medial side where the radius lies subcutaneously. The extensor muscles of the carpus and digit lie dorsally and laterally while the flexors are on the palmar aspect (Fig. 2.25).

Extensors of the digit

The *common digital extensor muscle* originates from the distal extremity of the humerus and the proximal extremity of the radius. Its tendon passes downwards over the dorsal surface of the third metacarpal bone and of the fetlock joint. Part of the tendon attaches to the proximal aspect of the dorsal surface of the proximal phalanx. A little below the middle of the proximal phalanx it is joined by branches of the suspensory ligament, which greatly

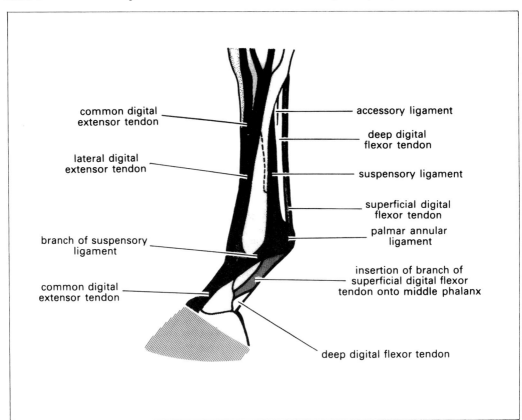

common digital extensor tendon

lateral digital extensor tendon

branch of suspensory ligament

common digital extensor tendon

accessory ligament

deep digital flexor tendon

suspensory ligament

superficial digital flexor tendon

palmar annular ligament

insertion of branch of superficial digital flexor tendon onto middle phalanx

deep digital flexor tendon

Fig. 2.25 The tendons and ligaments of the left front leg, lateral aspect.

increases its width. It then passes over the pastern joint and inserts on the proximal aspect of the dorsal surface of the middle phalanx and the extensor process of the distal phalanx. At the fetlock joint a bursa is located between it and the joint capsule.

The *lateral digital extensor muscle* arises from the distal humerus and the lateral and proximal aspect of the radius. Its tendon passes downwards on the dorso-lateral surface of the third metacarpal bone and over the dorsal aspect of the fetlock joint to insert on the eminence on the proximal aspect of the dorsal surface of the proximal phalanx.

Flexors of the digit

The *superficial digital flexor muscle* arises from the distal extremity of the humerus. Proximal to the carpus it is joined by a strong fibrous band, an accessory ligament, from the radius. Its tendon passes down the palmar aspect of

the metacarpus in common with the deep digital flexor tendon. At the fetlock joint it widens, still covering the deep digital flexor tendon, and here both tendons are supported and retained by the palmar annular ligament as they pass over the intersesamoidean ligament. Towards the distal extremity of the third metacarpal the tendon divides to form a ring, which permits the passage of the deep digital flexor tendon, and finally inserts on the eminence on either side of the distal extremity of the proximal phalanx and of the proximal extremity of the middle phalanx.

The *deep digital flexor muscle* originates from the distal extremity of the humerus, the proximal extremity of the ulna and the palmar surface of the radius. In the metacarpal area its tendon lies between the superficial digital flexor tendon and the suspensory ligament. Towards the middle of the metacarpus it is joined by a strong fibrous band, an *accessory*

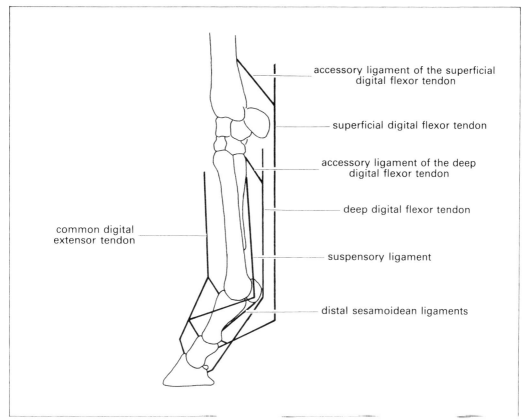

accessory ligament of the superficial
digital flexor tendon

superficial digital flexor tendon

accessory ligament of the deep
digital flexor tendon

deep digital flexor tendon

common digital
extensor tendon

suspensory ligament

distal sesamoidean ligaments

Fig. 2.26 The suspensory apparatus of the front leg.

ligament, which is a continuation of the palmar ligament of the carpus.

The tendon descends over the intersesamoidean ligament, passes through the opening formed by the division of the superficial digital flexor tendon, and then continues over the flexor surface of the distal sesamoid bone to insert on the solar surface of the distal phalanx.

Suspensory apparatus

As well as flexing the limb the digital flexor tendons and accessory ligament aid the suspensory ligament and distal sesamoidean ligaments in supporting the fetlock joint during weight bearing. Collectively these structures are known as the suspensory apparatus and form part of the stay apparatus which helps the horse to remain standing with the minimum of muscular effort (Fig. 2.26).

Muscles of the hind limb

In the hind limb the major extensor tendon is that of the long digital extensor muscle and is very similar to the common digital extensor tendon in the front limb. The lateral digital extensor tendon fuses with the long digital extensor tendon about a third of the way down the metatarsus. The tendons of the flexor muscles and the suspensory ligament are very similar to the front leg but the accessory ligament of the deep flexor muscle is longer and thinner or sometimes altogether absent.

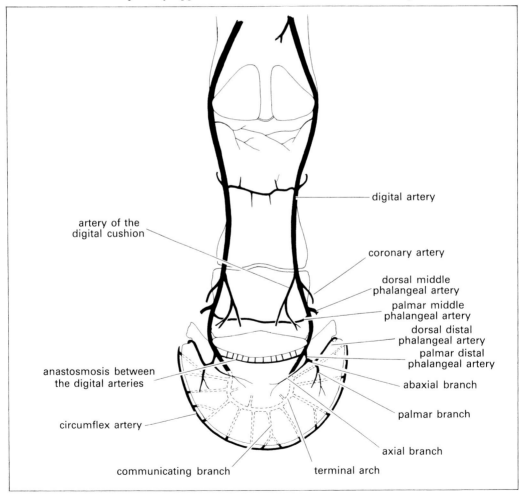

digital artery

artery of the digital cushion

coronary artery

dorsal middle phalangeal artery

palmar middle phalangeal artery

dorsal distal phalangeal artery

palmar distal phalangeal artery

anastosmosis between the digital arteries

abaxial branch

palmar branch

circumflex artery

axial branch

communicating branch

terminal arch

*Fig. **2.27** Arteries to the foot, palmar view.*

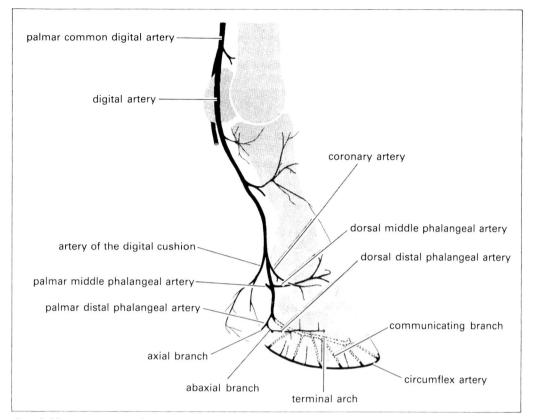

Fig. **2.28** *Arteries to the foot, side view.*

2.5 Blood vessels

Blood carries oxygen and nutrients to the tissues and takes away waste products. The organs of circulation of the blood are the heart and the blood vessels.

The *heart* is a muscular pump.

The *arteries* are thick elastic-walled tubes which carry the blood from the heart to the tissues. If cut, bright red blood escapes in a pulsating stream.

The *capillaries* are the microscopic end branches of the arteries. It is in the millions of capillaries that exchange of nutrients and gases takes place between the blood and the tissues.

The *veins* are thin-walled tubes which convey the blood back to the heart from the capillaries. In large veins valves are present which ensure that blood flows towards the heart but not away from it. If cut, dark red blood escapes in a steady flow.

Arteries of the front leg and foot

The *palmar common digital artery* conveys blood to the lower leg and foot. It descends the metacarpus medial to the flexor tendons and just above the fetlock it divides into the *medial and lateral digital arteries* (Figs 2.27–2.29).

The medial and lateral digital arteries pass down over the abaxial surfaces of the proximal sesamoid bones and descend along the edges of the flexor tendons to reach the distal phalanx where they enter the solar foramen on each side of the solar surface and unite to form the *terminal arch.*

Each digital artery gives off the following branches to the foot:

The *artery of the digital cushion* descends down and divides into two branches. The *abaxial branch* supplies blood to the bulbs, bar, angle of the heel and the corium of the heel region. The *axial branch* supplies the corium of the bar and frog.

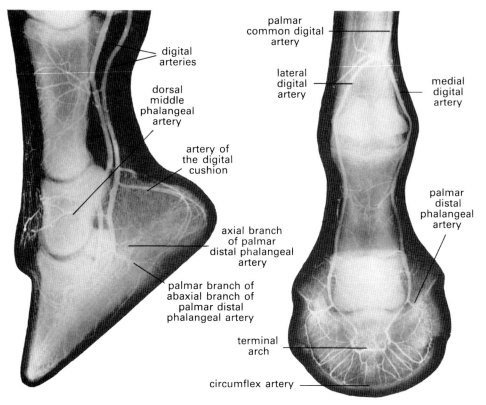

Fig. 2.29 Arteriogram of the horse's foot.

The *coronary artery* supplies the coronet including the coronary corium.

The *dorsal middle phalangeal artery* supplies the proximal and distal interphalangeal joints and the coronet.

The *palmar middle phalangeal artery* joins the same vessel of the opposite side to form a direct connection between the medial and lateral digital arteries. It gives off some vessels to the dorsal border of the navicular bone.

A small branch of the digital artery runs within the distal impar ligament of the navicular bone and anastomoses with the similar vessel of the opposite side. This distal anastomosis between the digital arteries provides the majority of the blood to the navicular bone.

The *palmar distal phalangeal artery* arises distal to the navicular bone and divides into two branches. The *axial branch* supplies the corium of the apex of the frog and of the sole. The *abaxial branch* again divides into two

branches. A *palmar branch* supplies the corium of the sole and contributes to the circumflex artery. A *dorsal branch* passes through the notch of the palmar process of the distal phalanx to the parietal groove as the *dorsal distal phalangeal artery*.

The dorsal distal phalangeal artery supplies blood to the laminae of the quarters and heels before passing through a foramen in the distal phalanx to join the terminal arch. It gives off small vessels which anastomose proximally with the coronary artery and distally with the circumflex artery.

Approximately ten small *communicating branches* radiate out from the terminal arch through foraminae of the distal phalanx and form the *circumflex artery* at the solar border.

Arteries of the hind leg and foot

In the hind leg the *dorsal metatarsal artery* conveys the blood to the lower leg and foot. It descends in the groove on the lateral aspect of the metatarsus between the third and fourth metatarsal bones. A little above the button of the fourth metatarsal bone it passes to the plantar aspect where it divides into the lateral and medial digital arteries which have the same arrangement as in the front leg.

Veins of the front and hind leg and foot

The veins of the foot comprise several distinct networks of freely communicating vessels called *venous plexuses* and several large distinct veins (Figs. 2.30–2.32).

The *circumflex vein* drains blood from the corium of both wall and sole.

The *terminal vein* within the solar canal drains the deep venous network of the distal phalanx. Emerging through the solar foramen the medial and lateral terminal veins pass proximally on the axial aspect of the cartilages and join with the inner venous plexus to form the medial and lateral *digital veins* which drain all the blood from the hoof.

The *coronary vein* and the *subcoronary vein* drain blood from the coronary venous plexus into the digital veins.

The *palmar hoof vein* drains blood from the heel area into the digital veins.

The *sole venous plexus* drains into the circumflex vein, the palmar hoof vein and the inner venous plexus of the digital veins.

The *frog venous plexus* is distinct from that of the sole though they communicate through numerous branches. It drains mainly into the palmar hoof vein.

The *wall venous plexus* is less extensive than that of the coronary area or sole, possibly because the laminar epidermis does not proliferate to the same degree. It drains into the coronary vein and circumflex vein at the toe and additionally into the palmar hoof vein at the heels.

The *inner venous plexus*, medial and lateral, is situated axially to each cartilage. It drains blood from the corium of the sole and frog up into the digital veins.

The *coronary venous plexus* receives blood from the coronary corium and drains into coronary and subcoronary veins.

Drainage of the navicular bone occurs via an anastomosis between the terminal veins which runs within the distal impar ligament.

The medial and lateral digital veins ascend the limb in front of the corresponding digital arteries.

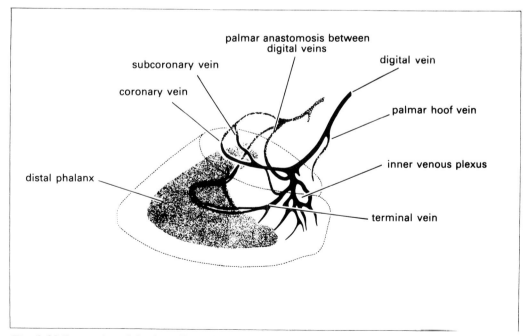

Fig. **2.30** *Deep veins of the foot. (Reproduced by permission of M.C. Mishra and D.H. Leach)*

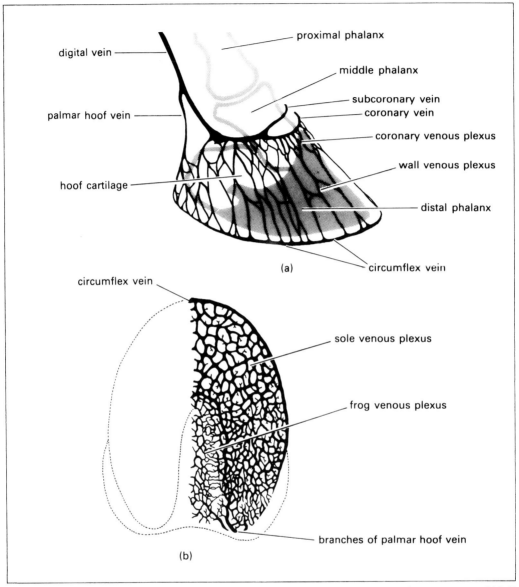

Fig. 2.31 Superficial veins of the foot: (a) side view; (b) solar view. (Reproduced by permission of M.C. Mishra and D.H. Leach)

The veins of the hind leg are similar to those of the front leg.

Valves are present mainly in three areas: the tributaries of the coronary and subcoronary veins, the palmar hoof vein and its tributaries, and in the digital vein.

Most of the veins of the foot are valveless since weight bearing is used for effective venous return from the digit. When the foot takes weight the blood pressure in the veins is raised and they empty. When the foot is raised the pressure is reduced and the veins fill.

The extensive venous network in the foot probably provides a hydraulic network which helps absorb and distribute concussion.

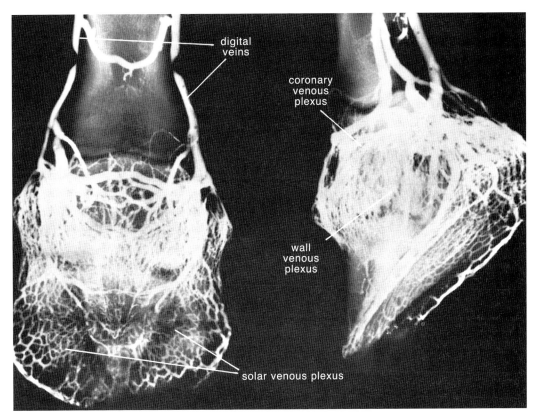

digital
veins

coronary
venous
plexus

wall
venous
plexus

solar venous plexus

Fig. 2.32 Venogram of the horse's foot.

2.6 Nerves

The nervous system coordinates the various parts of the body. It has two parts: the central nervous system (CNS) and the peripheral nervous system.

The CNS consists of the brain and spinal cord.

The peripheral nervous system consists of the nerves. Nerves are bundles of fibres, each of which conducts electrical impulses to or from the CNS.

Sensory nerve fibres conduct impulses to the CNS in response to stimulation of nerve endings. Different nerve endings are sensitive to different stimuli such as heat, cold, pressure and pain.

Motor nerve fibres conduct impulses from the CNS to muscles causing them to contract and to move the limbs.

Some nerves are mixed nerves containing both sensory and motor fibres. Nerves in the leg contain mostly sensory fibres. This is only to be expected as there is virtually no muscle in the leg.

Nerves of the front leg and foot

The *medial palmar nerve* (Fig. 2.33), which is a continuation of the median nerve, passes down the metacarpus on the medial aspect of the superficial digital flexor tendon, with the palmar common digital artery. Towards the middle of the metacarpus it gives off a communicating branch which passes obliquely down over the flexor tendons to join the lateral palmar nerve. At the fetlock joint the medial palmar nerve is called the *medial digital nerve* and divides into two branches:

(i) The *dorsal branch of the digital nerve* passes dorsally and divides into two branches which spread out into the corium of the foot, innervating the extensor process and the coronet at the toe and the dorsal aspect of the distal interphalangeal joint.

(ii) The *palmar branch of the digital nerve* descends along the edge of the flexor tendons and supplies the distal phalanx, distal sesamoid bone, digital cushion and corium of the sole.

The *lateral palmar nerve* is formed by the combining of the terminal ulnar nerve with a terminal branch of the median. It descends down the metacarpus along the lateral border of the deep digital flexor tendon behind the lateral metacarpal vein. Just above the button of the fourth metacarpal bone it is joined by the communicating branch from the medial palmar nerve. At the fetlock joint the nerve is called the *lateral digital nerve* and divides in an identical manner to the medial digital nerve.

Nerves of the hind leg and foot

In the hind leg the medial and lateral *plantar nerves* result from the bifurcation of the tibial nerve. They descend in the metatarsal region, one on each side of the deep digital flexor tendon and accompanied by a metatarsal vein. There is a communicating branch as in the front leg. Below the fetlock the nerves are identical to those of the front leg.

The nerve supply to the sensitive structures of the foot originates from the terminal branches of the digital nerves.

Valuable as this nerve supply is in keeping the horse informed of the type of ground over which it is travelling, it is not essential to progression as all the nerves to the foot can be severed without seriously affecting the horse's movement.

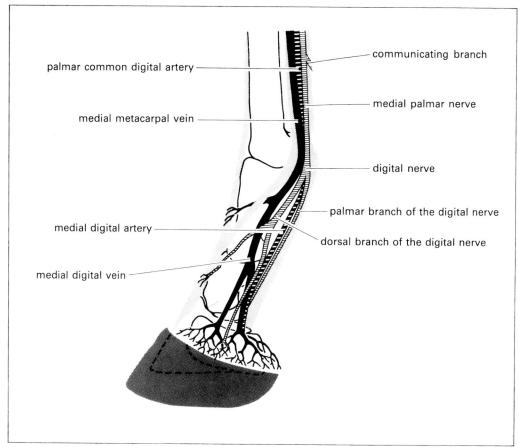

Fig. 2.33 Nerves of the front leg and foot, medial aspect.

palmar common digital artery

medial metacarpal vein

medial digital artery

medial digital vein

communicating branch

medial palmar nerve

digital nerve

palmar branch of the digital nerve

dorsal branch of the digital nerve

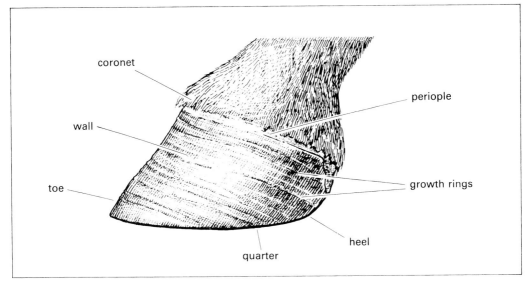

Fig. 2.34 The hoof, side view.

2.7 The hoof

The hoof is the covering of horn at the end of the digit and is a continuation of the outer layer of the skin, the epidermis. It is also known as the insensitive foot, and the structures within it as the sensitive foot. The coronet is the prominent junction between the skin and the hoof.

Epidermis has several layers. The inner layer is the germinative layer, which is attached to the corium and consists of undifferentiated cells which multiply to form the succeeding layers. There are a variable number of these layers as the cells pass through successive stages of keratinisation, a process whereby a cell becomes filled with keratin, a protein. The bulk of the hoof is composed of the outer layer, the horny layer, the cells of which are fully keratinised and are dead.

There are no blood vessels or nerves in the epidermis and the inner living layers obtain nutrients by diffusion from the corium.

The hoof serves the normal functions of epidermis in protecting the underlying sensitive structures from friction, extremes of heat and cold (horn is a poor conductor of heat), dehydration and infection. The specialised functions of weight bearing, reducing concussion and preventing slipping are considered

as a part of the functions of the whole foot at the end of the chapter.

The hoof comprises the wall, bars, white zone, sole and frog.

The wall and bars

The wall is that part of the hoof which is seen when the foot is on the ground. It is cone shaped and for description is divided into toe, quarters and heels, although no natural divisions exist (Fig. 2.34).

The wall does not form a complete circle but is reflected inwards and forwards at an acute angle at the heels to form the bars (Fig. 2.35 a-b). The bars appear on the ground surface of the foot as ridges between the sole and the frog. By not completing the circle of the wall they allow for expansion of the foot. Being part of the wall they take weight and provide extra bearing surface and strength at the heels.

The external surface is convex from side to side and slopes obliquely downwards. The slope is steeper at the quarters and heels than at the toe. The external surface is smooth and crossed by a number of ridges, commonly referred to as growth rings, which run parallel to the coronet and indicate variations in the growth rate of the wall (Fig. 2.34).

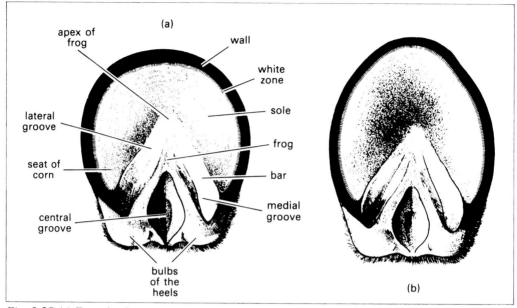

Fig. 2.35 (a) Front hoof, ground surface.

(b) Hind hoof, ground surface. A hind hoof is more pointed at the toe, straighter at the quarters and the sole is more vaulted than in a front hoof.

The proximal or coronary border is hollowed out to form the large coronary groove which lodges the coronary corium and the smaller perioplic groove which lodges the corium of the periople. These grooves merge at the heels.

The internal surface is concave from side to side.

The wall has an outer, middle and inner layer.

The outer layer or periople develops at the coronet as a layer of soft horn, light in colour, which bridges the junction between the skin and the hoof (Fig. 2.34). It is thickest proximally and gradually disintegrates as it moves down with the remainder of the wall, but at the heels it forms a cap which blends with the frog. When the hoof is dry the periople is not obvious, but when the feet are wet it is very conspicuous. It can then be seen that in the lower half of the wall the periople has been completely worn away. Thus its importance in protecting the hoof and reducing evaporation is limited. The main function of the periople is to bridge the junction between the skin and the hoof wall, keeping out dirt and infection.

The middle layer or stratum medium forms the bulk of the wall. It is produced at the coronet and grows distally. It is formed of thousands of hair-like tubules which give rigidity, cemented together by intertubular horn (Fig. 2.36). Each tubule is produced from the germinative cells of the epidermis on a papilla of the coronary corium (Fig. 2.37). These tubules have a multiple spiral structure which gives them strength. The keratinised cells which compose the tubules are arranged in concentric spirals in alternately opposite directions.

The tubules of the innermost area of the stratum medium are larger than the outermost tubules. The average water content of the stratum medium is 25% but it is higher (32% +) in the innermost area than in the outermost area (15%). This makes the inner part of the stratum medium softer and more yielding which reduces the tensile stress on the laminae and distal phalanx on weight bearing.

The intertubular horn is produced by the germinative cells in the areas between papillae. It has a much less specialised structure than tubular horn.

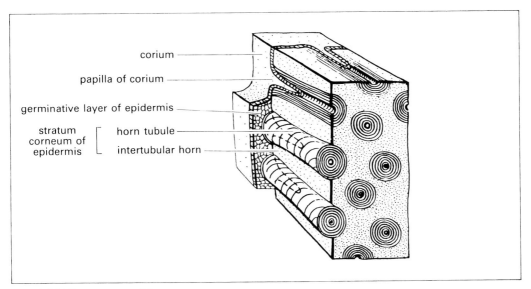

Fig. 2.36 The structure of horn.

The colour of the stratum medium is governed by the colour of the skin at the coronet. If the skin is white it contains no pigment and in consequence the horn below it is white. White horn has the reputation of being weak and brittle but experiments have not confirmed this. It is probable that the presence of pigment confers increased resistance to abrasion.

The inner layer consists of 500 to 600 primary horny laminae which extend from the coronary groove to the bearing surface (Fig. 2.38). Each primary horny lamina bears 100 to 200 secondary horny laminae. These insensitive epidermal laminae dovetail with the sensitive laminae of the corium to establish a very strong union which can support the weight of the horse (Fig. 2.39).

The primary horny laminae are produced at the lower border of the coronary corium. The secondary horny laminae are produced by the germinative layer of the epidermis on the laminar corium.

It is interesting to note that as the horny laminae grow downwards there is a continual movement between them and the fixed sensitive laminae. It has been thought that the horny laminae are able to move over the sensitive laminae by the division of cells in the secondary

horny laminae producing small amounts of horn which enables them to move but keep their attachment. Recent research suggests that the primary horny laminae move over the secondary horny laminae by making and breaking specialised attachments between cells.

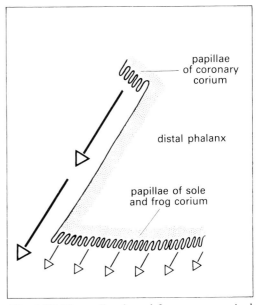

Fig. 2.37 The wall, sole and frog grow as a single functional unit.

47

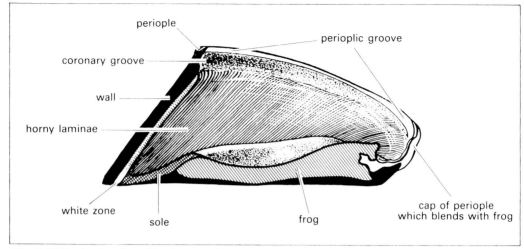

Fig. 2.38 Sagittal section of hoof, internal surface.

The wall is of equal thickness from the proximal to the distal border, but is thicker at the toe than at the heels. The distal border comes into contact with the ground and here its inner surface is united with the outer border of the sole. This union is indicated on the ground surface of the foot by a well-defined white zone.

The white zone

The white zone is the union between the wall and the sole (Fig. 2.35). Between the horny laminae on the internal surface of the wall there is a soft yellowish horn which is produced on papillae on the ends of the sensitive laminae. Thus the white zone consists of both the light-coloured horny laminae and this horn filler.

The white zone is an important anatomical feature and a most helpful guide for the farrier. It indicates the thickness of the wall and the position of the sensitive structures, which together with the slope of the wall enable the farrier to assess the position and angle to drive

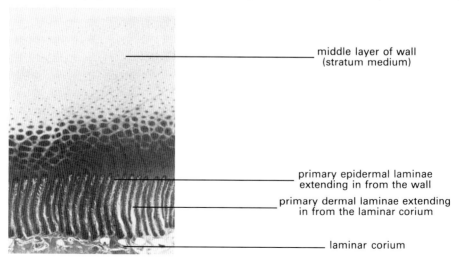

Fig. 2.39 Histological section of the laminae to illustrate the interdigitation of the horny and sensitive laminae.

the nails to prevent pricking or pressing on the sensitive foot.

The sole

The sole constitutes the greater part of the ground surface of the hoof and presents two surfaces and two borders (Fig. 2.35).

The external or ground surface is arched or vaulted. This feature is more pronounced in the hind than in the front feet, but is subject to wide variation in different breeds. The area between the wall and the bars is referred to as the 'seat of corn'.

The internal surface is convex and conforms to the concavity of the sole surface of the distal phalanx (Fig. 2.38). It is covered with numerous minute holes which lodge the papillae of the corium of the sole.

The parietal border is convex and thick and is joined to the wall by the white zone.

The central border consists of a deep notch which is occupied by the bars and frog.

The soles of heavy draught horses are generally flatter than those of riding horses and ponies. The thickness of the sole varies considerably; in some horses they are firm and rigid, whereas in others they are thin and yield to pressure. Growth of the sole differs from that of the wall because it exfoliates or flakes off when it reaches a certain thickness. The sole is softer than the wall probably due to its higher moisture content, which is about 33%.

The frog

The frog is a wedge-shaped mass of soft elastic horn which occupies the angle between the bars and the sole (Fig. 2.35). It is described as having four surfaces, a base and an apex.

The external or ground surface has a shallow central groove into which open the ducts of sweat glands in the digital cushion.

The lateral and medial surfaces are united with the sole and bars above and are free below and form the central borders of the medial and lateral grooves.

The internal surface has a central ridge called the frog stay (Fig. 2.38). On each side of the frog stay the surface is depressed. The whole surface is moulded to the digital cushion and perforated by minute holes which lodge the papillae of the corium.

The base is depressed centrally by the central groove and is prominent on each side forming part of the bulbs of the heels.

The apex is a blunt point which fills the centre of the concave border of the sole. It extends to just in front of the middle of the ground surface of the hoof.

The frog contains more moisture than any other part of the hoof – about 40% – which accounts for its soft pliable state. Like the wall and sole it is composed of tubular and inter-tubular horn.

Excessive growth of the frog is controlled by its being worn away by friction with the ground and by flakes of it separating.

The frog provides protection to the distal interphalangeal joint and the deep digital flexor tendon, plays an important role in the anti-concussion mechanism of the foot and in preventing slipping.

To function satisfactorily the frog must be healthy and normal in size and to attain this it must be free from thrush and contact the ground during weight bearing.

The ergot

The ergot is a small mass of horn at the palmar and plantar surface of the fore and hind fetlock respectively. It is the vestigial equivalent of the metacarpal and metatarsal pad of the dog and cat. The *ligament of the ergot* runs distally from the ergot to the digital cushion.

2.8 The corium

Corium or dermis is the deep layer of mammalian skin. The corium of the foot is a continuation of the dermis of the skin and forms a continuous layer over the entire foot. It contains blood vessels and nerves and provides nutrition to the hoof as well as attaching it to the deeper structures of the foot. It is divided into five regions: the perioplic and coronary corium, the laminar corium and the corium of the sole and frog (Figs. 2.40–2.41).

The *perioplic corium* is situated immediately above the coronary corium and lies in the perioplic groove. It possesses fine papillae which supply nutrition to the periople and on which the horn tubules of the periople develop from the germinative layer of the epidermis.

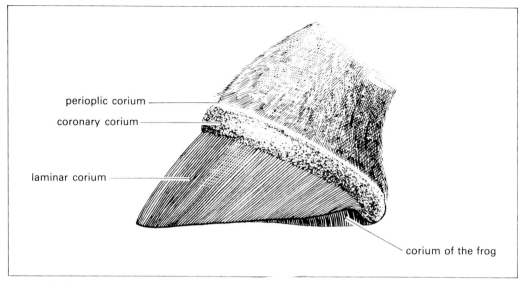

Fig. **2.40** *Hoof removed to show the sensitive foot, side view.*

The *coronary corium* is the thick part of the corium situated above the sensitive laminae and lying in the coronary groove. Its surface is covered with long papillae which supply nutrition to the wall and on which the horn tubules of the wall develop from the germinative layer of the epidermis (Fig. 2.42). The primary horny laminae develop at the lower border of the coronary corium.

The *laminar corium*, which bears the primary and secondary sensitive laminae, extends from the coronary corium to the solar border of the distal phalanx. It is attached on its deep surface to the periosteum on the parietal surface of the bone and to the lower part of the cartilages. The sensitive laminae dovetail with the horny laminae of the wall to which they supply nutrition (Fig. 2.39). The laminae at the toe

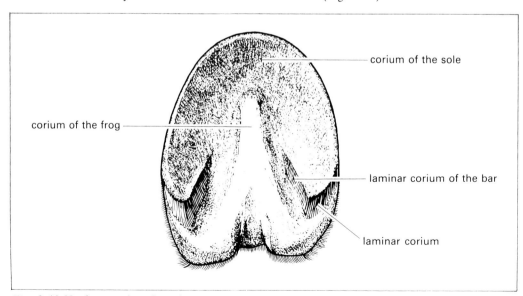

Fig. **2.41** *Hoof removed to show the corium, palmar view.*

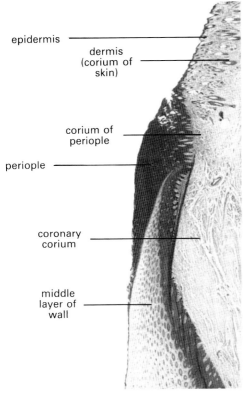

epidermis

dermis
(corium of
skin)

corium of
periople

periople

coronary
corium

middle
layer of
wall

Fig. 2.42 Histological cross-section of the coronet.

are longer than those of the heels, where they turn inwards to form the sensitive laminae of the bars.

It is interesting to note that the weight of the horse is supported by the union of the horny and sensitive laminae. At stages of the gallop, for example, when the horse is supported by one limb only, its whole weight is taken by the dovetailing of these delicate structures. In relation to body size the horse's foot is small but due to the interleaving of 500 to 600 primary laminae and about 72,000 secondary laminae it encloses an area of approximately 8 square feet (0.74 square metres), thus keeping the functional surfaces of the internal foot within small proportions without affecting its strength.

The *corium of the sole* corresponds in shape to the horny sole. It is firmly adherent to the periosteum of the solar surface of the distal phalanx and on its free surface has long papillae which supply nutrition to the sole and on which the tubules of the horny sole develop (Fig. 2.43).

The *corium of the frog* supplies nutrition to the epidermis of the frog. It has long papillae. It is related above to the digital cushion (Fig. 2.44).

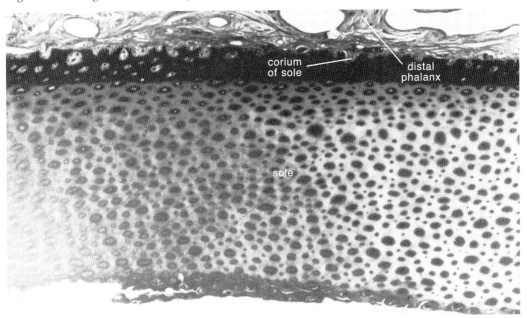

corium
of sole

distal
phalanx

sole

Fig. 2.43 Histological cross-section of the sole.

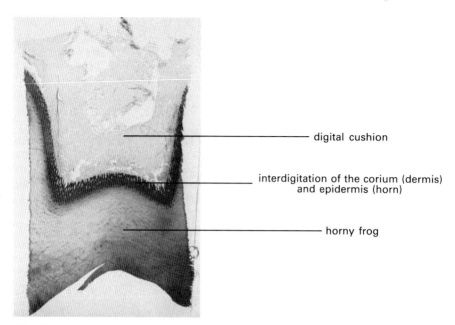

digital cushion

interdigitation of the corium (dermis)
and epidermis (horn)

horny frog

Fig. 2.44 Histological cross-section of the frog.

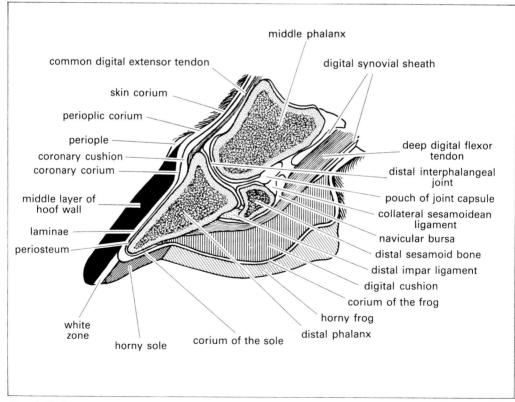

middle phalanx

common digital extensor tendon

digital synovial sheath

skin corium

perioplic corium

periople

coronary cushion

coronary corium

deep digital flexor
tendon

distal interphalangeal
joint

middle layer of
hoof wall

pouch of joint capsule

collateral sesamoidean
ligament

laminae

navicular bursa

periosteum

distal sesamoid bone

distal impar ligament

digital cushion

corium of the frog

horny frog

white
zone

horny sole

corium of the sole

distal phalanx

Fig. 2.45 Sagittal section of the foot.

2.9 The digital cushion

The digital cushion is a wedge-shaped fibro-elastic pad occupying the back part of the foot and filling in the hollow of the heels (Fig. 2.45). It is firm yet yielding and possesses four surfaces, a base and an apex.

The dorsal surface is applied to the deep digital flexor tendon. The palmar surface is moulded on to the corium of the frog. The lateral and medial surfaces are related to the cartilages. The apex lies distally and is adherent to the deep digital flexor tendon at its insertion. The base lies under the skin and is divided by a depression into two rounded masses forming part of the bulbs of the heels. Sweat glands are present within the digital cushion whose ducts open into the central groove of the frog.

The digital cushion plays an important role in reducing concussion.

2.10 The physiology of the foot

The foot is a specialised structure which supports weight, limits concussion and prevents slipping.

Changes in the shape of the hoof
When weight is taken on to a normal hoof the following changes take place. They are most pronounced at the moment of maximum dorsal flexion of the fetlock joint:

1) The heels move outwards (expand) both at the proximal and distal border. Average expansion for each heel is about $\frac{1}{60}$ in. (0.4 mm) at the walk, $\frac{1}{50}$ in. (0.5 mm) at the trot and $\frac{1}{40}$ in. (0.6 mm) at the canter. Expansion is less when the frog does not come into contact with the ground. Indeed, if a frog is so small that it does not come into contact with the ground, then when weight is taken it is pressed downwards by the phalanges. This results in the cartilages being drawn inwards which will contribute to the development of a contracted foot.

2) At the toe the proximal border sinks (contracts) (Fig. 2.46). Average contraction is about $\frac{1}{50}$ in. (0.5 mm).

3) The sole sinks, especially in the centre. Average descent is about $\frac{1}{125}$ in. (0.2 mm),

more in flat feet (up to $\frac{1}{25}$ in. or 1 mm).

4) The height of the hoof is reduced.

5) The distal phalanx sinks and rotates backwards slightly corresponding with the changes in the hoof.

Weight-bearing mechanism
Weight is transmitted through the foot to the bones of the limb. Most of the weight passes from the ground to the hoof wall and through the laminae to the distal phalanx. The distal phalanx is in effect suspended from the hoof wall by the laminae.

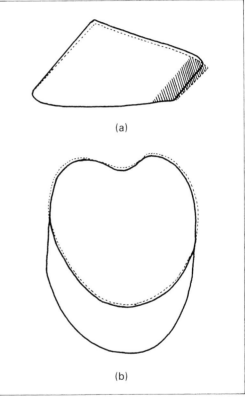

(a)

(b)

Fig. 2.46 Diagram to show the area over which the wall expands, the retraction of the anterior coronary edge of the hoof and the sinking of the heels (Lungwitz). (a) The unbroken line indicates the shape of the foot; the dotted line illustrates the retraction of the coronary edge in front and sinking of the heels. The shaded part illustrates the area which expands. (b) The dotted line shows the change in shape the hoof undergoes under the influence of the weight of the body.

The function of the sole is to protect the sensitive structures above it, to support weight and to bear weight around its parietal border. It will be noted that the sole is less dense and friction-resistant than the waall. The vaulting of the sole is clear evidence to show that it is not intended to bear weight except at its parietal border.

Anti-concussion mechanism

The effects of concussion are minimised by the structure of the limbs and the movements of the foot when it comes to the ground and as the weight of the horse passes over it. When examining the part played by the foot in reducing the concussion of weight bearing, it must be considered as a whole because its various structures are interdependent. The importance of the anti-concussion mechanism

of the foot is readily appreciated when it is realised that a little more than one quarter of a horse's weight is supported by each front limb when it is standing, and at certain stages of the gallop the whole of its weight is supported by one foot.

The foot is protected from concussion by the yielding articulation of the distal interphalangeal joint, the slight descent of the distal phalanx and the sole, the elasticity of the frog and digital cushion, the flexibility of the cartilages and the expansion of the wall at the heels.

When the foot comes to the ground the weight is taken by the wall and frog (Fig. 2.47). The frog is compressed and expands, more especially if it is well developed and the horse has low heels. This results in pressure on the digital cushion and the bars and these in turn press on the cartilages which yield and press

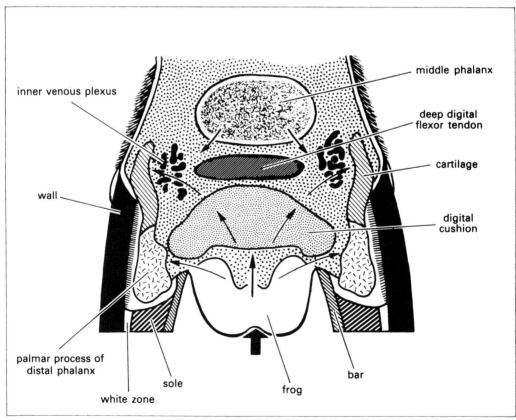

Fig. 2.47 Frontal section of the foot. When the foot takes weight the frog is compressed. This results in pressure on the bars and digital cushion. These in turn press on the cartilages which yield and is followed by expansion of the foot at the heels.

apart the wall at the heels. When weight is taken off the foot, the frog and digital cushion contract and the cartilages and the wall return to their resting positions.

The intermittent pressure which causes expansion also assists circulation of the blood within the foot, aiding venous return and possibly also assisting arterial circulation to the laminar corium. The extensive venous plexuses of the hoof probably act as a hydraulic shock absorber.

Anti-slipping mechanism

The sole is concave and, like a saucer, due to its concavity and rim, it grips firmly when pressed into the ground.

The frog, which is wedge-shaped, with a groove running down its centre and each side, digs into the ground.

The combination of a saucer-shaped sole and a wedge-shaped frog assists the horse to maintain its balance and prevents slipping when it turns, stops or accelerates sharply.

CHAPTER 3

THE HORSESHOE AND HORSESHOE NAILS

3.1 The horseshoe

Materials for making horseshoes

Horseshoes have been made from a variety of materials which include rubber, vulcanite, plastic, brass and copper but wrought iron and mild steel are the most suitable.

Wrought iron is almost pure iron containing approximately 0.04% of carbon. When heated it is easily worked and can be easily fire welded. It has a characteristic fibrous appearance.

Steel is an alloy of iron and carbon. Mild steel is low carbon steel and contains 0.2 to 0.3% of carbon. When mild steel is heated it becomes ductile and malleable and if rapidly cooled it is rendered extra hard and brittle. It can be fire welded but not as easily as wrought iron. Shoes made from mild steel have been reputed to wear very smooth and break easily. These disadvantages are not borne out in practice.

Mild steel becomes harder to forge as it cools than wrought iron which is soft enough to be worked at a black heat. However, mild steel is of a more consistent quality than wrought iron, is cheaper, easier to machine and is now universally used, wrought iron being no longer manufactured.

Flat mild steel bar and concave fullered mild steel bar are the two materials in general use for making horseshoes.

Aluminium alloys, which are about one third of the density of iron and steel, are used when a light shoe is required that will not be subjected to a lot of wear, such as for race-horses and show ponies.

Appendix 1 gives cross-sections and sizes of commonly available forms of steel bar.

The design of horseshoes

The type of shoe fitted varies according to the horse and the work it is expected to perform, but a number of basic design features are common to all shoes (Fig. 3.1).

A horseshoe, like a hoof, is described as having a toe, quarters and heels.

From toe to heel on each side is called a branch.

The whole substance of the shoe, that is the width and thickness of the metal, is referred to as the web.

The width of the web is called the cover. Thus a shoe with a wide web is said to have plenty of cover.

Two front or hind shoes make a pair. A pair of each makes a set.

A remove is a shoe which has been taken off and put back on again. A refit is a shoe which has been removed, refitted and put back on again.

A shoe has two surfaces and two edges. The foot surface of the shoe is in contact with the hoof. The ground surface of the shoe is in contact with the ground. There is an inner edge and an outer edge.

The *width* of the web is related to the natural bearing surface of the foot and should cover the wall, white zone and outer border of the sole. The average cover of a shoe is about twice the thickness of the wall but it should be a little wider at the toe where wear is greatest and a little narrower at the heels so as not to impinge on the frog. A shoe which is too wide predisposes to grit and stones lodging under it, is more likely to be sucked off in mud, and when worn is conducive to slipping.

The *thickness* of the shoe is related to its size.

If too thick the shoe raises the foot too far from the ground which reduces normal frog pressure. In addition excessively large nails are required, which split the hoof.

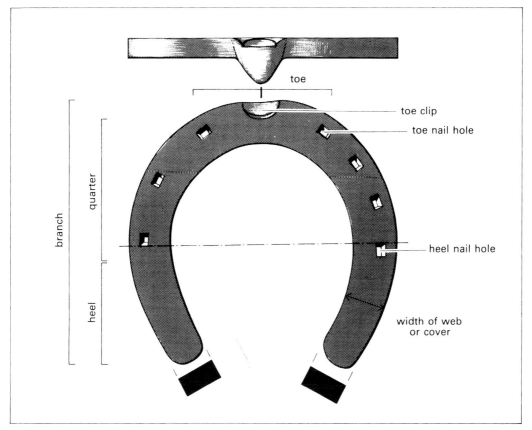

Fig. 3.1 Front shoe, plain stamped, ground surface. Note the traditional pattern of the nail holes; in each branch three nail holes are in front of an imaginary line which divides the shoe into two a little below the midline. In the outside branch is a fourth nail hole just behind this line.

Shoes should normally be of uniform thickness to preserve the balance of the foot. If the toe is too thick it puts strain on the flexor tendons and is conducive to stumbling. If the heels are too thick the frog is raised too far from the ground.

The *foot surface* of the shoe contacts and supports the hoof. There are several varieties:

A *flat foot surface* (Fig. 3.2) provides a firm base for the foot to rest on and is suitable for all normal feet.

A *seated-out foot surface* (Fig. 3.3) has the inner foot surface sloped to relieve pressure on the sole. Seated-out shoes are used for horses with flat and dropped soles and for brittle hooves where the wall is broken away at its distal border leaving the sole prominent.

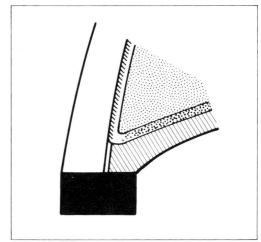

Fig. 3.2 Cross section of a shoe with a flat foot surface.

Seated-out shoes have the disadvantage that grit and stones accumulate under them and in heavy going are liable to be sucked off.

A *foot surface sloped inwards* (Fig. 3.4) has the same advantages as a seated-out foot surface in relieving pressure on the sole and may also be useful in the correction of a flaring hoof. However, it is likely to lead to contraction of the foot. With concave fullered shoes it is easier to slope the foot surface inwards than to seat it out deeply.

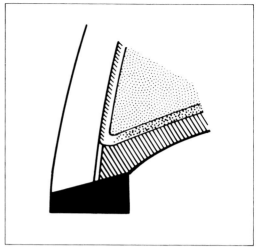

Fig. *3.5* *Cross-section of a shoe with the foot surface sloped outwards.*

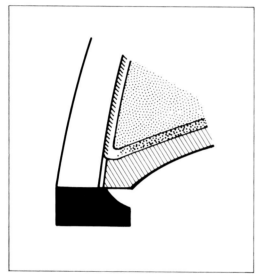

Fig. *3.3* *Cross-section of a seated-out shoe.*

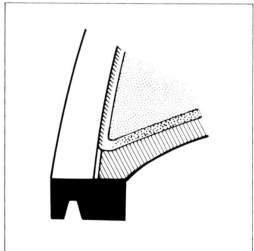

Fig. *3.6* *Cross-section of a fullered shoe.*

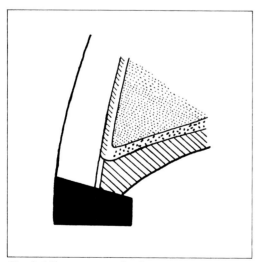

Fig. *3.4* *Cross-section of a shoe with the foot surface sloped inwards.*

A *foot surface sloped outwards* (Fig. 3.5) was introduced to prevent contraction of the foot by contributing to expansion. In practice this is not attained and it predisposes to lameness.

The *ground surface* of the shoe has to be considered in relation to the foothold it provides, its wearing properties and its support for the nails.

A *plain stamped shoe* (Fig. 3.2) has a flat ground surface which is broken only by the nail holes and wears well.

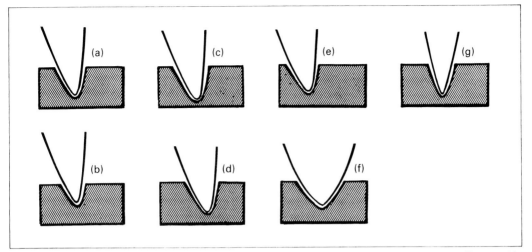

Fig. 3.7 Fullering: (a) correct; (b) too shallow; (c) too deep; (d) too coarse; (e) too fine; (f) too wide; (g) too narrow.

A *fullered shoe* (Fig. 3.6) has a groove round the ground surface. This improves the foothold and helps to prevent slipping, but does not wear as well as a plain foot surface. As the nail holes are usually stamped in the fullering the nail heads are supported only on two sides, but this has the advantage that the exactness of their fit can be seen and their removal is easier.

Fullering can be put in a shoe by hand with a fullering iron but in most cases fullered shoes are made either from concave fullered bar or are machine made. Fullering is said to be complete when it extends around the shoe from toe to heel, or incomplete when it is confined to the region of the nail holes leaving the toe and heel plain. When close to the outer edge of the shoe it is called fine fullering and when further from the outer edge it is called coarse fullering (Fig. 3.7).

A *concave shoe* (Fig. 3.8) has the inner ground surface sloped to conform with the natural concavity of the sole. This makes it lighter than a plain stamped shoe with the same cover and thickness, gives a better foothold and reduces

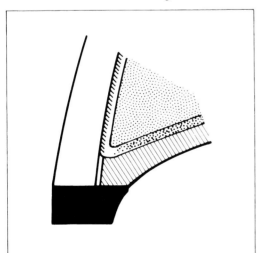

Fig. 3.8 Cross-section of a concave shoe.

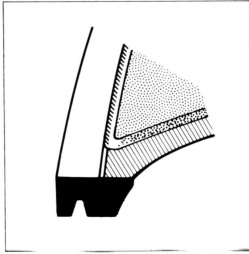

Fig. 3.9 Cross-section of a concave fullered shoe.

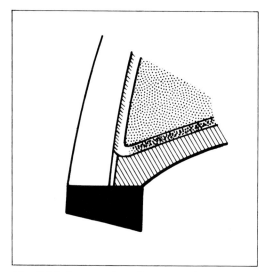

Fig. **3.10** *Cross-section of a convex shoe.*

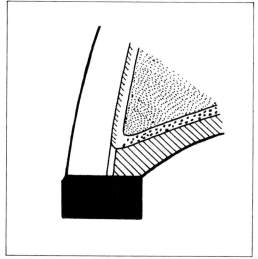

Fig. **3.12** *Cross-section of a boxed-off shoe.*

suction in heavy going, though it will tend to wear out faster.

A *concave fullered shoe* (Fig. 3.9) combines the advantages of concaving and fullering and is the most popular general-purpose shoe in the United Kingdom for all except draught horses.

A *convex shoe* (Fig. 3.10) has the inner edge thicker than the outer edge by as much as ¼ in. (6 mm) so that the ground surface slopes inwards. This shoe is for horses which wear

out their shoes quickly. The inner edge is worn first and saves the outer edge and the nail heads for later wear. Convex shoes are little used these days.

The *outer edge* of the shoe is normally upright.

A *bevelled shoe* (Fig. 3.11) has the outer edge sloped to conform to the slope of the wall of the hoof, making the foot appear larger.

Boxing off or *semi-bevelling* (Fig. 3.12) is where the upper part of the outer edge is sloped to take away the sharpness of the rim. All shoes should be boxed off to a small degree. Boxing off may be exaggerated when the shoe is fitted full.

The *weight* of the shoe is important and generally the lighter the shoe the better but obviously it must be related to wear.

The extent to which heavy shoes can tire a horse is all too frequently overlooked. The shoes for a heavy draught horse weigh about 5 lbs (2.25 kg), and therefore, if a horse takes thirty strides per minute it has to make the necessary effort to raise 150 lbs (67.5 kg) for each leg, a total of 600 lbs (270 kg) for all four legs. At the end of an average day's work of four hours at the walk this comes to over 60 tons (60 tonnes). When it is realised that this extra weight of shoe is at the end of a long arm lever, it is easier to appreciate the expendi-

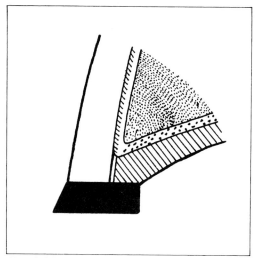

Fig. **3.11** *Cross-section of a bevelled shoe.*

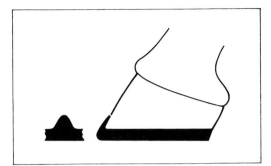

Fig. 3.13 Toe clip correctly angulated, low and broad.

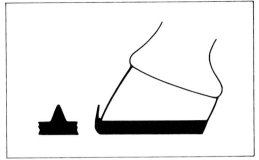

Fig. 3.14 Toe clip incorrectly drawn, too upright, narrow and pointed.

ture of effort necessary for a horse to perform a day's work and the contribution made by heavy shoes to the stresses on the limbs and to fatigue.

There can be a number of features of horseshoes additional to the basic design such as clips, calkins, etc.

Clips

A clip is a thin triangular projection drawn from the outer edge of a shoe at the toe, quarter or heel.

A good clip should be broad and low, not exceeding in height double the thickness of the shoe, and should have the same slope as the wall, against which it accurately rests (Fig. 3.13). A narrow pointed clip does not give adequate support and should the shoe become loose it may be trodden on and puncture the sole (Fig. 3.14). Care must be taken when drawing a clip that the foot surface behind it is kept smooth and level. With concave fullered bar a clip should be equal in width at the base and in height to the thickness of the bar.

The surface of a clip is flat and, therefore, for a clip to be accurately fitted it may be necessary to reduce the curvature of the wall slightly with a stroke of the rasp. If fitting hot the clip can be allowed to bed itself (but not bury itself) into the wall. The removal of a piece of the wall for the reception of a clip (Fig. 3.15), or drawing a clip vertical and hammering it into position after the shoe has been nailed on (Fig. 3.16), are undesirable practices which can injure the hoof.

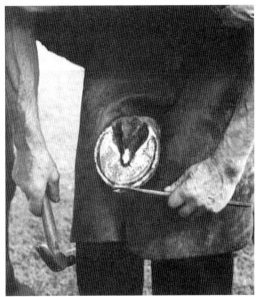

Fig. 3.15 The removal of a piece of wall for the reception of a clip is an undesirable practice.

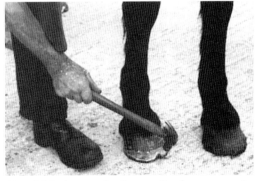

Fig. 3.16 A correctly drawn clip does not require to be hammered into position.

61

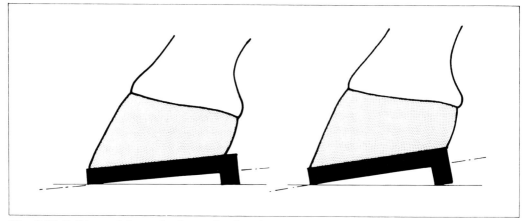

Fig. **3.17** *Calkins unbalance the foot and reduce frog pressure. The higher the calkins and the further forwards they are placed the more serious the effects.*

If a single toe clip is drawn it is placed at the centre of the toe, but when two clips are drawn they are placed one on each toe quarter between the first and second nail holes.

Clips resist shearing forces on the shoe and thus support the nails. Clips also aid in fitting a shoe, as once bedded into the hoof they provide a fixed point from which the branches of the shoe can be shaped to fit the outline of the hoof. Clips also help to steady the shoe while the nails are driven.

For riding horses a single toe clip is traditional for front shoes and two quarter clips for hind shoes. The quarter clips on the hind shoes enable the toe of the shoe to be set back a little to reduce the danger of injury from over-reaching, and they give the shoe more resistance to being displaced sideways than a single toe clip would do. Many horses wear

the toes of their hind feet so heavily that a toe clip soon wears away.

Heel clips are sometimes used on surgical shoes.

Calkins

A calkin is a projection formed by either turning down or welding a piece of steel to the heel of a shoe. Calkins provide a good foothold on soft ground and country roads and assist draught horses to back and hold back loads, but are of little advantage on modern roads.

Calkins, by raising the heels, reduce frog pressure and unbalance the foot. The higher

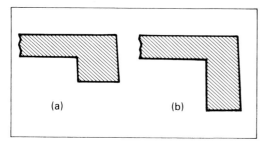

Fig. **3.18** *(a) A good calkin – low, broad and square, set at right angles and not more than twice the thickness of the shoe; (b) a poor calkin – too high and too narrow.*

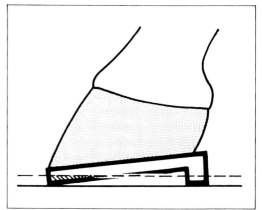

Fig. **3.19** *Calkins result in excessive wear at the toe. The dotted line illustrates that a lot of steel is wasted because the toe is worn through before the shoe is worn out.*

the calkins or the nearer the toe the calkins are placed the more serious the effects (Fig. 3.17). Calkins should be low, broad and square, set at right angles, not more than twice the thickness of the shoe and the same height at each heel (Fig. 3.18 a-b).

Inevitably calkins result in excessive wear at the toe which is worn through before the shoe is worn thin, thus wasting a lot of steel (Fig. 3.19). To counter this the toe can be made thicker, but unless the branches are made correspondingly thinner it only increases the weight of the shoe. The maximum wear of a shoe with calkins is obtained by rolling the toe, thus bringing more of the branches into wear, but it makes the preparation of the hoof and fitting the shoe more difficult.

It is not customary to fit calkins on front shoes, but when they are used, on draught horses for example, it is in conjunction with a toe piece to preserve the balance of the foot. Riding horses shod behind with calkins should have the inside calkin replaced by a wedge heel to prevent brushing injuries.

Care must be taken to ensure that the calkin and wedge heel are equal in height and that the calkin is not too high, as it tends to catch and twist the foot.

Toe pieces

A toe piece is a rod of mild steel welded across the toe of a shoe (Fig. 3.20). To make a toe piece, the length required is cut half through but not detached. Next, the toe piece to be and the toe of the shoe are brought to a white heat. The toe piece is placed in position across and a little behind the toe, welded with a few light blows and broken off. A more reliable method for welding on a toe piece is to use an electric welder.

In some areas it is customary for draught horses to be shod with a toe piece and calkins. The toe piece not only provides a firm foothold to start loads but also remedies the unnatural balance of the foot caused by the calkins. In addition as the wear of the branches between the toe and the heels is reduced a lighter shoe can be fitted.

Wedge heels

Wedge heels designed to raise the angle of the hoof can be gradual increases in thickness as in a navicular shoe, or more sloping wedges as in a spavin shoe. Wedge heels designed to give grip are more pointed projections as in the calk and wedge heels used for hunting.

Rolled toes

A rolled toe is where the web is turned up at the toe to ease breakover and prolong the wear of the shoe (Fig. 3.21).

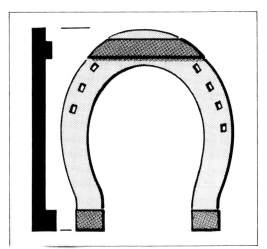

Fig. **3.20** *Draught horse shoe with toe piece and calkins.*

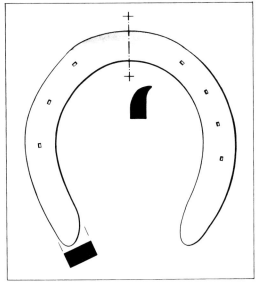

Fig. **3.21** *Rolled toe shoe. Half the width of the web is turned up at the toe.*

Set toes

A set toe is similar to a rolled toe but the web is turned up sharply and in profile forms a sharp angle rather than a curve (Fig. 3.22).

Bars

A bar joins a shoe across the heels (Fig. 3.23) and can be designed either to press on the frog, thus taking weight from the hoof wall at the heels, or to clear the frog, thus relieving it completely of weight bearing.

The back edge of the ground surface of the bar can be sloped to reduce concussion when the heels come to the ground and to reduce the chance of it being struck by a hind shoe and pulled off.

Continuous pressure as from the bar of a shoe is abnormal and in time results in atrophy of the frog. Thus the commonly accepted view that the bar shoe stimulates growth of an atrophied frog is erroneous. The usefulness of a bar shoe is in taking weight off areas of the wall by transferring it to the frog or to the opposite heel. A bar can also help to protect the bulbs of the heel from bruising. For these reasons a bar shoe is suitable for treating weak heels and corns, but it must not be overlooked that there is a limit to the continuous pressure which the horny frog can sustain without pain and injury to the sensitive foot.

A bar shoe has a number of disadvantages. It is heavier than an ordinary shoe and therefore requires more nails to secure it, provides a poorer foothold and makes it difficult to pick out the clefts of the frog thus encouraging the development of thrush.

Stud holes

Holes are punched or drilled in shoes to take drive-in studs or plugs. If tapped they can take screw-in studs (Fig. 9.6) or in special circumstances they may take bolts to secure a plate or bar.

Hard surfacing

A layer of weld may be applied to a shoe to increase wear, or borium (tungsten carbide crystals in a mild steel flux) may be applied to increase both wear and foothold (Fig. 3.24).

3.2 Nail holes

The *size and shape* of a nail hole should be an exact counterpart of the head and neck of the nail though a little smaller to allow the head to project slightly when the nail is driven home.

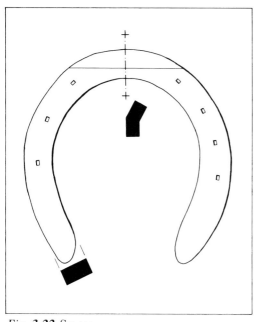

Fig. 3.22 Set toe.

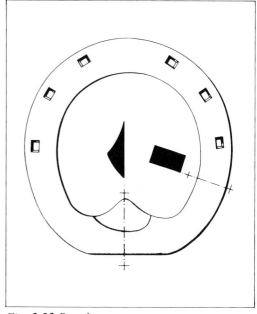

Fig. 3.23 Bar shoe.

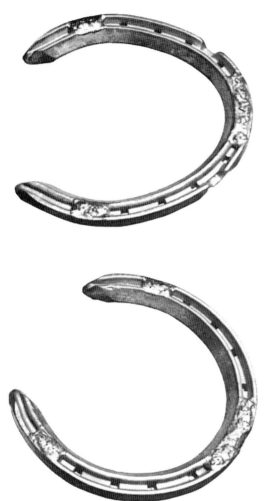

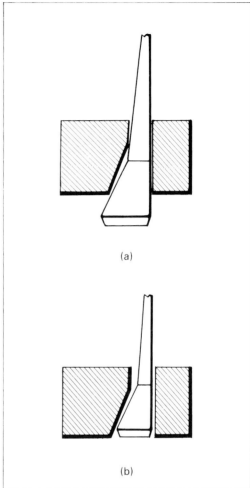

(a)

(b)

Fig. 3.24 Shoe treated with horseshoe borium. (Photograph supplied by Adgrip, Plympton, Devon)

Fig. 3.25 (a) Nail hole too small. The nail head projects excessively and quickly wears away, leaving too little head to carry the nail. (b) Nail hole too large. Nail head has no hold which results in slack and a loose shoe.

If the nail hole is too small the nail head will project excessively and wear away leaving too little to secure the shoe (Fig. 3.25a). If the nail hole is too large then slackness occurs as driving and clenching the nail tightly is difficult (Fig. 3.25b).

Sometimes, by back pritchelling, the neck of the nail hole is made a little larger than that of the nail. This enables the pitch of the nail to be varied when driven. Seemingly this is an advantage but slackness occurs below the head of the nail which results in the shoe becoming loose before it has worn thin (Fig. 3.26a). On the other hand, if the neck of the nail hole is on the small side, it may be assumed that a really secure fit will be obtained when the nail is driven home. This is not the case as the shoe strips or pinches the neck of the nail, which breaks (Fig. 3.26b).

A nail hole stamped in a fullered shoe supports the head of the nail on two sides, but in a plain stamped shoe the head is supported on all four sides and, given a good fit, the nail is immovable.

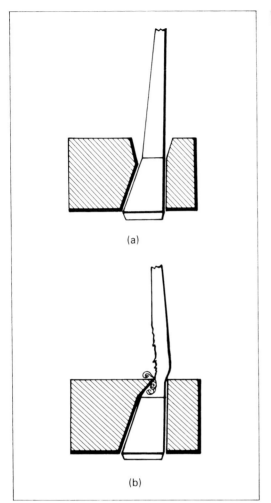

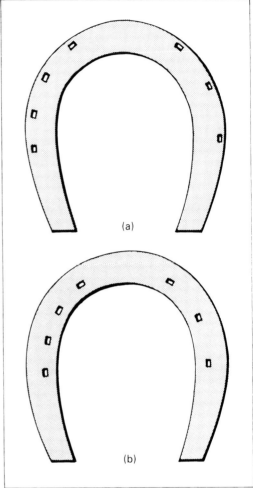

Fig. 3.26 Back pritchelling: (a) excessive – neck of nail hole too large which gives no support and results in nail slack; (b) insufficient – leaves a sharp rim which either strips or pinches in the neck of the nail and results in it breaking.

Fig. 3.27 (a) Fine nail holes. (b) Coarse nail holes.

The *position and angulation* of a nail hole determines the course taken by the nail as it passes through the hoof. A nail hole near the outer edge of a shoe is called fine, and away from the outer edge is called coarse (Fig. 3.27 a-b). A nail driven through a fine nail hole may split the horn and has to be driven excessively high to obtain a good hold, whereas through a coarse nail hole it goes close to the sensitive foot and may lead to a nail bind or a prick. Nail holes require to be fine when a shoe is

fitted close and coarse when it is fitted full. The angulation of a nail hole is referred to as its pitch. The holes at the toe are pitched to conform with the slope of the wall whereas those towards the heel are more upright (Fig. 3.28 a-c). Nail holes pitched too upright or outwards (Fig. 3.28d) are unsatisfactory as the nail obtains very little hold.

Nail holes should be evenly spaced ¾–1¼ ins (2–3 cm) apart, and distributed in the front half of front shoes and the front two thirds of hind shoes.

The position of nail holes in practice will depend upon the condition of the hoof to which the shoe is to be nailed and can vary

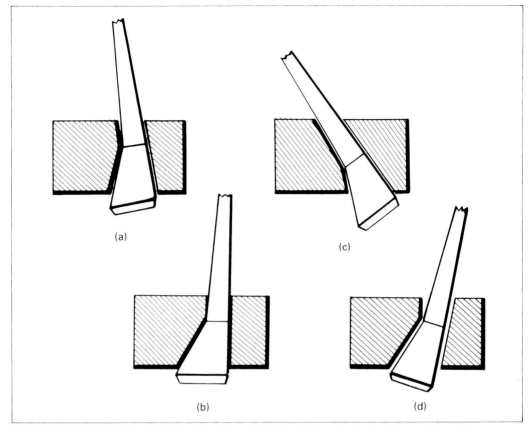

(a)

(c)

(b)

(d)

Fig. 3.28 Nail holes: (a) slightly angulated or pitched nail hole suitable for the toe; (b) upright nail hole suitable for quarters and heels; (c) excessively pitched nail hole which may lead to a pricked foot; (d) outwardly pitched nail hole, unsatisfactory, provides little hold.

from the conventional pattern if hoof defects are present.

The *number* of nail holes is traditionally seven. A front shoe with seven nail holes has three stamped in the inner and four in the outer branch. In each branch three holes are stamped in front of an imaginary transverse line dividing the shoe into equal parts. The heel nail hole in the outer branch is placed just behind this line and in consequence the four nail holes in the outer branch are spaced closer together than the three in the inner branch (Fig. 3.1).

It is common practice to punch five nail holes in small shoes, six or seven in medium-sized shoes and seven or eight in heavy draught horse shoes and racing plates. It is a good idea to punch more nail holes than will actually be used to give a choice in positioning the nails. In most cases this will enable the farrier to drive sufficient nails to secure the shoe avoiding weak parts of the wall. The better the position of the nails the fewer will be needed and the less the hoof will be damaged.

3.3 Machine-made horseshoes

Machine-made shoes have regularity of form and a true foot surface with regularly placed nail holes. They save the farrier valuable time by reducing manual labour. A good machine-made shoe is not as good as a good hand-made shoe but because machine-made shoes are of consistent quality they are preferable to all but the most carefully made hand-made shoes.

Shoes are manufactured either by bending a length of bar around a block or are drop stamped by a heavy hammer in a die.

Machine-made shoes are of three basic types: concave fullered, threequarter fullered and plain stamped. These shoes are made in a whole range of styles, weights and sizes and can be supplied with heels cut and rounded and clips drawn (Figs. 3.29 a-b, 3.30 a-b).

The chief disadvantage of machine-made shoes is their nail holes. All are stamped at the same pitch, which tends to be upright, and in the same position in every shoe of the same pattern and size. Upright nail holes make it difficult to drive nails up a sloping hoof. To overcome this defect it may be necessary to

back pritchel the holes with the disadvantages this entails. When making a shoe by hand the nail holes can be stamped in the best position and at the best pitch to suit the particular hoof. However, extra nail holes can always be punched in a machine-made shoe if required.

3.4 Horseshoe nails

Hand-made horseshoe nails are a relic of the past, except for the occasional frost nail. Today machine-made nails are in general use and are more perfect in all respects than the best hand-made nails.

Machine-made nails are smooth and polished and made from the best mild steel.

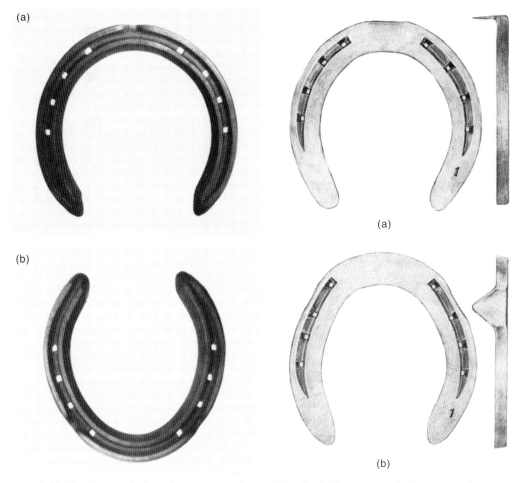

(a)

(b)

(a)

(b)

Fig. 3.29 Machine-made horseshoes, concave fullered: (a) fore; (b) hind.

Fig. 3.30 Machine-made horseshoes, threequarter fullered: (a) fore; (b) hind.

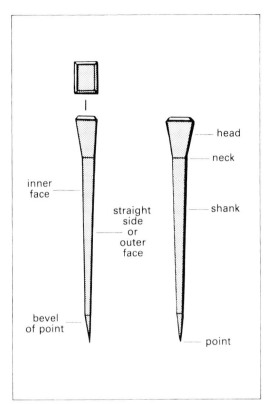

Fig. 3.31 Horseshoe nail, European type.

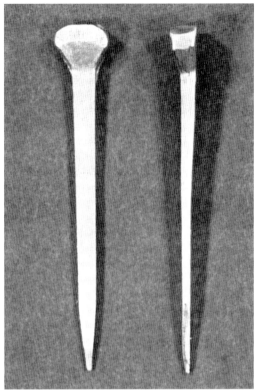

Fig. 3.32 Horseshoe nail, US type.

They are hard enough to be driven through the hoof without buckling but are sufficiently flexible not to snap when the point is turned over, or break when the shoe is subjected to shearing forces.

There are two basic types of horseshoe nail, the European (E) type (Fig. 3.31) which has a long tapering head and is designed for thicker bar stock, and the US type (Fig 3.32) which has a shorter head and is more suited to thin bar stock.

The head, neck, shank and point of a horseshoe nail are all designed to meet its special requirements.

The *head* is wedge-shaped, with the outer surface flat and the inner sloped to the neck. The inner surface of the head is marked to identify the inside of the nail, which must always face the inside when driven. Nail heads of this shape in accurately shaped nail holes will secure a shoe firmly until the shoe has worn out. Nails with flat heads can only secure

a shoe as long as their heads have not worn off.

The *neck* is the junction between the head and the shank.

The *shank* extends from the neck to the point, has two surfaces and is twice as wide as it is thick.

The *point* is bevelled on the inner face. When the nail is driven the bevel forces the point towards the straight side of the shank. Therefore the nail must always be driven with the bevel to the inside so that the point will turn away from the sensitive foot and emerge on the outside of the wall (Fig. 3.33).

The size of E horseshoe nails is denoted by numbers ranging from 2 to 14 (Fig. 3.34). The numbers correspond to the weight in pounds of 1000 nails. For example, 1000 nails of size 6 weigh 6 lbs. Therefore the higher the number the larger the nail. The difference in length between successive sizes is approximately 1/8 in. (3 mm).

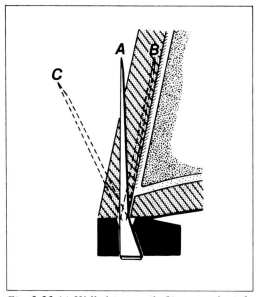

Fig. 3.33 (a) Well-driven nail; (b) too much pitch; (c) pitched outwards.

The size of nail chosen depends largely on the thickness of metal used and thus only indirectly on the size of the horse. Sizes E2 – E4 can be used with up to 3/8 in. (9 mm) thick shoes. Sizes E4 – E6 can be used with shoes of 7/16 in. (11 mm) thickness and sizes E6 – E8 are needed with 1/2 in. (12.5 mm) thickness.

Racing plate nails are of the US pattern and are commonly available in 1 1/2 in. (US 3.5), 1 5/8 in. (US 4) and 1 3/4 in. (US 4.5) sizes with a choice of large (regular or ASM) or small (city) heads.

To secure a shoe with nails can be considered an undesirable practice and in consequence alternative methods have been investigated. Numerous ideas have been tried, ranging from special toe and quarter clips to metal bands. Without exception all these methods have failed to prevent the loss of shoes and the metal bands wear grooves in the hoof. No nail-less shoe has been invented which can be attached so securely to the foot

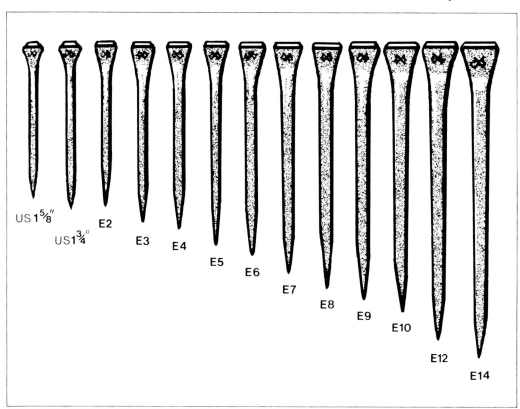

Fig. 3.34 Sizes of Mustad nails (actual size).

either by mechanical means or by adhesives to make it a practical proposition.

For all practical purposes properly driven nails cause no harm to the foot and obtain a more than adequate hold to secure the shoe. Caulton Reeks (1906) records three cases of avulsion of the entire hoof. The horses were engaged in shunting and the heel of a shoe was either caught between two converging rails or trapped by a wagon wheel. The horse sensing its foot trapped made a violent effort to release it and pulled it out from the imprisoned hoof. The effectiveness of correctly driven nails to secure a shoe requires no further support.

CHAPTER 4

STYLES OF HORSESHOEING

4.1 Thoroughbred racing (flat racing, hurdling and steeplechasing)

Racehorses require the lightest shoe possible to protect the foot and provide a good foothold, but it must be strong enough not to twist, bend or break.

For racing, concave fullered shoes made of aluminium alloy are used, called racing plates (Fig. 4.1). The alloy is specially heat treated to give extra hardness without becoming brittle.

For training, slightly heavier and stronger concave fullered shoes made of mild steel are used, called training plates (Fig. 4.2). Some horses racing on the flat may be shod with steel shoes behind and some steeplechasers may race with steel shoes all round.

Racing plates
There are a number of varieties of the basic alloy racing plate:

(i) Some have two grooves and are claimed to give a better foothold.
(ii) Some have a steel strip inserted around the toe to increase their wear (Fig. 4.3).
(iii) Some have a synthetic rim pad bonded to

*Fig. **4.2** Steel training plate.*

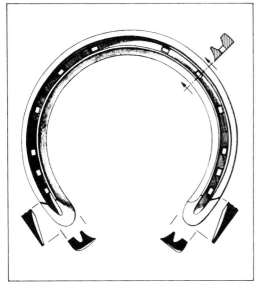

*Fig. **4.1** Racing plate, aluminium alloy, machine made. Front shoe with sloping or 'pencilled' heels.*

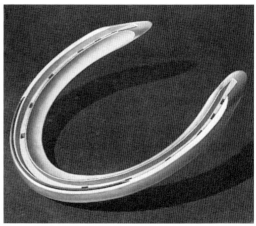

*Fig. **4.3** Steel-inserted racing plate.*

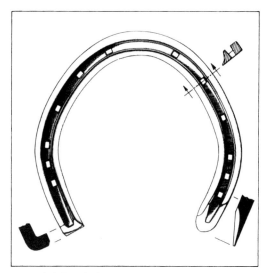

Fig. **4.4** *Hind shoe with a calkin on the outside heel.*

the foot surface with the idea of absorbing concussion.

(iv) Hind shoes are available as either full-sized or threequarter shoes, the latter having a short inside branch to avoid the risk of brushing injuries.

(v) Hind shoes are available with or without calkins at the outside heel (Fig. 4.4).

Racing plates come in a selection of widths of web from ½ in. (12 mm) to ⅞ in. (22 mm).

Racing plates have very sloping or 'pencilled off' heels. Front shoes are fitted close and short to prevent brushing and the shoe being wrenched off. Racing plates are fitted cold. At the time of writing, racing plates are not available with clips.

Front and hind plates are secured with six to eight nails, with the heel nails placed well back to prevent the shoe from spreading or bending.

A set of racing plates weighs from 6–10 oz (170–280 g).

Training plates
Training plates are mild steel concave fullered shoes. Front shoes may have a toe clip and have sloping heels which are fitted close and short. Hind shoes may have a toe clip or two quarter clips and may have a calkin on the outside heel. As for racing plates each is

secured with six to eight nails but the heel nails are not placed quite so far back.

A set of training plates weighs from 12–16 oz (340–450 g).

The size of calkin permitted is governed by the Jockey Club rule no. 149 which relates to shoeing for racing, and states:

> 'No horse shall enter the parade ring or run in shoes which have protrusions on the ground surface other than calkins on the hind, limited to ¼ in. in height. The use of American type toe-grab plates or with a sharp flange is forbidden whether or not modified in any way.'

It should be noted that the term 'protrusion' includes nail heads. Nail heads should be long enough only to hold the shoe and the use of large nail heads to provide extra grip is prohibited. (¼ in. = 6.5 mm)

4.2 Standardbred racing (trotting and pacing)

Trotters and pacers are normally shod with light mild steel shoes. Trotters and pacers race at speeds at which it would be natural to canter or gallop. There is a strong tendency for a trotter to change its gait to a pace and for a pacer to change its gait to a canter. In addition

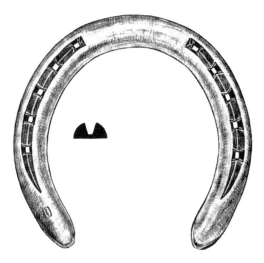

Fig. **4.5** *Trotter shoe of half round section, plain stamped.*

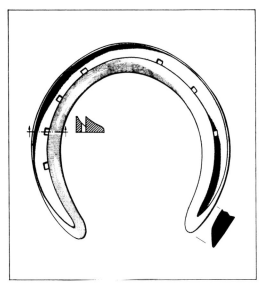

Fig. 4.6 Hunter shoe, hand made and unclipped. Front shoe, concave fullered with sloping heels.

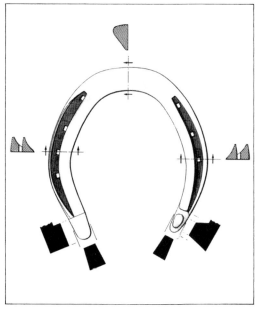

Fig. 4.7 Hunter shoe, hand made and unclipped. Hind shoe, concave fullered with rounded toe and calkin and wedge heels.

both types of horse have a strong tendency to interfere.

Subtle changes in the balance of the feet and in the weight and character of the shoes can have a significant influence over both the tendency to change gait and the tendency to interfere.

Shoes may have a concave, flat or half-round (Fig. 4.5) ground surface and may be plain stamped or fullered.

4.3 Hunters, show jumpers, polo ponies and hacks

Hunters have to jump, gallop and turn at speed. A shoe is required which provides a good foothold and remains secure on heavy going. Concave fullered shoes are most satisfactory.

Front shoes (Fig. 4.6) have a toe clip and the inner branch is sometimes fitted close to prevent brushing injuries. The heels should be a little shorter than the bearing surface, by about ⅛ in. (3 mm) and at the same angle as the heels of the foot to reduce the chance of being struck and wrenched off.

Hind shoes (Fig. 4.7) have the toe squared slightly and two quarter clips. These features allow the toe to be set back to prevent over-reach injuries. The heels are more upright and

fitted a little longer than the foot. It has been fashionable for the shoe to have a wedge heel and calkin. Studs are also popular, especially on the outside branch of the hind shoes. Hunters should be reshod every four weeks because the close fitting does not allow for growth of the hoof which will soon overgrow the shoe, wearing down the heels, becoming unbalanced and causing corns.

Show jumpers have to be able to twist and turn at speed and to pull up sharply. Competitions are held both out of doors and in indoor arenas and horses have to meet the challenge of changes in the siting of obstacles and variations of pace. These problems are met by shoeing show jumpers with concave fullered shoes fitted hunter-style with the heels tapped to take studs. The position of the studs and the types used are very much a matter of personal preference, the going and the performance required of a horse in a particular competition or jump-off.

Polo ponies require a shoe which provides a good foothold for pulling up and turning sharply at the gallop, when it brings its weight back on to its hocks and uses its hind legs as a pivot.

The shoe fitted has to comply with the Hurlingham Polo Club rules as laid down under the section 'Equipment for Ponies' and which states:

'(i) Rimmed shoes are allowed, but the rim may only be on the inside of the shoe.
(ii) Frost nails and screws are not allowed, but a calkin, fixed or movable, is permissible provided this is placed only at the heels of the hind shoes. The fixed or movable calkin shall be limited in size to a ½ in. cube.'

NOTE: The movable calkin is allowed so that when it becomes worn it can be replaced by a fresh one without reshoeing. The essence of this permission is that the movable calkin should resemble, as far as possible, the recognised form of fixed calkin, and does not permit the fixing of any fancy-shaped spike, nor the placing of the calkin anywhere except near the heels of the hind shoes (½ in. = 12.5 mm).

The polo or rimmed shoe (Fig. 4.8) is fashioned in a special tool. The ground surface has a sharp rim round the inside edge which gives an excellent grip on turf. The polo shoe

is rarely used today.

Polo ponies are generally shod with concave fullered shoes fitted hunter-style and with the heels of the hind shoes tapped to take studs.

Hacks are rarely used for more than a few hours each day and do a lot of road work. For this reason they require reasonably heavy shoes. Shoes can be threequarter fullered or concave fullered. Often concave fullered shoes in front and threequarter fullered shoes behind are used.

The shoes are fitted long and full, about $\frac{1}{16}$ in. (1.5 mm) full from quarter to heel and $\frac{1}{8}$ in. (3 mm) long. The heels of the shoes are more upright than for a hunter shoe. A single toe clip in front and two quarter clips behind are usual, the latter enabling the toe of the hind shoe to be set a little under the hoof to prevent over-reaching injuries, ease breakover and prolong the wear of the shoe.

If horses are found to slip on the roads, which will depend largely on local conditions, then tungsten carbide cored plugs or nails are used in one or both heels of each shoe to secure a good foothold. Calkins and studs should be avoided as they will unbalance the feet by raising the part where they are situated when the horse is on firm ground but sinking into soft ground. Hacks should be reshod every five to six weeks.

A set of shoes for a hunter, show jumper, polo pony or hack weighs about 4 lbs (1.8 kg).

Riding ponies are shod similarly to either hunters or to hacks according to their uses.

4.4 Driving horses and ponies

Carriage horses tend to wear their shoes harder than saddle horses and especially the toes of the hind shoes.

At one time the double fullered Rodway shoe was popular but it did not meet its expectations of providing a better foothold and increased wear. Carriage horses are traditionally shod with plain fullered shoes in front and plain stamped shoes behind with calkins, but today they are often shod with concave fullered shoes in front and threequarter fullered shoes behind.

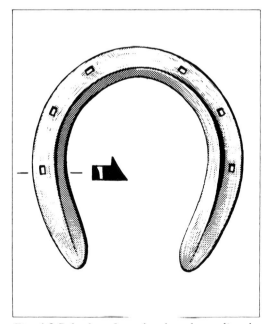

Fig. 4.8 Polo shoe, front, hand made, unclipped.

Front shoes have the heels left long and fitted a little wide but not extending more than ¼ in. (6 mm) beyond the bearing surface and at an upright angle.

Hind shoes require plenty of cover at the toe to combat wear and may have a calkin at each heel or a square stud.

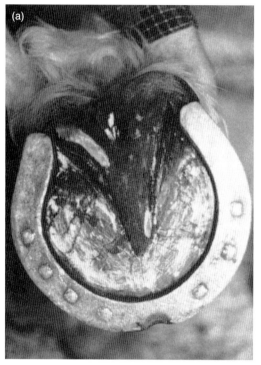

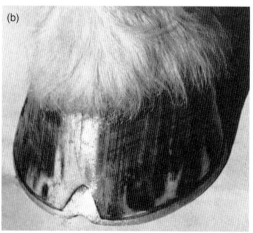

Fig. 4.9 a-b Draught horse shoe, hand made. Front shoe, plain stamped, on a Suffolk Horse.

Driving ponies are shod with the same pattern shoes as those for carriage horses. For driving competitions the heels of the hind shoes may be tapped to take the studs of choice to suit the terrain.

4.5 Draught horses

Draught horses, if worked, have to haul, start and back loads. The type of shoe fitted varies with the district and the road surface.

For all general purposes plain stamped shoes are satisfactory (Fig. 4.9 a-b). As draught horses work at a slow pace brushing is not a problem and, in consequence, the heels of both front and hind shoes can be fitted moderately long and wide.

In some parts of the country it is the practice to shoe heavy draught horses behind with a toe piece and calkins (Fig. 4.10). This method of shoeing provides a good foothold, especially on paved streets, and maintains a normal balance of the foot but deprives the frog of normal weight bearing.

On the smooth surfaces of modern roads toe pieces and calkins provide no extra grip or foothold and once a horse has become accustomed to this type of shoe it takes some time for it to adapt to a flat shoe.

A set of shoes for a draught horse weighs from 16–20 lbs (7–9 kg).

Bevelled shoes (Fig. 4.11) are fitted for shows and the sale ring to make the foot look larger. Bevelled shoes are rarely used for normal work due to their increased weight, the extra time it

Fig. 4.10 Hind shoe with toe piece and calkins.

Fig. 4.11 Bevelled front shoe, hand made.

takes to make them, and the injuries that their prominent sharp edges can cause.

4.6 Hackneys

Hackney horses and ponies have a naturally high action (Fig. 4.12), with great flexion of the limb joints. This is exaggerated by cultivating long hooves and using heavy shoes.

The shoes are plain stamped and the web is wider at the toe where the weight is thus concentrated. Front shoes (Fig. 6.177) have upright heels, hind shoes (Fig 6.178) often have calkin and wedge heels. Both front and hind shoes have a strong toe clip.

Fig. 4.12 Walton Searchlight, champion Hackney stallion 1958–60.

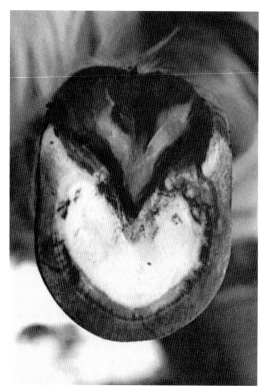

Fig. 4.13 Donkey front foot, ground surface.

Maximum individual shoe weight allowed including nails is 1½ lbs (680 g) for a pony under 14 hands and 2 lbs (907 g) for a horse. For yearlings the maximum weights are 8 oz (227 g) and 12 oz (340 g) for ponies and horses respectively.

There is no maximum length but extremely long hooves would not find favour. Average lengths of the hooves at the toe are about 3½ ins (9 cm) for both front and hind feet for a pony and 4 ins (10 cm) for a horse. Pads may be fitted to make the shod foot longer but are not widely used. It is important to maintain a normal hoof pastern axis.

Shoes are fitted slightly full, about $^1/_{16}$ in. (1.5 mm), from quarter to heel and slightly long, about ¼ in. (6 mm). Larger than normal nails are needed to secure such thick shoes. Seven nails are usual for a horse and six for a pony.

Shoes receive little wear and may last a season, being refitted every four to six weeks. At the end of the showing season the shoes are removed and the hooves trimmed back to a normal length. The horses or ponies may then either go unshod or be fitted with ordinary shoes.

(a)

(b)

Fig. 4.14 Mule shoes; (a) front shoe; (b) hind shoe with calkins. Note the heels are turned outwards to conform with the shape of the bearing surface.

This style of shoeing is predominant but not mandatory and horses should be treated as individuals, for instance some Hackneys go better in concave fullered shoes.

It is important to keep a record of the details of the shoes fitted so that changes may be made if required by the trainer.

4.7 Mules and donkeys

The anatomy and physiology of the mule or donkey's foot is essentially the same as for the horse.

In comparison with the horse the mule's foot is long and narrow. The wall, which is relatively thicker with the horn more dense, is rounded at the toe, gradually becomes thinner as it comes in at the quarters and then expands at the heels. The hoof is upright and may be almost vertical at the quarters, has a very concave sole and a large frog.

A donkey's foot is similar but may be even more exaggerated (Fig. 4.13).

When mules and donkeys are worked both under load and in draught without shoes then their feet require attention every three or four weeks to have the edge of the hoof rounded off with a rasp to prevent splitting or flaring and to keep the foot balanced.

In wet weather and when working on modern roads, shoeing is necessary. A mule or a donkey shoe is usually a plain stamped shoe which is narrower and lighter than the pattern used for horses (Fig. 4.14 a–b). To conform with the shape of the bearing surface the heels of the shoe are turned outwards and it is customary for them to be extended beyond the heels. The shoes are retained with four to six nails and since the wall at the quarters and heels is almost vertical the nail holes are punched upright.

CHAPTER 5

TOOLS AND EQUIPMENT

Shoeing tools are used to remove the shoe, prepare the foot and nail on the shoe. Forge tools are used at the fire and the anvil to make and fit the shoe.

5.1 Clothing

Clothing should not be any looser than necessary for freedom of movement. Nothing should be loose enough that tools, hot metal, clenches or machines can tangle with it. Shoes should be stout, preferably with steel toecaps and with support and protection for the ankles. Cloth hats will serve to keep hot sparks out of the hair and, though they will not prevent concussion, may well prevent a cut to the head from the forefoot of a rearing foal.

Apron

A farrier's apron is made of chromed leather. It is designed to protect the legs from hot metal and sparks when working in the forge and from hooves, shoes, clenches and the sharp edges of the farrier's own tools when shoeing. An apron should be in good condition. If not, it should be replaced. Chaps are preferred by some farriers especially in cold weather.

Safety glasses

Eye protection is essential when working at the forge fire and with electrical grinders and welders. Safety glasses of a variety of designs are cheap and widely available.

5.2 Shoeing tools

Shoeing hammer (driving or nailing-on hammer) (Fig. 5.1)

This hammer weighs 10–12 oz (280–340 g). It is used for driving nails, striking the buffer and forming the clenches. It has a short curved claw for withdrawing nails and twisting off their points.

Fig. 5.1 Shoeing hammer.

Buffer (clench cutter) (Fig. 5.2)

This tool is about 6 ins (15 cm) long. Many farriers make their own from an old rasp.

The chisel-shaped end, which is about 1½ ins (4 cm) wide, is used with the shoeing hammer to cut off or straighten the clenches before removing the shoe. It can also be used for removing flakes of the horny sole.

*Fig. **5.2** Buffer.*

The pointed end is used for punching out nails which have broken off in the hoof. It can also be used for raising the head of a nail from the fullering sufficiently for it to be gripped with the pincers and withdrawn. It can also be used to pick out the feet.

Pincers (Fig. 5.3)
These pincers have handles about 12 ins (30 cm) long and jaws 1 in. (2.5 cm) wide. They are used for raising the branches and levering off the shoe, withdrawing nails, cutting off any excess of a wrung-off nail, and to turn the clenches.

Toeing knife (Fig. 5.4)
This knife is often made by the farrier from an old rasp. It is about 10 ins (25 cm) long with 2½ ins (6 cm) of one end ground sharp. This is used for trimming feet by driving it through the wall with a mallet or the shoeing hammer. A mallet with a nylon head is safer than the shoeing hammer which may cause the toeing knife to break and splinters to fly. Skill and care are needed when using a toeing knife because it can easily twist in the hand and cut into the sensitive foot. This is particularly liable to happen when trimming the feet of young

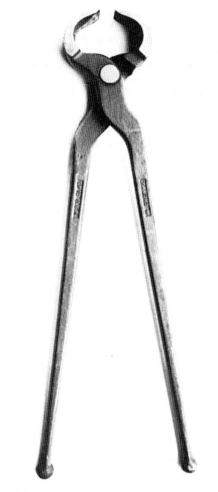

*Fig. **5.3** Pincers.*

stock which are difficult to control and sensitive to hammering.

Hoof cutter (hoof trimmer, hoof nipper or hoof parer) (Fig. 5.5)
This tool has handles about 12 ins (30 cm) long with a pincer-like head having both jaws

*Fig. **5.4** Toeing knife.*

Fig. 5.5 Hoof cutter.

sharp. It is easier and safer to use than the toeing knife and in consequence most farriers use it for removing excess wall. Hoof cutters should not be used to grip nails. They should require little sharpening and last a long time.

Drawing knife (Fig. 5.6)
This knife has a blade about ½ in. (13 mm) wide with a slight curve. The point is bent over to the inside of the curve for safety. The handle is made of wood, horn or plastic. Originally the knife was designed for paring down the sole, a harmful practice which has now been discarded.

It is used for removing loose flakes of sole and ragged pieces of frog and easing the seat of corn. Also it is used to remove horn for the reception of a clip, a practice that is not recommended.

The back of the blade is used for cleaning out the sole and grooves of the frog. The butt of a horn handle or the point of the knife can be used to manipulate a hot shoe onto the foot when it is being fitted. The blade of a knife will lose its hardness if heated and so it is advisable to keep one knife for trimming and another for fitting if the point of the knife is to be used in this way.

Searcher (Fig. 5.7)
This is a knife similar to the drawing knife but with a narrower blade. It is used for searching the foot, paring the horn around puncture wounds and easing corns.

Both the drawing knife and searcher are available in right- and left-handed patterns.

Rasp (Fig. 5.8)
A rasp must be long and wide to help obtain

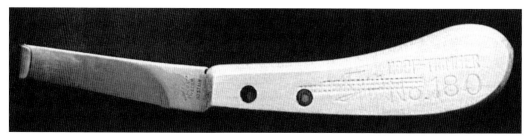

Fig. 5.6 Drawing knife.

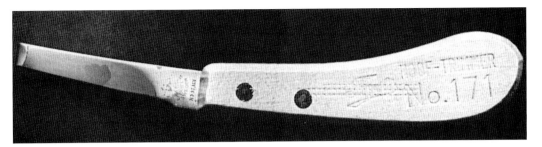

Fig. 5.7 Searcher.

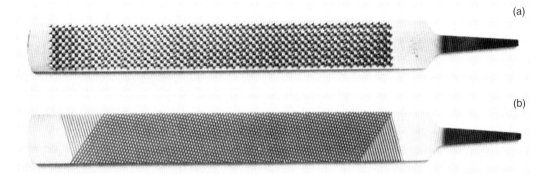

Fig. 5.8 Tanged rasp: (a) coarse side; (b) file side.

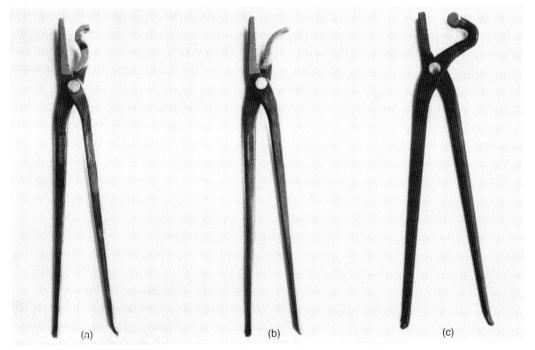

Fig. 5.9 Types of clenching tongs: goose-necked, standard and pony model.

a level bearing surface. The standard farrier's rasp is 14 ins (35 cm) long with one face coarse cut and one face file cut and the two sides are serrated. The point at the end which fits into the handle is called the tang.

A blunt-ended or half-file rasp has each face divided into two sections whose cutting edges face in opposite directions. It is shorter than a tanged rasp and thus more portable. It is useful for trimming foals' feet.

Rasps are used for trimming and levelling the hoof wall, filing the clenches and hot rasping and finishing off the shoe. New rasps should be reserved for trimming the hoof. As they lose their edge they are used for filing the clenches and finally for hot rasping.

Half-round file
A half-round file is useful to smooth away coarse rasp marks on hooves. A large file with a tang to which a handle can be fitted is best. When the file loses its sharpness it can be used for finishing shoes.

Clenching tongs (Fig. 5.9)
Clenching tongs are specially designed for turning and bedding the clenches. They are particularly useful when working on young or sensitive horses which resent hammering. Three basic types can be purchased: the standard clencher, the pony clencher and the goose-neck clencher. There is little difference between the uses of each type.

Nail puller (Fig. 5.10)
This is a tool for removing nails from a fullered shoe when the heads cannot be gripped with pincers.

Fig. *5.11* Tool box.

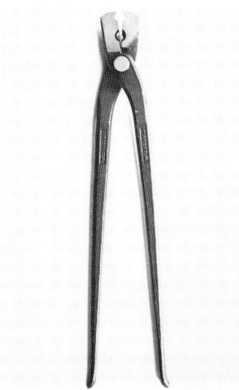

Fig. *5.10* Nail pullers.

Fig. *5.12* Joiner's bag.

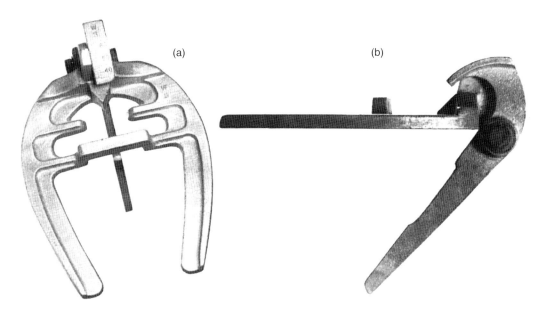

(a)   (b)

Fig. 5.13 Hoof gauge.

Tool box

There are almost as many designs of tool box as there are farriers. Large wooden boxes (Fig. 5.11) are useful for carrying a wide selection of shoeing tools and usually have compartments on the top for nails which makes for less bending down when nailing on shoes. However, the larger the box the heavier it is and the more dirt and rubbish it accumulates. Boxes also represent a safety hazard in that either a person or a horse may fall over them.

A canvas joiner's bag (Fig. 5.12) is lighter and safer and is favoured by racehorse shoers. A piece of canvas about 24 ins (60 cm) by 18 ins (45 cm) on which tools can be carried is economical, clean and safe.

Ruler

A metal ruler is essential for measuring the feet and the length of bar to be cut off to make a shoe. Stainless steel or brass are the best materials as they do not rust. A 2 ft (60 cm) folding ruler is the most useful.

Divider

A divider is used to measure the length of the hoof at the toe.

Hoof gauge (Fig. 5.13)

A hoof gauge is used to measure the angle of the hoof wall at the toe. Several types are available.

Motorised burr

An electric mini drill with a burr attachment can be used for opening out cracks in the hoof. A selection of models are available that can be run from either mains, a car battery or both.

5.3 Forge tools

Turning hammer (Fig. 5.14)

This is the standard hammer used by the farrier at the anvil. It weighs 2–3 lbs (1–1½ kg), has one face flat and the other round and is fitted with a hickory or ash shaft about 1 ft (30 cm) long. Hickory is better quality than ash.

The flat face, which is actually slightly convex, is used when forging a flat surface and the round face for a concave surface. Either face can be used for striking tools but most farriers prefer to use the flat face for this purpose.

There are several variations of the standard turning hammer. The cat's head hammer (Fig.

85

Fig. **5.14** *Turning hammer.*

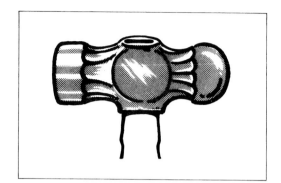

Fig. **5.16** *Ball pein hammer.*

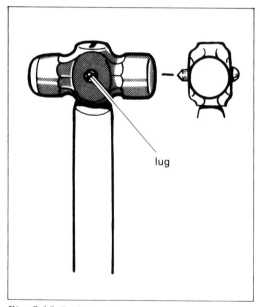

lug

Fig. **5.15** *Cat's head hammer.*

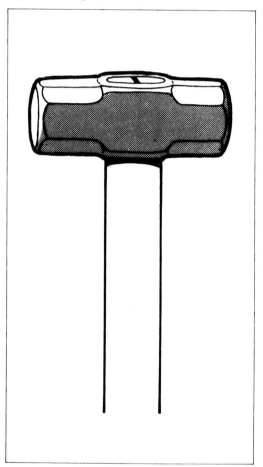

Fig. **5.17** *Sledge hammer.*

5.15) has a lug on each side of the head, one rounded and one pointed. A ball pein hammer (Fig. 5.16) has the round face replaced by a ball. A cross pein hammer has the round face replaced by a wedge.

Sledge hammer (Fig. 5.17)
A sledge hammer weighs about 9 lbs (4 kg) and has a 3 ft (90 cm) shaft. The most common variety is the double-faced sledge.

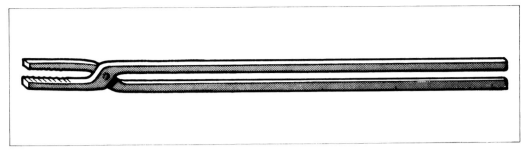

Fig. **5.18** *Fire tongs.*

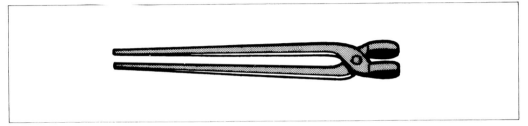

Fig. **5.19** *Shoe tongs.*

It is wielded by the striker under the direction of the farrier for heavy work such as making draught horse shoes and where more than two hands are helpful such as for tooling and fullering.

Fire tongs (Fig. 5.18)
These tongs are designed with 4 in. (10 cm) jaws and 24 in. (60 cm) long handles which enable the farrier to manipulate hot metal without having to be too close to the fire.

Tongs of all varieties are usually made from mild steel.

Shoe tongs (Fig. 5.19)
These tools are used by the farrier at the anvil for holding hot metal. They have shorter handles than fire tongs, about 12 ins (30 cm), and jaws from 1–2 ins (2.5–5 cm) long. This ratio of length of handle to jaw, coupled with the handles being parallel when in use, results in a most effective grip.

Different tongs are needed for different thicknesses of material. Those with jaws which shut close are called inside shoe tongs and those with jaws wider apart for handling thicker material are called outside shoe tongs.

Some farriers use shoe tongs for carrying a fullered shoe to the foot instead of a carrier

pritchel when fitting hot shoes. The tongs grip the outside edge of the fullering.

Hollow bit tongs (Fig. 5.20)
These are shoe tongs designed for gripping bar lengthways, having jaws which are elongated and semi-circular in cross-section.

Hot set (Fig. 5.21)
This is a chisel-shaped tool, about 4 ins (10 cm) long with a cutting edge ⅝ in. (16 mm) wide.

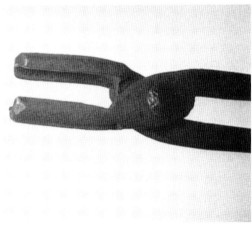

Fig. **5.20** *Hollow bit tongs.*

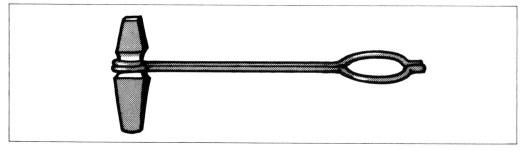

Fig. 5.21 Hot set.

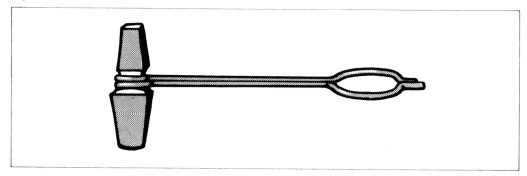

Fig. 5.22 Cold set.

It is used for cutting heated steel bars and is fitted hammer fashion on a handle. It is struck by an assistant with a sledge hammer.

Cold set (Fig. 5.22)
This tool is similar to the hot set but is larger and has a sharper edge. It is used for cutting mild steel bars cold.

When using either a hot set or a cold set the work is placed on the table of the anvil to preserve the anvil face.

Stamp (Fig. 5.23)
This is a punch set hammer fashion on a handle. It is used for making nail holes. Its

point must be the same shape as the head of the nail when stamping plain bar. When stamping fullered bar the nail head will rest in the fullering and therefore the stamp must be narrower to prevent marking the sides of the fullering, its point conforming to the neck of the nail.

The stamp is held in position by the farrier and either struck by the striker with a sledge hammer or by the farrier himself using the turning hammer.

Fuller or fullering iron (Fig. 5.24)
This is a blunt chisel set hammer fashion on a handle. It has one face flat and the other

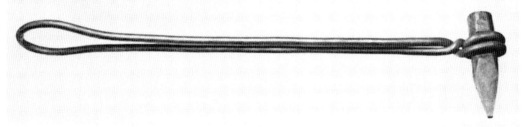

Fig. 5.23 Stamp.

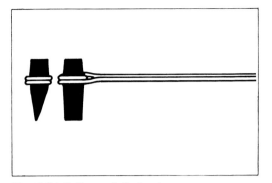

Fig. 5.24 Fuller or fullering iron.

bevelled and is used to make a groove in the shoe, which is called fullering. When in use the bevelled face is directed to the outside of the shoe. The fuller is held by the farrier and struck by the striker with a sledge hammer.

Guide fuller (Fig. 6.140)
A guide fuller can be used to mark the path for the fuller when working with tooled bar. It has the basic form of a fuller with a notch in one face which thus creates two blades. The inner face of the larger blade rests against the outside of the tooled bar while the smaller blade makes a shallow groove on the top of the bar.

The hot set, cold set, stamp, fuller and guide fuller are called 'top tools' because they are laid on top of the work and then struck with the hammer.

These tools can be made with an oval hole through the centre to take a wooden handle. This should be a slack fit to reduce jarring to the holder. A round hole should not be made as the tool will twist on the handle. Alternatively handles can be made out of thin (¼ in. or 6 mm) mild steel rod which is bent around the waist of the tool.

Hardie (Fig. 5.25)
This is a straight-edged tool, weighing up to 2 lbs (0.9 kg) shaped like a chisel and with a shank to fit the hardie hole on the face of the anvil. It is used to cut off lengths of hot mild steel bar which are placed over its edge and struck with the sledge hammer until they are cut through and broken off.

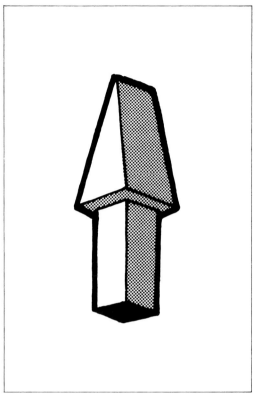

Fig. 5.25 Hardie.

Heel cutter or half round (Fig. 5.26)
This tool has a semi-circular cutting edge and a shank to fit the hardie hole on the face of the anvil. It is used for cutting off and trimming the heels of a shoe.

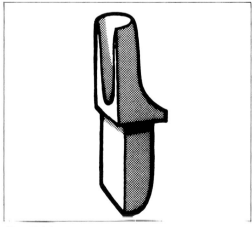

Fig. 5.26 Heel cutter or half round.

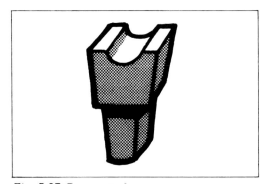

Fig. 5.27 Concave tool or swage.

Concave tool or swage block (Fig. 5.27)
This tool is a mould through which yellow hot steel, usually square bar, is drawn by the farrier while at the same time an assistant strikes it with the sledge hammer to shape it to the mould. The tool is used to make concave bar which can then be fullered. It has a shank to fit the hardie hole in the face of the anvil.

Heel crease
A heel crease is a mould the shape of a finished heel. Instead of forging and hot rasping heels they can be hammered at a yellow heat into the crease to form their shape.

The hardie, heel cutter, concave tool and heel crease are called 'bottom tools' because the work is placed on top of them and struck with the hammer.

Pritchel (Fig. 5.28)
This is a long steel punch, with a point which is an accurate reproduction of the neck of the nail. It is used to punch out the bottoms of the nail holes formed by the stamp. A pritchel used for carrying a hot shoe to the foot for fitting is called a carrier pritchel.

It is important that the point of a pritchel is of the exact shape and is used with care, not being allowed to overheat or being struck

Fig. 5.28 Pritchel.

against blackening metal. A pritchel is only as good as the steel from which it is made.

When making or shaping a pritchel the steel should not be allowed to reach a white heat or it will be spoiled. Nor should tool steel be hit when blackening or it will crack. Therefore the point should be heated to a light red heat before being hammered to shape, drawn to a fine taper and finally shaped with one or two upsetting blows on its point. Pritchels should be allowed to cool in air. Oil or grease can be used to cool the point while shoemaking to prevent it overheating.

Punch (Fig. 5.29)
The punch used by farriers is round and is used to make a hole through a shoe before enlarging it with a drift or tapping it to take a stud. It is used over the small round hole on the face of the anvil to avoid blunting the point and to prevent the branch of the shoe bending.

Fig. 5.29 Punch.

When punching fullered bar the punch is first driven into the foot surface of the shoe on the face of the anvil to start the hole. This results in a collar of metal forming around the hole in the fullering which ensures a tight-fitting stud. To shear out the bottom of the hole the shoe is turned over and the punch is then driven from the ground surface over the pritchel hole.

A bob punch has a rounded end and is used for clipping shoes.

Drift (Fig. 5.30)
This tool resembles a punch. It is shaped to conform to the neck of a drive-in stud and is used to enlarge a hole punched to take a stud.

Fig. 5.30 Drift.

Hot rasp

A hot rasp is a standard farrier's rasp which is used for rasping and filing steel, preferably with the steel at a light red heat. Usually it is a rasp that has been first used for dressing hooves, then for finishing the clenches and finally is used as a hot rasp.

Half-round file

A half-round file is useful for smoothing away coarse file marks on a shoe, usually at a black heat. A long file with a tang to which a handle can be fitted is best.

Centre punch/chisel

A centre punch or a chisel is used in conjunction with a ruler and a hammer for marking the centre of a bar when making a shoe.

Vise grips (Fig. 5.31)

Long-nosed vise grips (LN 15) can be used to carry a hot shoe instead of a carrier pritchel. They can be rapidly adjusted to hold most sizes of shoe. Vise grips have the advantage that they do not distort the nail holes and if they become loose they can be reattached to the shoe without going back to the anvil.

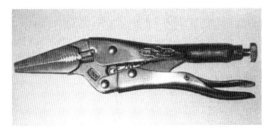

Fig. 5.31 Vise grips.

Wire brush

A wire brush is essential for cleaning hot metal of ashes, clinker and oxide scale.

5.4 Forges and forge fittings

Anvil (Fig. 5.32)

An anvil is made of high carbon steel fully annealed with the face flame hardened. Old anvils were made of wrought iron with a steel face welded on. The anvil has a square body and a rounded beak, and a full-sized anvil weighs from 2–3 cwt (100–150 kg).

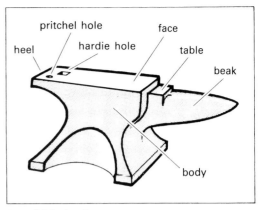

Fig. 5.32 Anvil.

The face or working surface measures about 2 ft by 6 ins (60 by 15 cm) and is used for drawing and welding. The beak is used for turning and shaping.

At the base of the beak is a small flat area, approximately ½ in. (1 cm) below the face, called the table. It is used when cutting steel with either the hot or cold set to keep the anvil face smooth and level. The opposite end of the anvil is called the heel and is made thinner so that the farrier can work on a shoe with one branch under the face.

On the face, towards the heel, are two holes which penetrate its entire thickness. One is a square hole, the hardie hole, which takes the shank of bottom tools such as the hardie or the heel cutter. The hardie hole measures up to 1¼ ins (30 mm) in diameter. The other is a small round hole, the pritchel hole, less than 1 in. (2.5 cm) in diameter, which is used to take the point of a pritchel, punch or drift when making holes in a shoe.

The anvil is fixed with its face 27–30 ins (70–75 cm) from the floor and pitched slightly away from the farrier so that scale and loose pieces of metal which scatter with each hammer blow will fall on the floor. The beak is to the farrier's left. It is placed in relation to the forge so that hot metal can be carried to it with the least time and effort.

The anvil may be set in a steel stand, but most farriers prefer to have them on a wooden base such as a section of a tree trunk which is set some 2 ft (60 cm) into the ground. The springiness provided by the wood gives lift to the hammer after each blow, which enables the farrier to strike more rapidly and with less effort and jarring.

Portable anvils weigh between 28–112 lbs (61–247 kg) according to personal preference. A steel stand is used.

Forge

Forges can be static or portable, and can use coal, coke or gas as fuel.

The static coal- or coke-burning forge (Fig. 5.33) can be made of cast iron, mild steel or brick. Air is blown through the fire from an electric fan which is controlled by a rheostat to give variable speed. The fan is connected

Fig. 5.33 Forge made of cast iron. There is a double hearth. The back is built of brick. There is a water-filled bosh and a tongs rack in front. Behind is an electric fan and a water-filled tank. The tank cools the tue iron. The fan is controlled by the rheostat above. The hood leads into a stainless-steel chimney.

to the back of the forge by a pipe in which is set a valve as an additional regulation to the flow of air. This pipe leads into a cast-iron tuyere or tue iron. This introduces the air to the fire, either from the bottom or from the back. Back draught is preferred by most farriers as the construction is simpler and the fire is easier to maintain. Bottom-draught forges do not absorb so much heat and therefore can be made lighter and more portable. The tue is made of cast iron because this has been found to last well. It is attached either to a cast-iron back plate or to a water-cooled tank which aids in dissipating heat. It can be detached and replaced when it is burnt out. Above the fire is a hood which tapers upwards into the chimney.

In front of the fire is a trough (bosh) filled with water and used for quenching hot metal and there may be a second trough for a supply of fuel. A bar attached to the side of the forge acts as a tongs rack.

The tools used to maintain a fire are the poker, which is used to open up the fire and remove clinker; the rake, which is designed for moving fuel on to the fire; and the fire shovel, which is used for banking up the fire and removing ashes.

Gas forges are of two types: the portable propane forge (Fig. 5.34 a-d) and the ceramic chip gas forge (Fig. 5.35). The ceramic chip gas forge is too heavy to be portable and is run off either mains gas or propane. Gas forges are much cleaner than the traditional coal and coke fires.

The portable propane forge is very useful for heating horseshoes for fitting in the field but often uses too much gas to be economical for routinely making shoes, nor can it bring metal to welding heat or heat a short length. It can be noisy but this rarely seems to upset horses.

The ceramic chip gas forge is quiet and economical to run. There is satisfactory heat control by adjusting the gas and air pressure. It is capable of bringing steel to welding heat.

Vice

A leg vice is best for blacksmithing as the shock of hammer blows is transmitted by the leg to the floor. It can be attached to a bench or to a special stand.

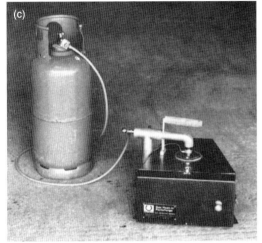

Fig. 5.34 Types of portable gas forge: (a) Alcosa; (b) Cottam; (c-d) Swan.

Fig. 5.35 Ceramic chip gas forge.

Bench

A strong steel bench is an essential item of equipment in a forge.

Guillotine

A guillotine is made of steel with hardened steel jaws and a long lever arm and is used for cutting cold mild steel bar. It has to be fixed to a stand which in turn has to be fixed to the floor.

Electric grinders

There are two basic types of electric grinder, the bench grinder and the angle grinder. A bench grinder, as the name implies, is mounted on a bench. An 8 in. (20 cm) bench grinder is more powerful and more useful than a 6 in. (15 cm) grinder. An angle grinder is hand held, the work being held in a vice. Safety glasses should always be worn when using a grinder.

93

Welding

An *electric arc welder* is a very useful tool in a workshop. The machines are generally too large and heavy to be transported by a farrier in his van. Mains electricity is required. Metal inert gas welding is a refined and relatively expensive system of electric arc welding that gives excellent results.

Oxy-acetylene welding equipment is not generally as suitable as electric arc welding for the relatively large thicknesses of metal used in making horseshoes. It can be used for delicate work and for applying borium to horseshoes. The equipment is more portable than electric welding equipment.

Many books and courses are available on welding. No-one should use welding equipment without proper training.

Fire welding is preferred where possible by examiners and judges of shoeing competitions because of the greater blacksmithing skill involved. However, there are some surgical shoes where electric welding may be not only more practical but essential.

CHAPTER 6

SHOEMAKING

Farriers acquire their own preferred techniques. The methods described will serve as a practical guide which can be modified by individuals in the light of experience.

Making each shoe is described in stages. The skilful farrier will complete several stages in one heat, while the beginner will require several heats to complete one stage.

The shoes described are specimen shoes. Their shape and pattern of nail holes is considered to be ideal. However, when actually shoeing horses the shape of the shoe should correspond with the shape of the (trimmed) foot and the nail holes punched where they will correspond with sound horn.

The rate at which a shoe can be made is limited by the steady cooling of the metal while it is out of the fire. The more that can be achieved at each heat the better. Thus speed is a great advantage. Time lost by not having tools to hand, by slow or awkward activity or in correcting mistakes will be compounded as the metal cools.

Time is also lost heating metal in the fire. Skill in managing the fire will make shoe-making easier. Each shoe in turn should be brought to the correct heat at the right moment. The more confident and skilful the farrier is at the anvil the easier it is to be aware of the fire at the same time, and faster progress can be made, less coal or coke used and fewer shoes will be destroyed by burning.

Safety glasses must be worn when working at the forge as there are dangers to the eyes not only from hot sparks but also from tools shattering when struck. The anvil face should be kept clean. A leather apron should be worn.

6.1 Managing a fire

Coal must be clean and free from slag. A fire can be built up easily with coal to form an oven. This is done by banking it up at the back of the fire and damping it well with water. Coal throws out a lot more face heat than coke.

Coke is also known as breeze. Coke beans about $\frac{3}{8} - \frac{5}{8}$ in. (9–15 mm) are the most suitable size. If the coke is too big there is difficulty in feeding the metal into the fire. Coke heats the metal more intensely than coal. There is no need to damp coke as the flame does not spread quickly. It is especially important to use safety glasses when using coke as it has a tendency to spit and explode.

To light a fire a hole should be scooped out in front of the tue nose. Remove clinker, dust and fine ash. Using wood, cardboard or straw for kindling light close to the blast hole. Slowly turn on the fan drawing a little fuel over the kindling and as the fire takes hold increase the blast and build up the fire. Coal is easier to light than coke.

In a *neutral fire* oxide scales form on the metal and about 1% of its weight is lost. Less scale will form if the metal is well up in the fire with a good bed of coals under it.

A *reducing fire* has a green tinge to the flame. All the oxygen from the blast is consumed in a reducing fire. A reducing fire is best for fire welding.

An *oxidising fire* has an excess of oxygen and is usually hollow. A lot of metal will be lost in an oxidising fire. An oxidising fire is of no use for fire welding.

Clinker always forms in a fire. It is formed from impurities in the fuel and from oxide scales from the metal. Hot clinker has the consistency of treacle. Clinker is formed in a molten state and runs to the bottom of the fire by the blast hole. The blast must be turned off for a few minutes from time to time to allow the clinker to solidify so that it can be lifted out in one piece with the poker. Cold clinker is brittle and black.

When a farrier places a length of metal in the fire it is referred to as taking a heat. The metal has to be heated to the correct temperature necessary for the work required. The number of heats required to complete a specific job vary considerably and to a great extent are dependent on individual skill.

At each heat the metal should be quickly brushed with a wire brush before being worked. This improves the finished shoe in cleanness of appearance and reduces sparks flying off which can easily burn the face and hands.

The *temperature* of hot steel is judged by colour. The terms used to distinguish the colours vary but the following explanation is a guide:

White or welding heat. The metal is white and tends to have a fluid appearance on its surface. It gives off sparks. This heat is required for fire welding. The temperature is about 1400°C (2500°F).

Yellow heat. The metal is very pliable and is easily worked. Yellow heat is suitable for most forge work. The temperature is about 1100°C (2000°F).

Red heat. Red heat is used for small adjustments in shaping and finishing off the shoe and for punching the nail holes. The temperature is about 800°C (1500°F).

Black or blue heat. The metal has a very faint glow. This heat is used for making minor changes in the shape of the shoe and for levelling it. The temperature is below 600°C (1100°F).

6.2 Forging exercises

Forging procedures used in shoemaking include drawing, bending, shaping, upsetting, welding and punching holes. The following exercises are useful ways of practising these procedures. They are designed as an introduction to working at the anvil. An apprentice should be proficient in these basic exercises before proceeding to make horseshoes.

Exercise 1: Drawing an edge
Take a piece of mild steel bar about 20 ins (50 cm) in length so that it can be held in the hand. Half-inch (12 mm) square section is suitable. Have the hammer ready on the anvil face. The anvil face should be clean.

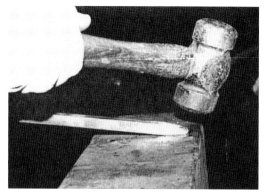

Fig. 6.1 Heat the end to a yellow heat. Brush. Hold the bar on the anvil face at a slight angle. Hammer along the hot length with firm overlapping blows with the flat face of the hammer. The bar should be turned over after every half-dozen blows so that it is hammered equally from both sides.

Fig. 6.2 As it is drawn out the width of the bar will increase in a fan shape. To keep the original width of the bar blows on both edges will be required.

Fig. 6.3 The job is finished off at a red heat when any hammer marks or irregularities are smoothed away with light overlapping blows.

Exercise 2: Square points

Take a piece of mild steel bar about 20 ins (50 cm) in length. Half-inch (12 mm) square is suitable.

Fig. 6.4 Heat the end to a yellow heat. Hammer along the hot length with firm overlapping blows on the anvil face. The bar should be given a quarter turn every half-dozen blows.

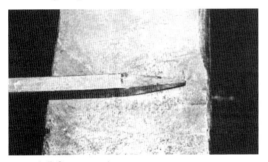

Fig. 6.5 Square point.

Exercise 3: Round points

To make a round point from either round or square bar first make a square point.

Fig. 6.6 Hammer along each corner to make an eight-sided point.

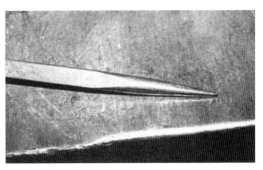

Fig. 6.7 With light blows smooth away all the edges to make a round point.

Exercise 4: Figure eights

Take 8 ins (20 cm) of ⁵⁄₁₆ in. (8 mm) round mild steel bar.

Fig. 6.8 Heat half the bar to a bright red heat. Make the first bend over the beak of the anvil.

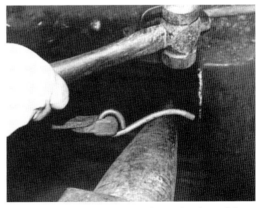

Fig. 6.9 Heat the other half to a bright red heat. Make the second bend over the beak in the opposite direction.

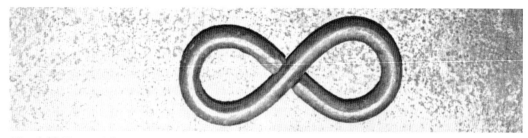

Fig. **6.10** *Figure eight.*

Exercise 5: Tongs

Cut off 5½ ins (14 cm) of ¾ in. (20 mm) square bar. Hollow bit tongs will be needed to hold the bar for the first stage.

Fig. **6.11** *Heat one half to a yellow heat and draw it out. The bulk of the drawing should be done over the beak of the anvil where the convex surface spreads the metal lengthways, rather than on the face of the anvil where the flat surface spreads the metal in all directions.*

Fig. **6.12** *Form about 9 ins (22 cm) of ⁵/₁₆ in. (8 mm) square, then round it to form the long round handle, the rein. Once the rein is formed it can be quenched and held in the hand for the succeeding stages.*

Fig. **6.13** *Heat the other end of the bar to a yellow heat. Flatten 1 in. (25 mm) of the end of the bar on the anvil face making a shoulder over the round edge of the anvil. The flattened end should be rounded with the hammer and measure 1 in. (25 mm) in diameter and ⁵/₁₆ in. (8 mm) thick.*

Fig. **6.14** *At a yellow heat the bar is given a quarter turn to the left and placed over the round edge at the far side of the anvil, moving the rein at a slight angle to the left. A second shoulder is forged and the middle section is flattened to ⁵/₁₆ in. (8 mm) thickness.*

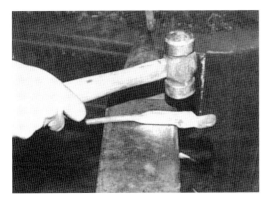

*Fig. **6.15** At a yellow heat the bar is given another quarter turn to the left and placed again over the rounded edge of the far side of the anvil. A third shoulder is forged 1 in. (25 mm) behind the last.*

*Fig. **6.16** The middle section is given a smooth rounded shape. The bar behind the shoulder is reduced to ⁵/₁₆ in. (8 mm) square, blending into the round rein.*

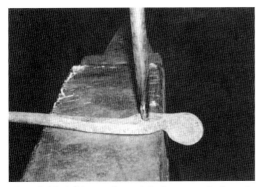

*Fig. **6.17** A ³/₈ in. (9 mm) hole is punched in the centre of the middle section. The hole is started at the edge of the anvil.*

*Fig. **6.18** The metal is turned over and the hole is completed from the other side over the pritchel hole.*

One half of a pair of tongs has now been formed. The other half should be made identically.

To make the rivet take a short length of ⁵/₁₆ in. (8 mm) round mild steel bar. An 8 ins (20 cm) length is ideal.

Take a short yellow heat at one end and upset it by holding the bar upright on the anvil face and striking with quick sharp blows on the other end, straightening the bar as it starts to buckle.

*Fig. **6.19** Place the thickened end over the far end of the anvil where the edge is sharp and with light blows towards the anvil and downwards, shape the head of the rivet; at the same time the anvil edge is making a shoulder. Rotate the bar slightly after each blow.*

Fig. **6.20** *When the first head is formed the bar is cut off where about ⁵/₁₆ in. (8 mm) will protrude above the tongs to form the other head of the rivet. The rivet and the tongs are heated to a light red heat and the rivet placed head down on the anvil face with the tongs over it.*

Fig. **6.21** *The end of the rivet is struck with light rapid blows of the flat face of the hammer from above which will spread it out and shape it similarly to the other head, though slightly smaller.*

Setting up the tongs: a pair of tongs can be used to handle comfortably a limited range of thicknesses of bar. For example, tongs might be set up as inside shoe tongs for ⁵/₁₆ in. (8 mm) bar in which case they will also handle ¼ in. and ³/₈ in. (6–9 mm) bar.

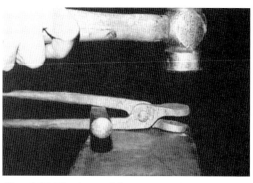

Fig. **6.22** *The jaws of the tongs are heated to a red heat. A cold piece of metal such as a pritchel is placed between the reins so that they keep a comfortable separation and the jaws are hammered together until they are the right distance apart.*

Exercise 6: Chain links

Cut off 7 ins (18 cm) of ³/₈ in. (9.5 mm) round mild steel bar.

Fig. **6.23** *Take a short yellow heat at one end.*

Fig. **6.24** *Upset the end of the bar. Little upsetting is required with thin bar as the weld can be made quickly keeping loss of metal to a minimum. The other end is also upset in the same way.*

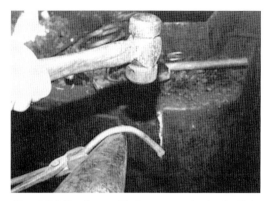

Fig. **6.25** *Bend to a U shape over the beak of the anvil.*

Fig. **6.26**

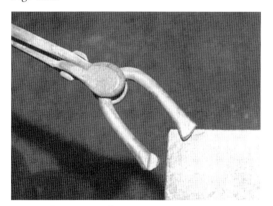

Fig. **6.27** *At a yellow heat hold one end at an angle just onto the edge of the anvil and hammer from above to make a shoulder ¼ in. (6 mm) before the end. From here there should be a slope towards a rounded point. This is called the scarf. The U is turned over and the other end is scarfed in exactly the same position as the first. Because the U has been turned over one scarf will face up and the other down so they will mate together.*

Fig. **6.28** *The ends are bent towards each other so the scarfs overlap.*

Fig. **6.29** *End view. The scarfs should be in as close contact as possible.*

Fig. **6.30** *Heat to a welding heat and hit with light blows on the face of the anvil. Then shape the welded section over the beak. The welded section should be slightly thicker than the rest of the ring.*

When joining chain links the finished links should be threaded over an unwelded link before closing the scarfs together.

Fig. 6.31 Chain link.

Some farriers use a flux for fire welding, usually borax or sand, but with a clean fire and a good technique flux is not necessary.

6.3 Cutting the correct length of bar

Measure the width of the trimmed foot and the length from the centre of the toe to either heel. Usually the length to each heel will be the same but if there is a difference the average is taken.

Concave fullered bar. Add the width and the length and a further 1½ ins (4 cm).

This rule can be altered according to the shape and size of the feet, the width of the bar used and the intended fit of the shoe.

For small feet as little as 1 in. (25 mm) and for large feet as much as 2 ins (5 cm) may be added to the length plus the width. For long narrow feet it is more accurate to use twice the length in the calculation rather than the length plus the width. A little less length will be needed if the foot is straight rather than rounded in shape across the quarters.

A slightly greater length of a narrower bar than a wider bar is required for the same foot.

Heels which are formed in a crease do not require as much bar as those which are finished by rasping.

These rules are for a conventional hunter shoe which is made to fit the exact outline and length of the foot. For a longer or fuller-fitting shoe more bar is required.

Another method of calculating the metal required is to use a tape measure. Measure from one heel round the circumference of the foot to the other heel. Subtract twice the width of the bar to be used and this will give the length required.

Flat bar. 1 in. (25 mm) is added to the width and length as the heels tend to be drawn more in the making. For carthorse shoes 2 ins (5 cm) is added.

Calk and wedge. For a calkin ½ in. (12 mm) is added. For a wedge nothing is added.

6.4 Making a front shoe from concave fullered bar

Fig. 6.32 Measure and mark the appropriate length of bar.

Fig. 6.33 Cut the bar. Here a cold set is being used.

Fig. **6.34** *Mark the centre. A length of an old three-sided file that has been normalised is commonly used. The bar is balanced fullering downwards across the file on the anvil face. When balanced a blow from the round face of the hammer from above will cause the edge of the file to mark the bar in the centre of the ground surface.*

Stage 1: Turning the toe

Shoes are generally made in pairs or in a set of four. The bars are placed in the fire fullering downwards so as not to collect dirt.

Fig. **6.35** *The middle third of each bar in turn is brought to a long yellow heat.*

Fig. **6.36** *The bar is held over the beak of the anvil and struck with the round face of the turning hammer on the inside edge with overlapping blows until the desired curve of the toe is formed. The bar is gripped by the tongs at right angles with the handles of the tongs held well into the body.*

Fig. **6.37** *If the bar starts to twist it should be levelled on the face of the anvil before continuing. When levelling try not to squash the bar between the hammer and the anvil.*

Fig. **6.38** *Final adjustments to the shape may be made over the beak and the bar is again levelled.*

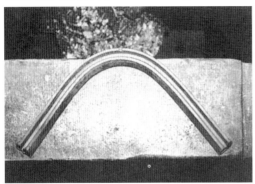

Fig. **6.39** *The toe bend should be formed so as to leave the ends of the bar at an angle of 90°.*

Stage 2: Forging the outside heel

The end of the bar should be at a yellow heat. The bar is gripped at the toe with the tongs in a straight line with the outside branch. The heel is worked at the far edge of the anvil or at the near edge of the hardie hole.

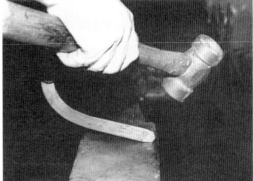

Fig. **6.40** *Hammer blows are directed at the inside edge, . . .*

Fig. **6.41** *. . . the outside edge, . . .*

Fig. **6.42** *. . . and the ground surface. The blows are directed into the bar and against the resistance of the left hand so that the heel is shaped rather than drawn out. It is important to get a full slope with the hammer – if not, it will be necessary to remove too much metal with the rasp.*

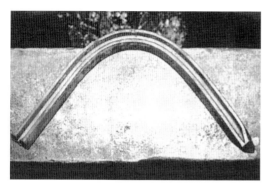

Fig. 6.43 Toe bend and outside heel formed.

Stage 3: Shaping the outside branch and punching the nail holes

A long yellow heat is needed from the end of the bar into the toe bend.

Fig. 6.44 The outside branch is turned over the beak of the anvil, starting from the toe bend, . . .

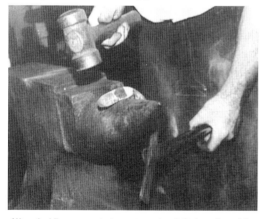

Fig. 6.45 . . . and dropping the left hand, taking the bend steadily towards the heel.

Fig. 6.46 If the bar starts to twist it should be levelled before continuing, and levelled again when the bend is completed.

The bar should still be at a red heat which is ideal for stamping and pritchelling the nail holes. If the metal is yellow the stamp and pritchel will overheat and lose their shape. If the metal is blackening the stamp and pritchel will be blunted, thickened, bent or broken.

The shoe is placed flat on the anvil face, fullering upwards. The stamp and pritchel are held at such an angle (pitch) that the angle of each nail hole corresponds with the slope of the hoof wall and thus the point of the nail will emerge on the foot surface at the outer edge of the white zone.

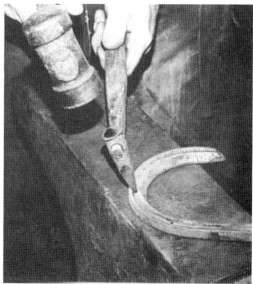

Fig. 6.47 The toe nail hole is the most pitched.

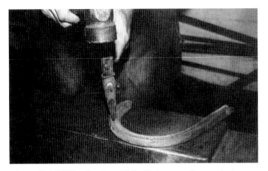

Fig. 6.48 The heel nail hole is nearly upright.

Care should be taken that the stamp is not held twisted in the fullering. The edges of the nail hole should be parallel with the edges of the shoe.

The stamp and pritchel are struck with the hammer. Two blows on the stamp should be sufficient to drive it *almost* through the thickness of the bar. Do not drive the stamp down on to the anvil face.

Stamp first at the cooler end of the branch, before it gets any cooler, to avoid distorting the stamp on blackening steel. When all the outside nail holes have been started with the stamp it is laid aside and the pritchel is used to shear out the bottom of each hole.

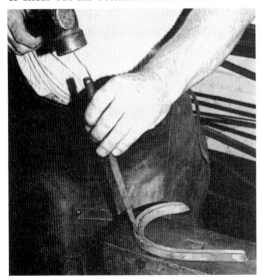

Fig. 6.49 The pritchel is struck over the pritchel hole on the anvil face. One confident blow should suffice.

Fig. 6.50 The shoe is turned over. If any of the small rectangular pieces punched out by the pritchel are still attached to the edge of a nail hole they are removed with light glancing hammer blows or with the coarse face of the hot rasp. If this is necessary it is a sign that either the stamp or the pritchel is the wrong shape or that the pritchel is losing its edge.

Fig. 6.51 The foot surface is now smoothed with overlapping blows on the face of the anvil.

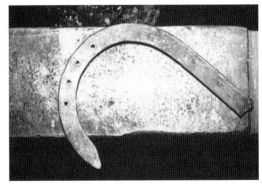

Fig. 6.52 The stamp will cause some bulging of the width of the bar. Too much bulging indicates that the stamp is too thick.

Fig. 6.53 After forming the nail holes the flat face of the hammer should be run round the outside of the branch over the beak of the anvil in overlapping blows to smooth out the bulges.

Fig. 6.54 The hammer is now run round the upper outside edge to box it off slightly.

These procedures tend to close the nail holes and so the pritchel should be passed again through each one.

The foot surface is again smoothed and levelled.

The nail holes should be checked to ensure that the chosen size of nail will fit.

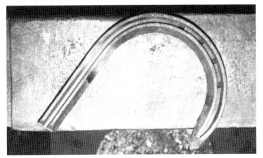

Fig. 6.55 Outer branch shaped and nail holes punched.

Stage 4: Forging the inside heel

This is the same as for the outside heel except that the fullering is closed from just behind the planned position of the last nail hole.

Fig. 6.56 A suitably long yellow heat is required. The bar is held with the inside edge on the anvil face and the fullering is closed with light overlapping blows from the flat face of the hammer.

Fig. 6.57 The foot surface will tend to become convex when the fullering is closed. The bar must be turned and smoothed with a few light overlapping blows.

Fig. 6.58 The heel is shaped.

Stage 5: Shaping the inside branch and punching the nail holes

The technique is the same as for the outside. Three holes are stamped, equally spaced.

Stage 6: Forming the toe clip

*Fig. **6.60** Completed bubble.*

*Fig. **6.59** A bubble is drawn with an oval bob punch. The punch is positioned in the fullering at the centre mark though slightly towards the inside to compensate for the inside branch having been drawn slightly more when the fullering was closed over. The punch is leant to point outwards and a couple of firm blows are struck on the face of the anvil which tend to push out the edge of the shoe. The shoe is then moved to the pritchel hole and a few more blows are struck with the punch positioned directly over the edge of the hole which pushes the metal further out and down.*

*Fig. **6.61** The bubble is placed over a good sharp right-angled edge of the anvil. A position is chosen that enables the hammer handle to be held below the level of the anvil face. The shoe is held at an angle and the bubble is struck with successive blows of the lower part of the flat face of the hammer bringing the shoe down against the side of the anvil as the bubble is trapped.*

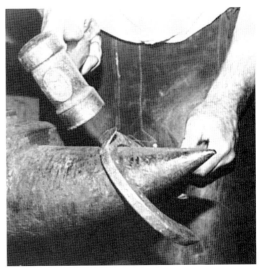

Fig. **6.63** *The base of the clip is smoothed into the edge of the shoe with light overlapping blows over the beak and in the same way the slope of the clip is set at the angle of the wall of the hoof.*

Fig. **6.62** *A slight gap is created between the shoe and the anvil as the end of the clip is drawn.*

Fig. **6.64** *Front view.*

Finally the shoe is brought up against the anvil again as the clip is given a few blows to smooth it.

It is crucial to hold the shoe steady with the left hand as the clip is drawn. If the shoe is allowed to slip down the side of the anvil or to turn like a steering wheel the clip will be distorted.

Fig. **6.65** *Side view.*

Stage 7: Hot rasping the heels

Each heel in turn is brought to a short yellow or red heat (a red heat will make for harder work but will result in less bending of the bar).

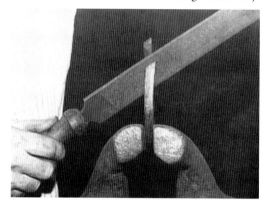

Fig. 6.66 The shoe is held firmly in a vice and the heels rasped with straight strokes, first with the coarse side, then with the file side of the rasp. The profile should be straight, the sides blending with the contours of the inside and outside of the branch. The outline from above and below should be roughly that of an equilateral triangle but with rounded sides.

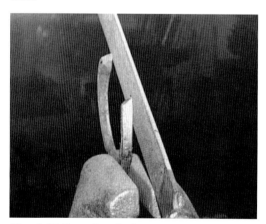

Fig. 6.67 Removing the burr.

The edges should be smooth. The branch is levelled on the face of the anvil.

Stage 8: Finishing off the shoe

The whole shoe should be heated to a red heat, any adjustments in shape carried out over the beak and the shoe levelled on the face of the anvil.

The round face of the hammer may be run lightly round the inside edge of the foot surface on the face of the anvil to seat it out very slightly: just enough to take away the sharpness of the edge to remove any pressure on the sole.

The nail holes should be checked again to ensure that the correct size of nail fits. If necessary they may be enlarged slightly with the pritchel or any burr at the foot surface removed by light back pritchelling.

Vigorous brushing will now improve the finished appearance of the shoe as will the use of a half-round file around the clips and heels, over the surfaces and round the edges.

Fig. 6.68 Completed shoe, ground surface.

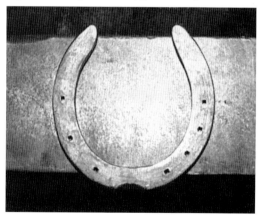

Fig. 6.69 Foot surface.

The shoe can now be quenched in water or allowed to cool in air. If quenched it will be harder and longer-wearing. If allowed to cool slowly it will be easier to carry out small alterations to the shoe when cold.

A good specimen front shoe has the following points. Branches are of equal length with the clip in the centre. The shape is circular round the toe and straighter from the widest points to the heels. The toe nail holes are in line with a tangent from the inside edge at the centre of the toe. There are four equally spaced nail holes on the outside and three equally spaced nail holes on the inside. The front edge of the outside heel nail hole and the back edge of the inside heel nail hole are midway from the toe nail hole to the end of the heel. The heels are in line with the toe nail holes. Nails of the chosen size should fit snugly in their holes with their heads just above the fullering and with the correct amount of pitch in their shanks.

The shoe should be level. The foot surface should be smooth, especially at the back of the clip, and should not slope inwards. Hammer marks should be indiscernible and the width of the bar should not have been reduced at any point, nor should it have any bulges. The upper outside edge should be bevelled slightly.

The height of the clip is equal to the width of its base and the width of the bar. The clip diminishes in thickness from its base to its point which is rounded. The clip is symmetrical and set at the angle of the hoof at the toe.

6.5 Making a hind shoe from concave fullered bar

The centre should be marked ¼ in. (6 mm) nearer to (what will be) the inside branch when the traditional outside heel is to be forged (this is drawn very little and fitted full as will be described). A rule and a hammer and centre punch are used for this. Experienced farriers may not make any mark, preferring to shape the toe bend by eye so that the outside branch is ¼ in. (6 mm) longer than the inside. This works for the hind shoe because its shape, not being an even curve as in the front shoe, clearly defines the centre of the shoe.

The outside heel of a hind shoe can be forged as for a front shoe if preferred, in which case the bar can be marked in the centre as for a front shoe.

Stage 1: Turning the toe

The toe is turned as for a front shoe but with a shorter, sharper bend to conform with the more pointed shape of a hind foot.

Fig. 6.70 The fullering is closed over the beak of the anvil. This is to ease breakover, prolong wear and reduce injury to the front leg in case of overreaching.

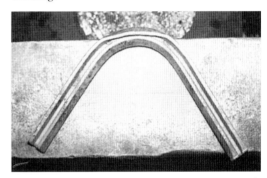

Fig. 6.71 The ends of the bar will be at an angle of 70°–80° to each other.

Stage 2: Forging the outside heel

Fig. 6.72 This consists of simply chamfering the inside. The slope of the heel is thus upright with the outside protruding, being boxed off by hot rasping on the foot surface so that the protrusion is not trodden on by another horse.

Stage 3: Shaping the outside branch and punching the nail holes

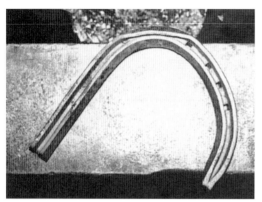

Fig. 6.73 This is the same as for a front shoe except that the quarters are straighter. The widest part of the shoe is two-thirds of the way back conforming with the usual shape of a hind foot. As hind hooves are generally less sloping all round than front hooves there should be less pitch in the nail holes.

Stage 4: Forging the inside heel

Fig. 6.74 This is the same as for a front shoe except that the heel is more upright.

Stage 5: Shaping the inside branch and punching the nail holes

This is the same as for the outside branch.

Stage 6: Making the quarter clips

Clips are drawn as for the front shoe but placed between the first and second nail holes on each branch. This permits the toe of the shoe to be fitted slightly under the toe of the hoof to prevent over-reach injury to the front leg.

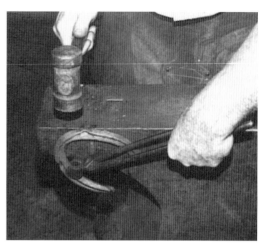

Fig. 6.75 For a right-handed person it is best to draw the right clip first to prevent it getting in the way when drawing the left clip. The clips are set to the angle of the wall.

Stage 7: Hot rasping the heels

The traditional outside heel is upright in profile, blending at the sides with the inside and outside of the branch. The foot surface is boxed off on the outside so that the bearing surface has the same triangular ending as for a front heel. The inside heel is the same as for a front shoe but more upright.

Stage 8: Finishing off the shoe

This is the same as for a front shoe. Because of the more convex sole of the average hind foot seating out is usually omitted.

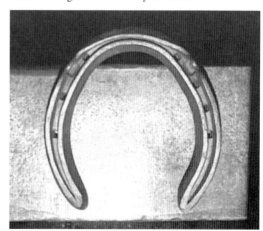

Fig. 6.76 Hind shoe.

6.6 Making a hind shoe with a calkin and wedge

A calkin and wedge are projections to prevent slipping. The refined shape of a wedge as compared with the simplicity of a calkin is determined by the wish to fit the shoe to the exact width and length of the inside heel of the hoof and to reduce the danger of injury from interference. This is a traditional shoe for hunters but it is time-consuming to make, difficult to fit as the heels once formed cannot be drawn or shortened, and unbalances the foot. The main value of the shoe is as a forging exercise. The bulk of the forging should be performed at a yellow heat.

Though making both wedge and calkin are described for simplicity in stages, in practice there can be considerable overlapping between the stages.

A. The wedge

Stage 1: Upsetting the end of the bar

It is best to hold the bar in the hand for this stage, though tongs may be used if preferred. It is *crucial* to have a *very short yellow heat*. At most 1 in. (25 mm) of the end of the bar should be yellow.

Fig. 6.77 The fullering is knocked over on the outside and the inside edge is also given a light blow on the face of the anvil so that one is starting with a more compact block of metal which is easier to upset.

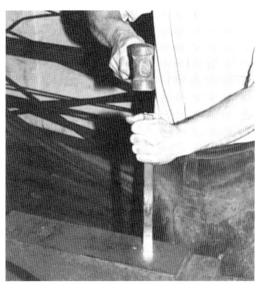

Fig. 6.78 The bar is held vertically on the anvil face with the fullering towards the farrier and struck with the hammer to upset the end. The hot section of the bar will be thickened by this operation so that a wedge can be drawn from it without loss of the width of the bar. If too long a heat is started with then a great deal of time and effort will be wasted in upsetting too great a length of bar and drawing it out again. If the bar starts to bend during upsetting it should be straightened before continuing.

Stage 2: Sloping the end of the bar

Fig. 6.79 At a yellow heat the end of the bar is now struck to slope the end of the wedge. The bar is held flat on the anvil with the end over the far edge. Hollow bit tongs are best for holding the bar at this and for the remaining stages. The basic shape of the wedge will now be formed.

Stage 3: Drawing the wedge

Fig. 6.80 The wedge is now drawn on the anvil face, being hit on both sides with the flat face of the hammer. The outside of the wedge should slope more than the inside. The first blows should be on the outside. The bar should be held with the foot surface upright on the anvil face when the first blows are struck. This will ensure that the inside of the wedge is started upright and not at too much of a slope which would be very difficult to change later. More blows should be struck on the outside of the wedge than on the inside.

Stage 4: Setting the wedge

Fig. 6.81 A clear demarcation is made at the front of the wedge and the bar is drawn up to this point by hammering over the far edge of the anvil. It is important to look at the underside of the bar while setting the wedge or a series of steps may be created or the wedge may not be cut in at the right place. The bar should be drawn to half its original thickness but the width of the foot surface should not be reduced except to the normal short taper of a heel at the end. The same overlapping blows from the flat face of the hammer used to set the wedge also level and smooth the foot surface.

Stage 5: Shaping the wedge

The wedge is finally shaped with further blows on the front, sides, back and top of the wedge. The better the forging the less hot rasping will be needed later.

Fig. 6.82 Side view.

Fig. 6.83 Ground surface.

Stage 6: Hot rasping the wedge

The wedge is brought to a red or yellow heat, the bar held firmly in a vice and the wedge rasped first with the coarse side, then with the file side of the rasp. The wedge should have a straight profile when viewed from the side and a rounded shape when viewed from above. The bar in front of the wedge should be rounded from side to side. There should be no sharp edges.

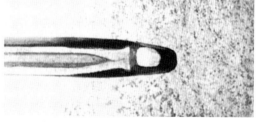

Fig. 6.84 A good wedge has a height equal to the width of the bar used. The slope of the front and back of the wedge should be equal and should be more than 45°. The slope of the inside should be approaching, but not quite, 90° and the outside should be slightly more sloping than the inside.

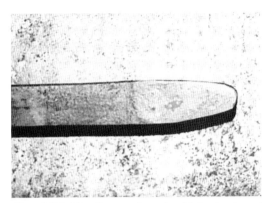

Fig. 6.85 The foot surface should be level and smooth and shaped like an ordinary heel, retaining most of the width of the bar until near the end.

B. The calkin

A short heat is not required as for forging the wedge. At least 2 ins (5 cm) of the end of the bar should be yellow. The wedge heel is held in hollow bit tongs to make the calkin. Alternatively the toe may be turned and ordinary tongs used to grip the shoe at the toe. The tongs are in line with the outside branch in both cases.

Stage 1: Bending the bar

Fig. 6.86 First close the fullering and take the sharp edge off the inside as in starting a wedge. This makes a more solid block which is easier to forge.

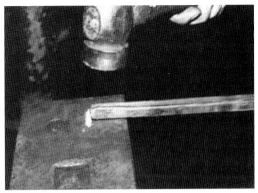

Fig. 6.87 One and a half inches (4 cm) are usually turned for a calkin. To assist this make a chalk mark on the anvil 1½ ins (4 cm) from the near edge. Line up the end of the bar with this mark, drop the left hand and strike the fullered surface with the hammer.

Fig. 6.88 The foot surface will be creased by the edge of the anvil 1½ ins (4 cm) from the end.

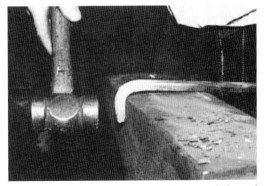

Fig. 6.89 The bar is then turned over and the end bent over the far edge of the anvil in line with this crease. It is important to get a good right-angled bend at this stage.

Stage 2: Hammering down the calkin

Fig. 6.90 The end of the bar which has been bent upwards is now forged into a solid block with blows on the end from the flat face of the hammer.

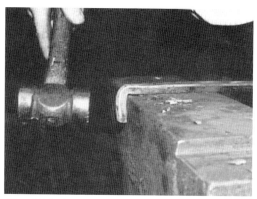

Fig. 6.91 If it starts to buckle or bend this must be corrected before continuing.

Fig. 6.92 A solid block.

Stage 3: Shaping the calkin

Fig. 6.93 The inside edge of the calkin is chamfered to correspond with the bar of the hoof as for a normal heel. The outside edge is left full as for the traditional outside heel and later boxed off with a rasp.

Fig. 6.94 The front edge is set at an angle to the bar to face forwards on the finished shoe. This is achieved by moving the bar towards the outside while hitting the back of the calkin over the far edge of the anvil.

Stage 4: Setting the calkin

Fig. 6.95 The calkin is set as for a wedge although not so deeply, over the edge of the anvil or the end of a half-round swage, and at an angle as described above.

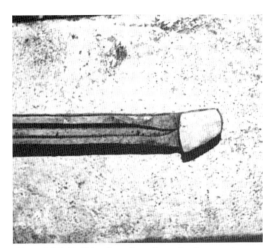

Fig. 6.96 Calkin forged and ready for rasping.

Stage 5: Hot rasping the calkin

The calkin is hot rasped to give it a smooth finish, take off the sharp edges, box off the outside foot surface and round the bar in front of the calkin from side to side. The calkin should have a vertical profile when viewed from the side and straight sides and rounded corners when viewed from above.

A good calkin should be equal in height to the wedge, which is of course equal in height to the width of the bar. The face of the calkin should have a slight slope from front to back so that it rests flat on the ground when the shoe is completed. The height of the calkin is measured at the back.

C. Completing the shoe

Fig. 6.97 The centre of the bar is marked using a ruler, hammer and centre punch.

Fig. 6.98 The toe and branches are turned, the nail holes punched and quarter clips drawn as for a normal hind shoe.

6.7 Making a plain fullered shoe

Fullering should be performed at a yellow heat, dipping the tool in oil or water to prevent it getting too hot and losing its shape. A lubricant on the fuller can be used, such as saddle soap which also serves to cool the fuller.

Because the fullering iron pushes out the outside edge of the bar, the more so the finer the fullering, the hammer should be run along the outside edge of the bar in preparation, chamfering it towards the ground surface, with the inside edge flat on the anvil face. This will also have the effect of creating a ridge along the outside of the ground surface which helps to guide the blade of the fuller. It is easier to start fullering a shoe before the bar is bent. Once the shoe is shaped the fullering can be completed to its final depth.

The farrier holds the fullering iron in one hand and the tongs and shoe in the other hand while the fuller is drawn towards the farrier with a rocking movement which keeps the rear of the blade of the tool in the groove as it is advanced.

When the shoe is levelled all blows should be directed to the inside of the fullering.

Front shoe

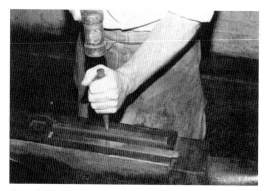

Fig. 6.99 Having cut the appropriate length of bar mark the centre on the inside of the ground surface.

Fig. 6.100 One half of the bar is heated and the outside edge is chamfered, keeping the inside edge flat on the anvil, from the end to 1½ ins (4 cm) past the centre mark.

Fig. 6.101 The bar is then fullered from the centre to the end, which will be the end nearest to the farrier. If the far end is fullered first the hand holding the fuller will be uncomfortably positioned over the hot bar. The far end can be fullered more comfortably when the near branch has been turned.

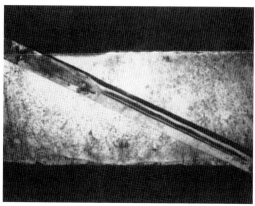

Fig. 6.102

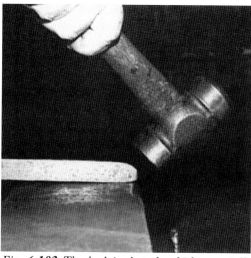

Fig. 6.103 The heel is shaped, which essentially involves chamfering the inside.

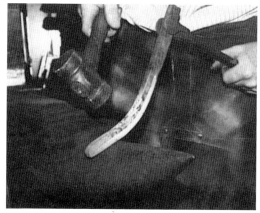

Fig. 6.104 The branch is turned.

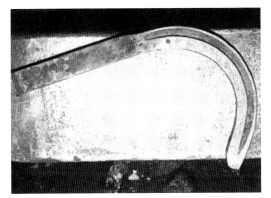

Fig. **6.105**

Fig. **6.108** *The heel is shaped.*

Fig. **6.106** *The other branch is then heated and the outside edge chamfered.*

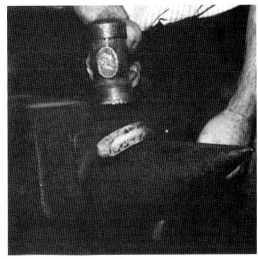

Fig. **6.109** *The branch is turned.*

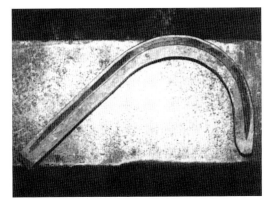

Fig. **6.107** *The branch is fullered from the heel to join the original fullering at the toe. The inside branch can be fullered slightly more finely than the outside branch.*

Fig. **6.110** *It is best not to fuller too deeply before turning each branch, and then to finish fullering with the branches turned.*

F—I

Fig. **6.111** *The groove should be as deep as possible without splitting the metal so the nail heads, which fit in the fullering, will not be worn away before the shoe is worn through. The fuller should not be struck when the metal is blackening as, apart from the damage this may do to the fuller, the bar may split.*

Fig. **6.112** *The nail holes are stamped and pritchelled, the bulges made by the stamp are smoothed out, the outside edge of the foot surface is bevelled slightly, the shoe is seated out slightly and the shoe is levelled.*

Hind shoe

Fig. **6.113** *The centre of the bar is upset slightly because the toe is not fullered and will otherwise be narrower than the quarters. The bar is straightened when it starts to buckle.*

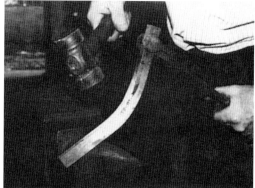

Fig. **6.114** *The toe is turned.*

Fig. **6.115** *A mark for one toe nail hole is made.*

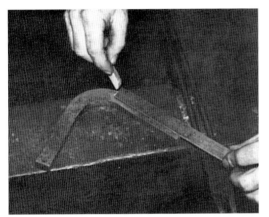

Fig. **6.116** *The outside toe nail is measured to be ¹/₄ in. (6 mm) further from the heel than the inside toe nail hole.*

Fig. **6.117** *The second toe nail hole is marked.*

Fig. **6.118**

Fig. **6.119** *Each branch is then heated and the outside edge chamfered.*

Fig. **6.120** *The branch is fullered and the heel is shaped.*

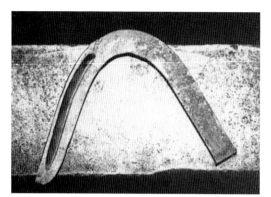

Fig. **6.121**

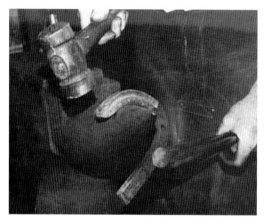

Fig. **6.122** *The branch is turned.*

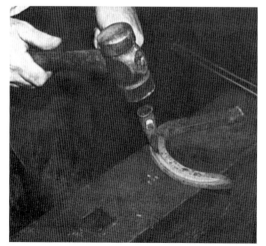

Fig. **6.123** *The nail holes are stamped and pritchelled in the normal way. The bulges made by the stamp are smoothed out and the upper outside edge is bevelled slightly.*

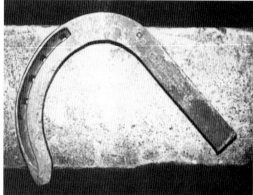

Fig. **6.124** *Outside branch completed.*

Fig. **6.125**

Fig. **6.126**

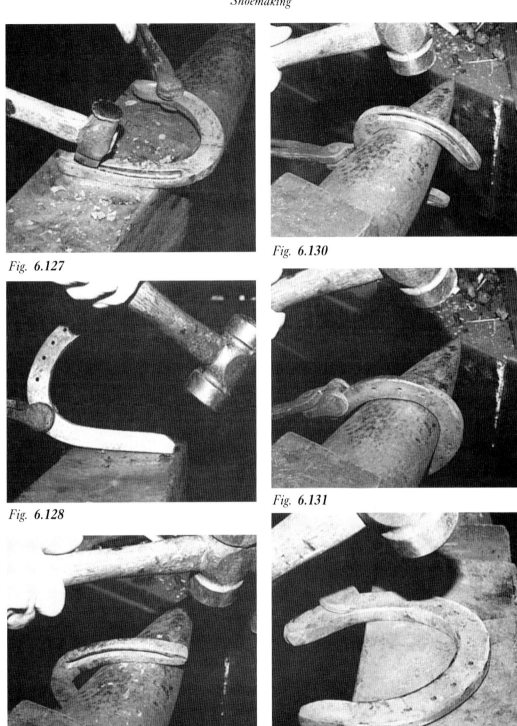

Fig. **6.127**

Fig. **6.128**

Fig. **6.129**

Fig. **6.130**

Fig. **6.131**

Fig. **6.132**

Fig. **6.133**

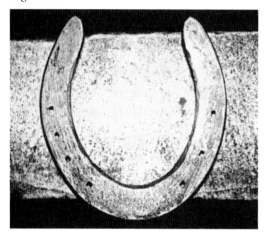

Fig. **6.134**

6.8 Making special shoes

Sidebone shoe (Fig. 6.135)
A sidebone shoe is made from flat bar and is plain stamped. Sidebones most commonly develop on one side, the lateral side, of the foot and the shoe described is for such a case.

A sidebone shoe is usually made from 1 in. x ½ in. (25 mm x 12 mm) flat bar. The length required is the same as for a normal shoe.

The toe is bent and the outside branch formed. The outside branch is then chamfered on the ground surface towards the outside, retaining the thickness of the inner edge. The chamfering, which has the effect of broadening the web, should be greatest at the heel and gradually reduced towards the toe.

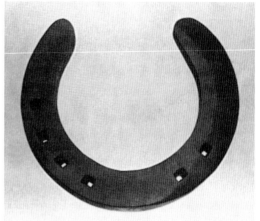

Fig. **6.135** *Sidebone shoe.*

Two nail holes are stamped in the toe quarter. The outside edge of the foot surface is boxed off heavily at the heel.

The inside branch is turned and four nail holes stamped in the first half.

Speedy-cutting shoe
A speedy-cutting shoe is made from square bar which is tooled and fullered. Tooling means putting the bar through a swage block to make concave bar.

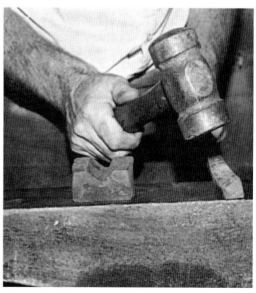

Fig. **6.136** *First one edge is chamfered so that the bar will fit deeper into the swage block.*

To calculate the length of square bar needed first add the width plus the length of the foot plus 1½ ins (4 cm). This is the normal way of calculating the length of concave bar for a shoe. The length of square bar which will produce this is then calculated. This will depend on the individual swage, but an increase in length of between a third and a half is usual.

For a medium-sized foot ⅝ in. (16 mm) square bar is put through a swage block to produce ¾ in. x ⁷⁄₁₆ in. (19 mm x 11 mm) concave.

The outside branch is formed first by tooling from the centre of the bar to one end.

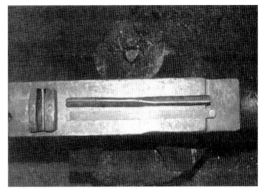

*Fig. **6.139** The bar is then turned around and the inside branch is tooled. The swage block is not turned around so that the concaving will be on the outside of the inside branch.*

*Fig. **6.137** The bar is hammered through the swage block.*

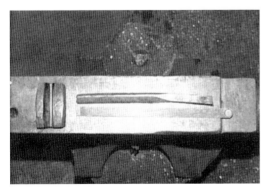

*Fig. **6.138** A centre mark is made by measuring off half the intended length of the tooled bar.*

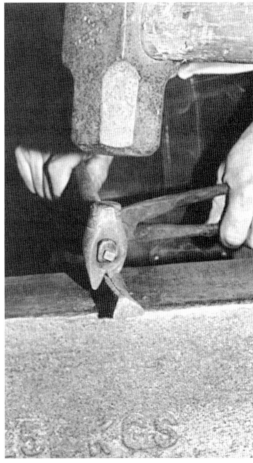

*Fig. **6.140** The outside branch is fullered. The fullering is first marked with a guide fuller.*

*Fig. **6.141** The fullering is continued with the fuller. The branch is turned. The inside branch is shaped straight across the toe quarter. This means that the heel will be too long and must be carefully cropped to balance the shoe.*

*Fig. **6.142** Two nail holes are stamped finely in the inside heel quarter. The shoe will tend to slide away from the stamp and so it is advisable to steady it on the anvil face with the sledge hammer held by the striker.*

*Fig. **6.143** Speedy-cutting shoe.*

Navicular shoe (Fig. 6.144)

A navicular shoe for a medium-sized foot is made from ¾ in. x ½ in. (20 mm x 12 mm) flat bar. The length needed is the same as for a normal shoe using the same bar.

Both heels are upset slightly. The toe is turned. The middle of the bar is drawn out on the flat of the anvil to thin it and widen it and the quarters are drawn so as to give a steady increase in thickness from toe to heels. The quarters are then fullered, the heels shaped and the branches turned, the fullering completed and the nail holes punched. Finally the toe is rolled.

When the shoe is nailed on the heads of the nails towards the toe will be more prominent than those further back and should be rasped down.

*Fig. **6.144** Navicular shoe.*

Spavin shoe (Fig. 6.145)

A spavin shoe is made from flat bar, usually 1 in. x ½ in. (25 mm x 12 mm). The length of bar required equals the length plus the

*Fig. **6.145** Spavin shoe.*

width of the hoof plus a further 1½ ins (4 cm) for each heel.

The toe is upset for thickness. The heels are then thickened by upsetting. Long sloping heels are forged. The toe is turned.

The quarters are thinned slightly since they will not be subjected to wear, and are fullered. The width of the branches must be retained to ensure ample bearing surface. The branches are turned and the nail holes punched. The toe is rolled.

Bar shoe from concave fullered stock
A bar shoe made from concave fullered stock uses the usual length of stock plus the width of the bar plus ½ in. (12 mm) to allow for the loss of metal in welding.

*Fig. **6.147** Bend the toe. Make the heel bends.*

*Fig. **6.148** Scarf the ends.*

*Fig. **6.146** The ends of the bar are upset slightly to allow for loss of metal in welding.*

*Fig **6.149** Make sure that one scarf faces up and one down so that they will mate.*

Fig. **6.150** *Scarfs completed.*

Fig. **6.153** *Draw out a frog plate on the anvil face with the round face of the hammer.*

Fig. **6.151** *Weld the bar.*

Fig. **6.154** *Shaping the bar over the beak. The nail holes are punched in the normal way.*

Fig. **6.152** *The back of the ground surface of the bar is chamfered.*

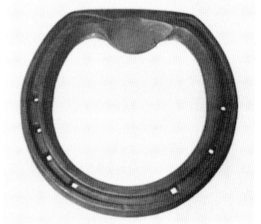

Fig. **6.155** *Concave fullered bar shoe.*

Bar shoe tooled and fullered

A tooled and fullered bar shoe is made from square bar stock. To calculate the length needed first add the width and the length of the foot plus the width of the bar, plus ½ in. (12 mm) to allow for the loss of metal in welding. This is the normal way of calculating the length of concave bar for the shoe. The length of square bar which will produce this is then calculated. For a medium-sized foot ⅝ in. (16 mm) square bar is put through a swage block to produce ¾ in. x ⁷⁄₁₆ in. (20 mm x 10 mm) concave.

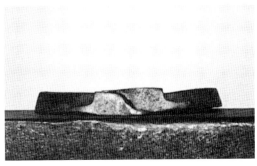

Fig. 6.158 End view of scarf. The bar is welded. The back of the ground surface of the bar is chamfered.

Fig. 6.156 The square bar is tooled except for ½ in. (12 mm) at each end.

The fullering is commenced while the bar is straight from the toe to the nearest end and the branch is turned. The bar is then fullered from the far end to the toe and this branch is turned. The heel bends are made.

Fig. 6.159 Drawing out a frog plate. The thickness of the bar should equal the thickness of the shoe.

Fig. 6.157 The ends are scarfed.

Fig. 6.160 The bar is shaped.

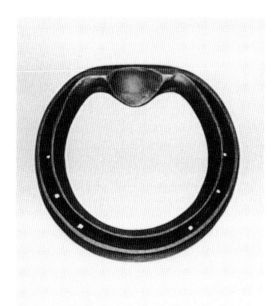

Fig. 6.161 Tooled and fullered bar shoe.

Fig. 6.162 The seating out is commenced on the straight bar.

Seated-out shoe (Figs 6.162–6.164)

A seated-out shoe is usually made from flat bar and is fullered. The length needed equals the length and width of the foot. No extra is needed since the bar is drawn considerably by the processes of seating and fullering. A shoe for a medium-sized foot is made from ¾ in. x ½ in. (20 mm x 12 mm) flat bar.

Fig. 6.163 Seated-out shoe, ground surface.

The seating out is commenced on the straight bar (Fig 6.162). The seating is done on the face of the anvil with the round face of the hammer and should extend to not more than half the width of the bar and from the toe to about half way along the quarters. The seating out is not too deep at this stage which makes it easier to turn the shoe. The bar will tend to twist and should be levelled and straightened frequently.

The outer edge is knocked over and the bar is fullered from the far heel to the toe. The other branch is then heated, knocked over and fullered from the toe to the heel.

The toe and branches are turned, heels shaped, the seating out and fullering completed and the nail holes punched.

The difficulty with making this shoe is that the seating out tends to destroy the fullering and vice-versa.

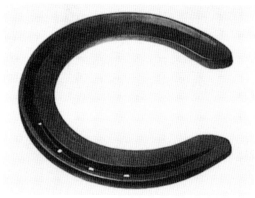

Fig. 6.164 Seated-out shoe, foot surface.

Seated-out bar shoe (Figs 6.165–6.166)

This shoe is made as for a seated-out shoe but allowing extra length equal to the intended width of the bar plus an extra ½ in. (12 mm) to allow for loss of metal in welding.

Fig. **6.165** *Seated-out bar shoe, ground surface.*

Fig. **6.167** *The bar is marked at the centre and at the positions of the first bend at each heel, which is calculated so as to leave the length plus the width of the hoof plus 1 in. (25 mm) for the branches of the shoe. Each end can be upset slightly to allow for loss of metal in welding. Each end is scarfed.*

Fig **6.166** *Seated-out bar shoe, foot surface.*

The first stages are similar to the stages of making a seated-out shoe. The fullering stops 2½ ins (6 cm) from each heel. Bend the toe. Scarf the ends. Bend in the heels. Weld. The bar is shaped over the beak of the anvil, the frog plate drawn out on the flat of the anvil, and the back of the ground surface is chamfered. The shoe is shaped. The fuller is run through again. The seating out is completed.

The centre of the toe is marked before the nail holes are punched. The nails are spaced widely so that a clip can go anywhere between them.

Fig. **6.168** *Each end is then bent to form the shape of the heels. First an 80° bend is made on edge at the mark, keeping the mark in the centre of the bend. This is done over the edge of the anvil.*

Patten shoe

A Patten shoe is made from ³/₄ in. x ¹/₄ in. (20 mm x 6mm) flat bar. To calculate the amount required add the length and the width of the foot to the width and twice the height of the bar plus ¹/₂ in. (12 mm) to allow for metal lost in fire welding. Remember that the width of the bar is greater than the width of the heels of the foot by about ¹/₂ in. (12 mm) to give the shoe stability.

*Fig. **6.169** Then the end is bent at right angles along the line of the outside edge of the branch. This is done in a vice, the bar being placed in the vice with the outside edge parallel to the jaws and protruding above them by ¹/₄ in. (6 mm), the thickness of the metal.*

*Fig. **6.170** The end of the bar is knocked over at right angles, the upper surface being level with the upper edge of the branch.*

*Fig. **6.171***

*Fig. **6.172** The final bend is made in the vice using a short length of flat bar of suitable thickness for the height of heel required. Here a length of ³/₄ in. (19 mm) square is used which will give the heel a height of 1in. (25 mm). The two heels are made in the same way but the first bend of the second heel must be in the opposite direction to which the other end of the bar is pointing.*

*Fig. **6.173** The toe bend is made and then the branches are bent so that the scarfs have come together in the centre of the bar. The bar is welded. The nail holes are stamped and the toe is rolled.*

*Fig. **6.174** Patten shoe, ground surface.*

*Fig. **6.175** Patten shoe, foot surface.*

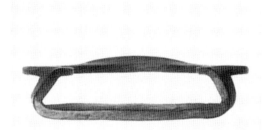

*Fig. **6.176** Patten shoe, rear view.*

Hackney shoes (Figs 6.177–6.178)

Hackney shoes are made from flat bar. The shoe is toe weighted, the toe being upset to thicken it. The length of bar needed is usually the length plus the width of the foot plus either 2 ins (5 cm) for a horse or 1 in. (2.5 cm) for a pony. This calculation applies to both front and hind shoes. This is the length of bar used for a normal shoe plus an allowance for upsetting the toe, in this case 1 in. (25 mm) for a horse and ½ in. (12 mm) for a pony. The heels of the front shoe are upright and thus are drawn very little although the whole branch is narrowed slightly. No allowance is made for a calk and wedge for the hind shoe since the branches are drawn out in front of the calk and wedge.

Thus a typical horse with a front foot 5¼ ins long and 5 ins wide (13.3 cm x 12.7 cm) would require 12¼ ins (31 cm) of bar and a typical pony with a foot 4¼ ins by 4 ins (10.8 cm x 10.2 cm) would require 9¼ ins (23.5 cm) of bar.

One inch by ½ in. (25 mm x 12 mm) flat bar is the average size used for horses and ¾ in. x ⅜ in. (20 mm x 10 mm) for ponies.

A *front shoe* is made by first upsetting the toe. The length of the bar is reduced by the amount allowed for. The toe is then turned. As with all shoes the outer edge will stretch

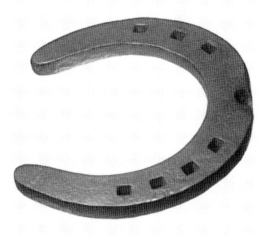

*Fig. **6.177** Hackney shoe, front.*

and the inner edge will thicken. Because the toe has been upset the outer edge is still relatively thick and the inner edge is reduced in proportion. Before turning each branch it is reduced in width gradually from the toe quarter back to the heel. The branches are then turned and the nail holes stamped.

A *hind shoe* with a calkin and wedge is of the pattern known as a roadster hind shoe. The toe is upset first as before. Secondly the wedge is upset and shaped, then the calkin is formed. The technique for making a calk and wedge from flat bar is the same as described for concave bar. The toe is then turned and the shoe completed.

Fig. 6.178 Hackney shoe, hind.

6.9 Working with aluminium alloy

Aluminium alloy is available in a wide range of sizes of flat and round bar. It is relatively soft and easy to forge. It cannot be welded in the forge fire although modern fluxes make it possible to weld at least certain types of aluminium alloy in a gas forge. All other forging procedures that can be performed with steel can be performed with aluminium.

Aluminium alloy is more expensive than steel and does not stand up to wear nearly as well. It is a better conductor of heat than steel. Its advantage is its lightness, being one third the density of iron and steel.

Aluminium alloy has a melting point of 660°C (1220°F) and so must be heated very carefully or it will be destroyed in the fire. To test the heat of aluminium alloy a spent match should be rubbed against the bar. If the match smoulders the aluminium is hot enough. When fullering aluminium or drawing it through a swage it tends to stick. To overcome this tools should have a smooth finish and if necessary be lubricated with soap.

Aluminium alloy can be heated enough to char the hoof, at least to show where the shoe does and does not contact the hoof but not sufficiently to burn it on to the hoof. This is a risky thing to do with an all but completed shoe and so it is usual to fit aluminium shoes cold.

Aluminium alloy is not hardened by quenching it in water. It is easy to file when cold. Racing plates are specially heat treated to give them extra hardness without becoming too brittle. This process cannot be duplicated in the forge. They can be satisfactorily shaped, nail holes stamped and pritchelled and clips drawn from them cold. If they are heated their extra hardness will be lost.

Tungsten carbide in an alloy matrix can be applied to aluminium alloy shoes to increase wear and traction, much in the same way that borium is applied to steel shoes, but the shoes tend to bend and spread when used and thus the process has limited value.

6.10 Working with tool steel

Tool steel is harder than mild steel. Modern tool steels come in a wide variety of alloys and may contain elements such as tungsten, chromium, cobalt, vanadium and titanium as well as carbon.

High speed steel is capable of being worked at a high temperature without losing hardness. It is used for tools such as drills and taps.

High carbon steel (cast steel) is most commonly used for blacksmiths' and farriers' tools. It contains from 0.5–1.5% carbon. The most useful type for stamps and pritchels is the AISI (American Iron and Steel Institute) designation S1 which contains 0.5% carbon plus chromium for hardness, tungsten for fatigue resistance, silicon and vanadium.

S1 combines good shock resistance with hot working properties, is economically priced and readily available.

High carbon tool steel should be forged at a yellow or light red heat. If overheated it becomes weakened, its crystal structure becoming irreversibly altered at high temperatures, and it also loses its carbon content. If struck at a black heat it will crack. A tool should be carefully annealed after forging otherwise it may shatter when struck. The tip of the tool only may then be hardened and tempered if desired.

Hardening and tempering are the processes by which high carbon tool steel is brought to the correct blend of hardness and elasticity for the work involved.

Hardening is attained by heating the steel to a high temperature and then quenching it rapidly in water or oil. This gives the steel maximum hardness but also makes it brittle. From this state the hardness is reduced to a suitable degree (tempered) by reheating.

One method of tempering is by colour. Heat is applied to the shank of the tool and thus is conducted to the blade. The blade is rubbed with a file or abrasive stone and the changing colours of the oxide film are used as an indication of temperature. The colours range from pale yellow through pale and dark straw, purple and blue as the temperature rises from 220°C (430°F) to 325°C (600°F). As the chosen colour is reached the tool is quenched. Generally tools used for cutting are tempered to a straw colour while tools which are hammered are tempered to a purple colour.

Modern alloys need to be brought up to the correct temperature in a furnace and 'soaked' at that temperature for long periods.

Annealing is a process by which high carbon steel is brought to a soft condition and internal stresses are released. The steel is heated to a red heat and allowed to cool slowly in the forge fire overnight.

Normalising is a quicker but less efficient method of annealing, the red hot steel being allowed to cool in air. The thicker the piece of steel the slower it will cool and the more effective normalising will be.

Case hardening is a process for hardening mild steel. Mild steel has a low percentage of carbon and cannot be hardened very much by quenching. It is, however, possible to produce a hard outer layer by increasing the carbon content. The mild steel is packed in a box containing charcoal and heated.

F—J

CHAPTER 7

THE PRACTICE OF SHOEING

Horseshoes are fitted to protect the foot and prevent it wearing away faster than the rate of growth. The shoe, as far as possible, should not interfere with either the normal function of the foot or the gait of the horse.

Before shoeing a horse the farrier must note the conformation of its limbs and feet, its action and the wear of its shoes or hooves. The horse should be seen walked and trotted on a clean level surface in good light. This information will enable the farrier to balance the feet and the gait and decide upon the type of shoe required.

Shoeing can often improve the gait of a horse whose conformation is less than perfect and whose hooves wear unevenly.

7.1 Management and control of the horse

Whether the farrier is dealing with a horse that he has shod on many occasions or a foal that has never had its feet attended to before, the same basic principles will apply.

The farrier must carry out his tasks in a quiet unhurried manner, if the horse has to be restrained it must be secured with a headcollar or halter and the rope tied with a quick-release knot or tied to baling twine which will break if the horse panics.

Whenever possible the horse should be held by an attendant with whom it is familiar. The attendant should stand on the same side of the horse as the farrier so that if the horse turns the farrier can keep by the attendant and will not be exposed to a kick from the hind feet. This is particularly important when dealing with young and nervous horses. There should always be plenty of room to safeguard the farrier and the attendant.

If a farrier is confident of his safety he may place the attendant on the opposite side of the horse to prevent the horse moving away from

him. Both attendant and farrier should be wary of a horse rearing and striking out with its front feet. Wearing a hat will not prevent concussion but may well prevent a cut to the head.

The majority of horses are quiet, easily managed and require no restraint. When restraint is required it must be the minimum necessary and should never extend to cruelty, which would only make the horse worse and more difficult to shoe the next time. Some horses become nervous due to the unusual noises of the forge and the glare of the fire but soon settle down and are easy to shoe outside or at their own stables. Others will stand quietly with their stable companions. At all times the leg should be held in a natural and comfortable position, care being taken not to abduct it as this puts the horse off balance. When the foot is put down it should be lowered gently, not dropped, and at the same time the farrier should step away from the horse.

Bad habits

A few horses develop bad habits and are difficult to shoe, but with patience and training the majority lose them. In many cases bad habits are overcome by firmness and an attendant at the head, often coupled with a feed and being shod after exercise. At times a good deal of self-control will be required.

Restlessness. When a horse will not stand still it is generally due to nervousness. In the majority of cases this can be controlled by an attendant at the head, its stable companion beside it, a feed or a combination of these measures. It is important for the farrier and the attendant not to react to a display of nervousness by shouting or becoming agitated as this will only prevent the horse from relaxing. Even soothing noises may have the wrong effect as the horse may associate such sounds with previous unpleasant experiences and become more apprehensive. There is nothing painful about shoeing and no reason to behave as if there is any pain.

Some horses do not like smoke, some horses do not like a hind leg brought forwards and others do not like to have a hind leg extended backwards. Other horses do not like a front leg held between the farrier's knees or may object to hammering. In cases such as these it is usually possible to adopt measures which do not upset the horse. This is preferable to engaging in a struggle.

Leaning. This is an annoying habit, but first altering the position of the horse's leg should be tried as it may be uncomfortable. If this fails then try giving with the horse to indicate that you will not support its weight, or dropping the foot, which will result in the horse having to make a definite effort to recover itself and prevent falling. After a few lessons it will quickly learn to stand properly on three legs.

Biting. This may be due to nervousness, in which case the horse only requires time to settle down in its new surroundings, but in others it is a vice. An inveterate biter requires to be muzzled or tied up short and always with an attendant at its head.

Kicking and striking. In many cases this is due to a nervous or spoilt horse. It can often be controlled by firmness, tying the horse up short with its head low, having an attendant at the head or applying a twitch.

Difficult to shoe

Horses classified as difficult to shoe are those which strike, kick, rear up, throw themselves about and become quite unmanageable. This is not always a vice. It may be due to extreme nervousness and bad handling when first shod. Many such horses can be retrained given time and patience and the bad habits will disappear. However, in all such cases it is impossible for the farrier, without applying adequate restraint, to shoe the horse and ensure not only his own safety but also that of the attendants.

The simplest methods should be tried first; an attendant at the head, a twitch applied and

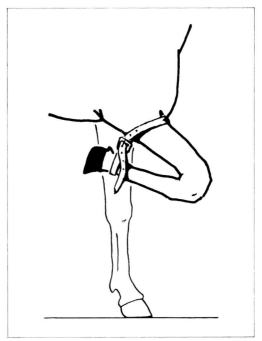

Fig. 7.1 Method of restraining a front leg by tying it up using a stirrup leather.

perhaps blinds. A twitch should only be applied to the horse's upper lip and removed immediately it is no longer required.

If these measures fail then try them coupled with tying up a front leg using a stirrup leather (Fig. 7.1) or restraining a hind leg with a single side line (Fig. 7.2).

These are the only practical methods available to the farrier unless stocks are available. Casting a horse with hobbles or side lines has little to recommend it. If a horse cannot be adequately restrained by the methods outlined, veterinary advice and assistance should be obtained. The use of tranquillizers or sedatives, either alone or combined with simple methods of restraint, will enable the most wild and vicious horses to be shod efficiently and safely. Care must be taken in handling a tranquillized or sedated horse as it may fall on the farrier.

Foals

Before foals have their feet attended to for the first time they should be halter broken and have received some preliminary training. They

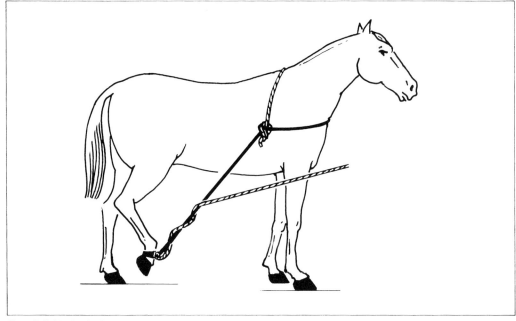

Fig. 7.2 Method of restraining a hind limb with a single side line.

should be accustomed to having their legs manipulated, feet picked up, feet brought forwards, standing on three legs and having their feet tapped lightly with a hammer. Time devoted to this training is well spent when one considers the number of times a horse is shod during its life.

In the majority of cases the only restraint required is an attendant at the head, but until the foal stands quietly it is a good plan to have it standing in the corner of a loose box and held against the wall. The foal should be held facing the wall when working on its hind feet, as it will tend to go forward, and backed into the corner when working on its front feet to prevent it running back.

7.2 Conformation

Conformation is the manner in which a horse is formed and depends on the length of its bones and the angles they make with one another at the joints. Conformation has a direct bearing on the distribution of a horse's weight and its action. Without studying a horse's conformation it is not possible to trim its feet correctly or to fit a suitable shoe.

Conformation should be distinguished from *posture*. Because of hoof imbalance or lameness a horse may adopt an abnormal posture and not walk or trot normally. For example, a horse may have perfect conformation but if the lateral sides of the hooves are longer than the medial sides it will adopt a base-wide and toe-out posture. A horse with corns will tend to adopt a base narrow posture to relieve the insides of the feet of pain, even though it may have good conformation. It should be possible to tell by careful examination whether a horse adopts a particular posture simply because of its conformation or because of hoof imbalance or lameness.

A horse must be examined at rest and in motion. First it should be examined standing on a level surface from the front, the side and behind. Next, to detect any abnormalities of gait, it must be walked in a straight line away from and back towards the observer. Finally it must be trotted to make sure it is not lame.

Defects of conformation cannot be altered once the growth plates have closed, but the adverse effects that arise may be controlled and alleviated by attention to a horse's feet and to shoeing. Attention to the feet is particularly important with young stock and corrective measures taken in good time will not only control the defect but may also result in considerable improvement.

Front limb conformation

When a horse is standing with its weight evenly distributed the front legs take between 60% and 65% of its weight.

A. Front View (Fig. 7.3)

Both limbs should be straight and parallel, and with the feet slightly separated. This provides a good base for support and prevents the horse striking itself when moving. A plumb line from the point of the shoulder divides the limb into two equal parts. The separation of the front and hind limbs is such that when viewed from the front they are in line with one another.

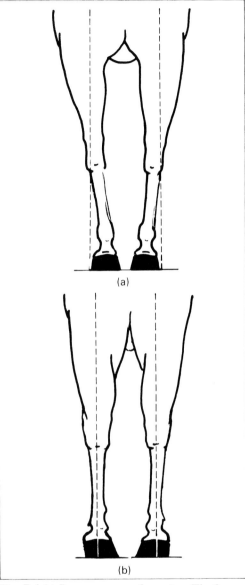

(a)

(b)

Fig. 7.4 (a) Base narrow conformation. The feet are placed close together. (b) Base narrow conformation complicated by the toes being turned in, which is referred to as pigeon-toed.

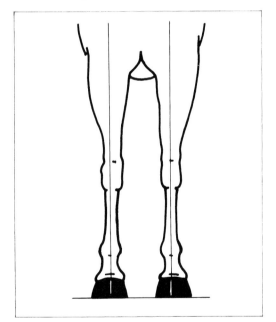

Fig. 7.3 Front view of normal front limbs. Both limbs are straight and parallel, and with the feet slightly separated.

Base narrow conformation (Fig. 7.4 a-b). The feet are placed close together and a plumb line from the centre of the shoulder falls towards the lateral side of the foot. It results in excessive strains being placed on the lateral sides of the joints and predisposes to articular

windgalls, sidebones and degenerative joint disease. The hoof tends to be wry, the medial side being longer and more sloping than the lateral side. More weight falls on the lateral side of the foot which can become excessively worn.

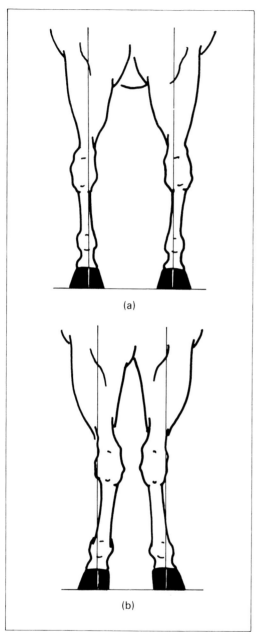

Fig. 7.5 (a) Bow legs; (b) knock knees.

Base narrow conformation is seen in broad-chested horses with well developed pectoral muscles. It can also be caused by limb deviation at the knee (bow legs) (Fig. 7.5a) or by rotation of the leg at the knee or the fetlock (pigeon toes).

Base narrow posture. A horse with none of the faults which cause base narrow conformation may be base narrow if the hoof is unbalanced by being longer on the medial than the lateral side. It will also be toe-in.

Base wide conformation (Fig. 7.6 a-b). The feet are placed wide apart and a plumb line from

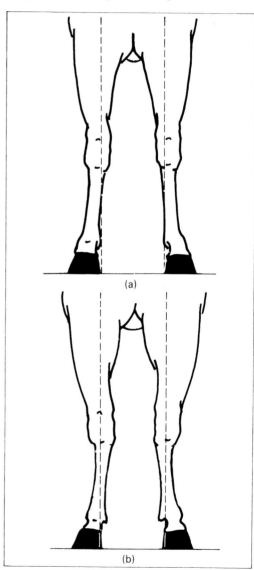

Fig. 7.6 (a) Base wide conformation. The feet are placed wide apart. (b) Base wide conformation complicated by the toes being turned out, which is referred to as splay-footed.

the centre of the shoulder falls towards the medial side of the foot. It results in excessive strains being placed on the medial sides of the joints and predisposes to articular windgalls, sidebone and degenerative joint disease. The hoof tends to be wry, the lateral side being longer and more sloping than the medial side. More weight falls on the medial side of the foot which can become excessively worn.

Base wide conformation is seen in narrow-chested horses. It can also result from limb deviation at the knee (knock knees) (Fig. 7.5b) or from outward rotation of the leg at the knee or fetlock (splay-footed).

Base wide posture. A horse with none of the faults which cause base wide conformation may be base wide if the hoof is unbalanced by being longer on the lateral than the medial side. It will also be toe-out.

B. Side view (Fig. 7.7)
A plumb line from the spine of the shoulder blade divides the limb from the elbow to the fetlock joint in half and touches the ground just behind the heels.

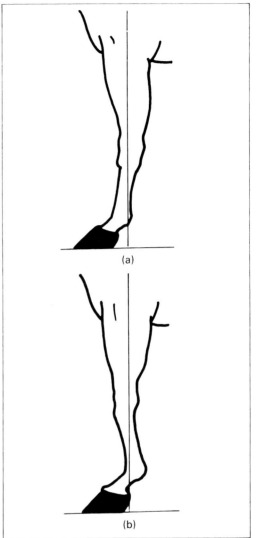

Fig. 7.8 (a) Calf knee; (b) bucked knee.

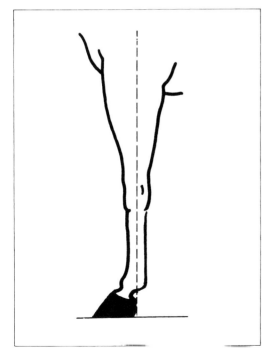

Fig. 7.7 Side view of a normal front limb.

Calf knee (Fig. 7.8a) is a backward deviation of the knee. This is a particularly bad conformation which puts stresses on the front edges of the knee joints and puts strain on the accessory ligament. Horses with this conformation when put to work seldom remain sound for long.

Bowing over at the knee (bucked or goat knee) (Fig. 7.8b) is a forward deviation of the knee. It is often associated with chronic contraction of the flexor tendons and results in stumbling

Hind limb conformation

A. Hind view (Fig. 7.9)
When a hind limb is observed from behind, a plumb line from the tuber ischii should divide the limb into two equal parts.

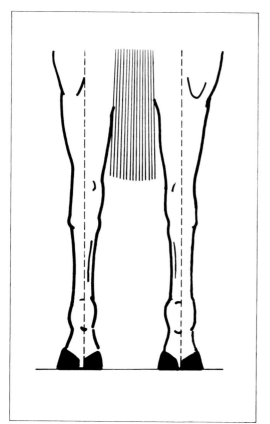

Fig. 7.9 Hind view of normal hind limbs.

Base narrow conformation (Fig. 7.10a). The feet are placed too close together which invariably results in the hock being turned out. This is called *bow legs*, is seen in heavy well-muscled horses, and results in strains on the lateral side of the limb.

Base wide conformation (Fig. 7.10b). The feet are placed too far apart which results in the hocks being too close together and pointing towards one another. This is called *cow hocks*. It results in excessive strains on the medial side of the limb, in particular the hock joint, which predisposes to bone spavin disease.

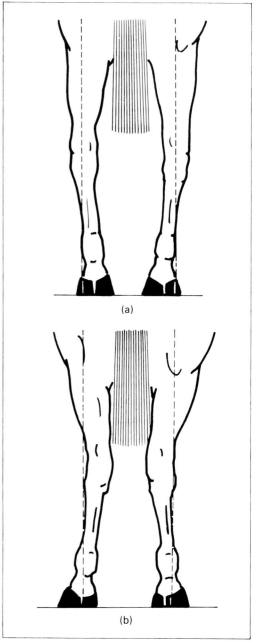

Fig. 7.10 (a) Base narrow conformation behind; (b) base wide conformation behind.

B. Side view (Fig. 7.11 a-b)
When a hind limb is observed from the side a plumb line from the tuber ischii should just touch the point of the hock, pass down the

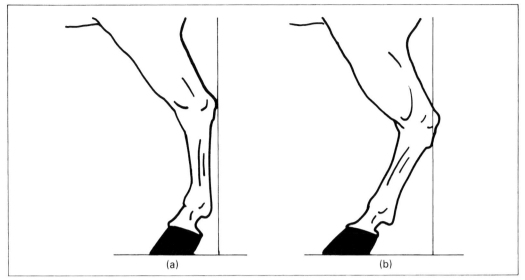

Fig. 7.11 (a) Side view of a normal hind limb. (b) Sickle hock. The hock joint is excessively angulated.

plantar aspect of the tarsus and metatarsus and meet the ground 2–3 ins (5–8 cm) behind the heels.

The most common defect of a hind limb when viewed from the side is an excessively curved or angulated hock joint. This is referred to as a *sickle hock* (Fig. 7.11b) and puts strain on the plantar aspect of the joint, predisposing

to a sprain of the plantar ligament. Sprain of the plantar ligament is called a *curb* and for this reason horses with sickle hocks are often referred to as having curby hocks.

Pastern foot axis

The *pastern axis*, when viewed from the front (Fig. 7.12a) or from the side (Fig. 7.14a) is an

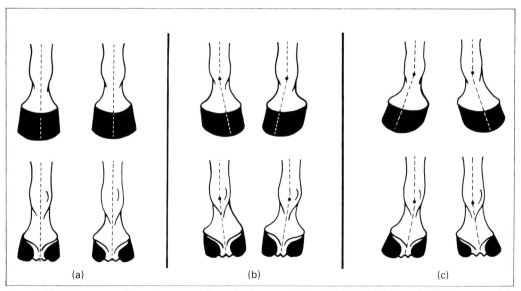

Fig. 7.12 The pastern foot axis in view from in front and from behind. (a) Normal; (b) toes turned in; (c) toes turned out.

imaginary straight line from the centre of the fetlock joint through the pastern which divides the proximal and middle phalanges into two equal parts.

The *foot axis* is a continuation of the pastern axis and extends from the coronet to the ground surface of the foot. When viewed from the front the foot axis passes to the centre of the toe and from the side the foot axis is at the same angle as the dorsal wall.

The *pastern foot axis* is the line formed by the pastern axis and the foot axis.

Balancing a foot means to trim and shoe a foot to obtain the correct length and the correct pastern foot axis.

A. Front view

Toe-in conformation (Fig. 7.12b). When viewed from the front the pastern foot axis slopes inwards. This is due to the conformation of the limb. Toe-in conformation often results from the same limb deviations that cause base narrow conformation. It is accompanied by a wry hoof, the medial side being longer and more sloping than the lateral side.

Toe-in posture. When viewed from the front the pastern foot axis slopes inwards. There is a wry hoof, the medial side being longer than the lateral side. This can be due to uneven wear or to trimming. There is no limb deviation as with toe-in conformation. The horse responds to the strain it feels by rotating the entire limb medially. The horse additionally compensates by adopting a more base narrow posture.

It is possible for toe-in conformation to be exaggerated by uneven wear of the hoof. If the medial side becomes excessively long the toe-in posture will be more marked than the true conformation. Conversely if a horse with toe-in conformation has its hoof trimmed to the shape of an ideal hoof with medial and lateral walls of equal length it will adopt a more normal posture but strains on the limb will be created leading to lameness (Fig. 7.13).

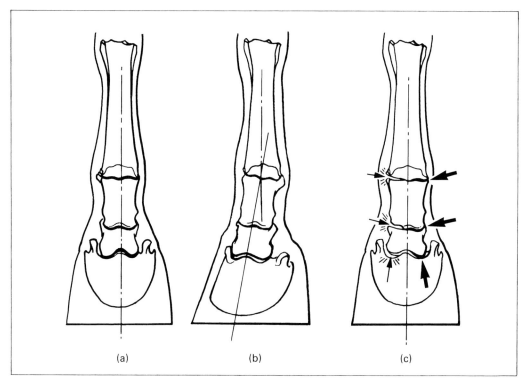

(a)   (b)   (c)

Fig. 7.13 (a) Ideal conformation; (b) a naturally wry hoof due to deviation at the fetlock; (c) 'correcting' a naturally wry hoof creates strains on the joints.

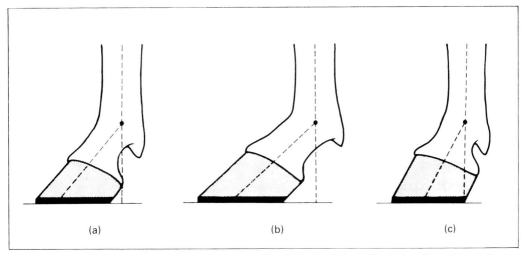

Fig. 7.14 Side view of a normal pastern foot axis for: (a) normal foot; (b) sloping foot; (c) upright foot.

Toe-out conformation (Fig. 7.12c). When viewed from the front the pastern foot axis slopes outwards. Toe-out conformation often results from the same limb deviation that gives a horse base wide conformation. It is accompanied by a wry hoof, the lateral side being longer and more sloping than the medial side.

Toe-out posture. When viewed from the front the pastern foot axis slopes outwards. There is a wry hoof, the lateral side being longer than the medial side. This can be due to uneven wear or to trimming. The horse responds by rotating the limb laterally and adopting a more base wide posture. There is no limb deviation as with toe-out conformation.

It is quite possible for toe-out conformation to be exaggerated by uneven wear of the hoof in much the same way as for toe-in conformation.

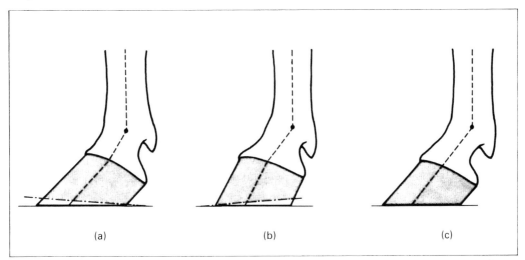

Fig. 7.15 Side view of a foot with an abnormal pastern foot axis due to: (a) excess horn at the toe, pastern foot axis broken back; (b) excess horn at the heels, pastern foot axis broken forwards; (c) pastern foot axis restored to normal by either lowering the toe or the heels.

145

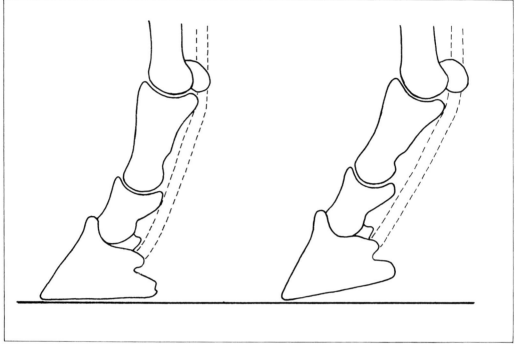

Fig. 7.16 Raising the heels causes a more sloping pastern.

B. Side view

Ideally when the horse is standing squarely on level ground the pastern foot axis is straight whether viewed from the front or from the side (Fig. 7.12a and 7.14).

The pastern axis is said to be *broken back* when the foot axis is more sloping than the pastern axis (Fig. 7.15a).

The pastern foot axis is said to be *broken forward* when the foot axis is steeper than the pastern axis (Fig. 7.15b).

The deep digital flexor tendon attaches to the distal phalanx and helps to support the fetlock joint. Raising the heels relaxes the tendon and causes a dropping of the fetlock and a more sloping pastern. Lowering the heels increases tension on the tendon and causes a raising of the fetlock and a steeper pastern (Fig. 7.16).

Hoof conformation

Front hoof. An ideal front hoof is rounded at the toe and perfectly symmetrical, with the slope of the inner quarter the same as the slope of the outer quarter (Fig. 7.17).

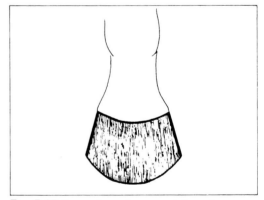

Fig. 7.17 Front view of a normal front foot.

The wall is thickest at the toe and gradually thinner toward the quarters, thickening again at the heels.

It should be borne in mind that when a hoof is trimmed level the wall at the toe is cut at more of an angle than elsewhere which makes it appear thicker than it is.

The sole is concave and the frog large and elastic with a shallow central groove and deep medial and lateral grooves.

The surface of the wall is not absolutely flat but broken by a wavy growth of horn which appears as a number of rings parallel to the coronet. These rings are a normal feature and indicate alterations in the rate of growth due to either changes in food or illness. It is important to differentiate growth rings from those associated with chronic laminitis, which are widely spaced at the heels and converging towards the toe.

The foot axis and the angle of the wall at the heels should correspond and be between 50° and 55° (Fig. 7.18 b-c).

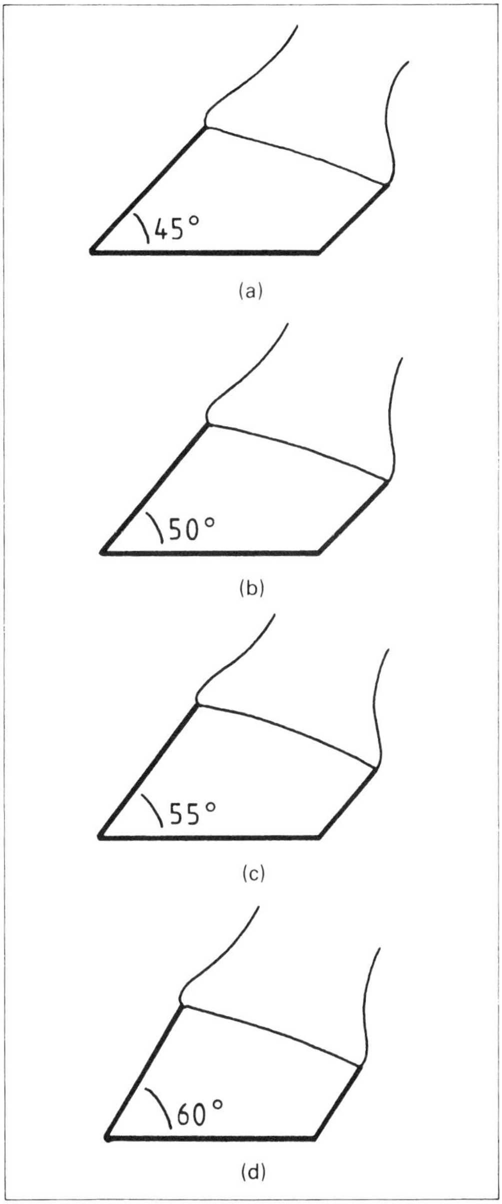

Hind hoof. A hind hoof is oval at the toe and widest toward the heels. In comparison with a front hoof the sole is more concave, the frog smaller and the slope of the wall at both the inner and outer quarters more upright. The foot axis and the angle of the walls at the heels should correspond and be between 50° and 55° as for a front foot.

Wry hooves. Wry hooves are hooves which are asymmetrical, the medial and lateral sides being of different lengths and slopes.

Naturally wry hooves (Fig. 7.19). It is often stated that the shape of the hoof is determined by the conformation of the limb. This is true of hooves which are wry in shape with defects

Fig. 7.18 Types of hoof: (a) sloping hoof; (b, c) normal hooves; (d) upright hoof.

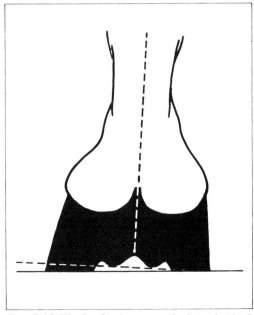

Fig. 7.19 The hoof is longer on the lateral side. If the horse has straight limb conformation the foot is unbalanced (unnaturally wry foot). If the horse has base wide or toe-out conformation the foot is correctly balanced (naturally wry foot).

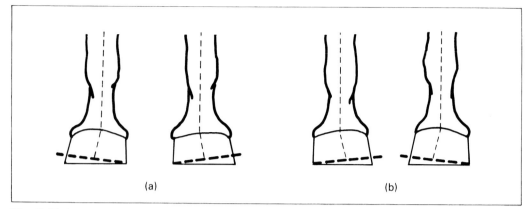

Fig. **7.20** *Unnaturally wry feet: (a) toe-out posture due to excessive length of the lateral hoof wall; (b) toe-in posture due to excessive length of the medial hoof wall.*

of conformation. With base wide or toe-out conformation the hoof wall will be longer and more sloping on the lateral side than on the medial side of the hoof. With base narrow or toe-in conformation the hoof wall will be longer and more sloping on the medial side than on the lateral side of the hoof. A naturally wry hoof cannot be remedied but can be prevented from getting worse by being properly trimmed.

Unnaturally wry hooves (Fig. 7.20 a-b). An unnaturally wry hoof is due to neglect. Attention to trimming the hoof and to shoeing will result in a gradual return to its normal shape.

If the ground surface of a hoof is not kept level there is an uneven distribution of the body weight which results in the wall being deflected.

Excessive length of the lateral wall results in it flaring out while the medial wall wears heavily and becomes upright or slopes inwards. Conversely, excessive length of the medial wall results in the medial wall flaring out while the lateral wall wears heavily and becomes upright or slopes inwards.

Unnaturally wry hooves will cause a horse to adopt an abnormal posture.

Sloping hooves (Fig. 7.18a). The angle of the foot axis and toe is less than 50°.

A horse with a *naturally sloping hoof*, long at the toe and low at the heels, has a straight pastern foot axis.

An *unnaturally sloping hoof*, caused by excess horn at the toe or lack of horn at the heels, has a pastern foot axis which is broken back. This can be corrected by lowering the toe, raising the heels or both.

Low heels. Low heels are associated with a very sloping pastern (naturally sloping hoof) or are caused by trimming or by weakness of the horn (unnaturally sloping hoof).

Weak heels. Weak heels are heels which curve inwards and forwards, weight being borne on the outside of the wall. Weak heels are caused by excessive weight bearing on the heels. This is usually because the quarters are not taking their share of weight having been allowed to flare out or grow over the shoe, become broken or rasped away, or a combination of these factors. Weak heels are always also low heels.

Flat feet. The sole lacks its normal concavity and is subject to bruising. Flat feet are commonest in the front feet of heavy draught horses and thoroughbreds, and in less severe cases of chronic laminitis. A normal foot can become a flat foot if its quarters are allowed to flare out and the heels to become lowered, or if the sole drops after laminitis.

Dropped sole. The sole is convex and below the bearing surface of the wall. It is a feature of severe laminitis and is due to pressure on the sole by the solar border of the rotated distal phalanx. Dropped soles are easily bruised, especially towards the toe.

Thin sole. This is an inherited condition and is usually accompanied by a thin wall. The conformation of the foot may be normal but the sole being thin yields under pressure and is easily bruised.

Upright hooves (Fig. 7.18d). The angle of the foot axis and toe is over 55°.

A horse with a *naturally upright hoof*, with a short toe and high heels, has a straight pastern foot axis.

An *unnaturally upright hoof*, caused by excess horn at the heels, has a pastern foot axis which is broken forwards. It can be corrected by lowering the heels.

Club foot. This is an accentuated upright foot with a foot pastern axis and toe angle of over 60°. As a rule when the condition is bilateral it is congenital in origin, but unilateral cases are more often associated with contracted tendons. A club foot should not be confused with a *buttress foot* which is characterised by a protrusion of the front of the wall at the coronet. Buttress foot is due to the proliferation of new bone as a result of degenerative joint disease or a fracture of the extensor process of the distal phalanx.

Contracted foot. A contracted foot is smaller than normal, narrower at the heel quarters and heels, has an excessively concave sole and an atrophied frog. It can result from prolonged disuse of the limb due to lameness or faulty trimming of the foot especially by opening up the heels and excessive paring of the sole. Methods of shoeing can also contribute, Calkins and studs reduce normal frog pressure and heel nails placed too far back reduce normal expansion of the foot. Thrush is a common cause of atrophy of the frog leading to contraction of the foot.

Brittle hooves. In some horses this condition is inherited. In the majority it is encountered in dry weather due to loss of moisture from the hoof. Dry horn tends to crack or split. White hooves appear to be more frequently affected probably because cracks show up more clearly as dark marks on a light hoof.

In wet weather especially in a hot climate the excessive moisture leads to softness, decay and disintegration of the horn which leads to broken hooves.

For both brittle and soft hooves a well-fitting shoe is very important so that a minimum number of nails can be used to retain the shoe securely while causing as little damage as possible to the hoof.

7.3 The horse's gait

To assess a horse's gait it is necessary to observe the horse at the walk and the trot, coming towards, going away from and past the observer on a level surface in good light. The horse should be on a loose rein or rope held at about 18 ins (50 cm) from the bridle or headcollar to ensure that nothing interferes with the free movement of the head.

A. Front view

A sound horse with good conformation of its limbs and balanced feet is seen to move its legs in alignment with its body. The toe is pointed forward and the foot set down flat (Fig. 7.21a).

Winging out (Fig. 7.21b, 7.22a). The foot moves forwards, outwards and then inwards in a circular movement. This results in the foot landing and breaking over on the outside toe causing excessive wear of the outside quarter. Winging out is normal in horses with a toe-in conformation (Fig. 7.20b).

Winging in (Fig. 7.21c, 7.22b). The foot moves forwards, inwards and then outwards in a circular movement. This results in the horse landing and breaking over on the inside toe which causes excessive wear on the inside quarter. Winging in is normal in horses with a toe-out conformation and is a cause of brushing.

Plaiting (Fig. 7.22c). The foot moves inwards to land in front of the opposite foot. It is seen in horses with base narrow conformation and is conducive to stumbling.

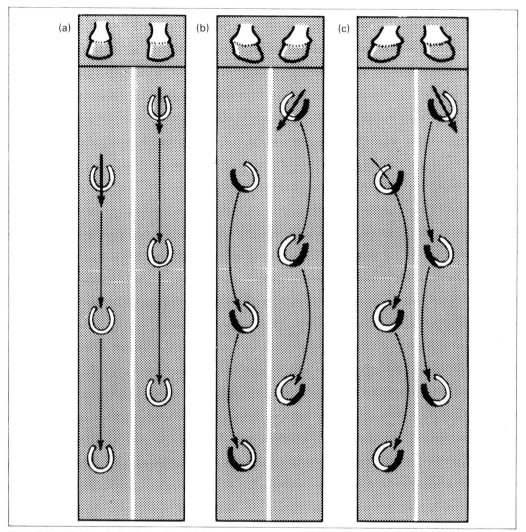

Fig. 7.21 Flight of the front feet: (a) normal flight; (b) winging out due to toe-in conformation; (c) winging in due to toe-out conformation.

B. Side view

Front foot action is characterised by the foot breaking over at the toe with the flight of the foot following a smooth arc which reaches its peak as it passes the opposite leg. The hind foot dips in mid stride (Fig. 7.23 a-b).

The length of the stride, the flexion of the joints in the first phase of the stride and the extension of the joints in the second phase of the stride should all be noted, as well as the co-ordination in raising a front foot to clear an approaching hind foot.

Factors which affect gait

Abnormalities of gait are caused by lameness, abnormal conformation or unbalanced hooves. Immaturity, lack of schooling, lack of fitness, fatigue, the rider, and uneven or heavy going also may cause or exaggerate an abnormal gait.

Lameness

When the leg on which the horse is lame moves and bears weight, pain is produced and to relieve pain the horse takes a shorter step or stride. At the walk the lame leg has the support of two other legs. At the trot the lame leg has the support of only one other leg, its diagonal, which makes the trot the best pace for detecting lameness.

Front leg lameness is best seen when the horse is moving towards the observer and is indicated by a nodding movement of the head. When the lame leg bears weight the head is raised and when the sound leg comes to the ground the head nods or drops.

Hind leg lameness is best seen when the horse trots away from the observer and is shown by the quarter on the lame side sinking more than the quarter on the sound side.

A horse that is lame in both front feet has a stiff or stilted action. It takes short strides, with decreased shoulder action and keeps its feet close to the ground. Lameness in both hind legs is indicated by a shortened stride, wobbling or straddling gait and difficulty in backing.

Conformation

Toe-in conformation. A horse with toe-in conformation tends to wing out.

Toe-out conformation. A horse with toe-out conformation tends to wing in.

Hoof and pastern angle. Hoof and pastern angle do not have a major effect on gait when the foot pastern axis is straight. The more uncomfortable ride given by a horse with upright conformation is due to the reduced sinking of the fetlock increasing concussion at least as much as to the way in which the hoof leaves or meets the ground. A sloping foot will go through a greater arc of flexion than a more upright foot. This is inevitable as the joints from the fetlock down are more extended while the foot is on the ground. Breakover will also tend to be delayed with a more sloping conformation and so flexion will be exaggerated due to the increased muscular and elastic energy involved.

Hoof and shoe balance

Foot pastern axis. A broken back pastern foot axis results in a shorter stride. The leg advanced has to be put down sooner as the distal interphalangeal joint of the supporting leg becomes increasingly hyperextended. There tends to be increased flexion of the limb during the stride as a response to the hyperextension during the support phase.

Hoof length. An excessively long foot results in increased flexion of all the joints of the limb, the knees and feet being lifted higher. This is because breakover is delayed which increases

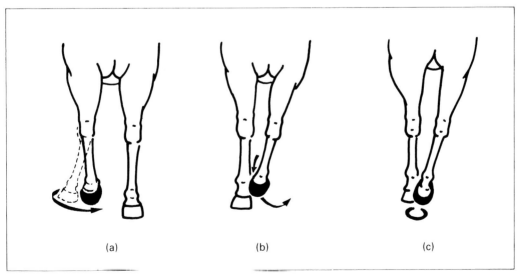

Fig. 7.22 (a) Winging out; (b) winging in; (c) plaiting.

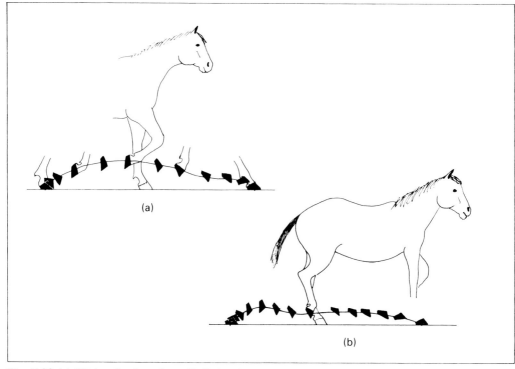

Fig. 7.23 (a) Flight of a front foot; (b) flight of a hind foot.

both the muscular and the elastic energy of flexion.

Medial to lateral hoof balance. If a hoof is not balanced in accordance with the limb conformation the hoof will be twisted towards the longer side while on the ground and when in flight it will tend to wing in the other direction as the leg untwists.

Shoe weight. The weight of the shoe increases flexion by its momentum reinforcing the upward movement of the foot in the first half of the stride. At the end of the stride the weight of the shoes tends to bring the feet nearer to the ground giving less elevation to the second half of the stride. Weight will exaggerate any tendency to wing in or out by increasing the centrifugal force involved.

7.4 Wear of the shoe

From the wear of the shoe much information can be gained regarding defects of confor-

mation and hoof imbalances, assisting in the preparation of the foot and the selection of the correct shoe.

Excessive wear. The wear of the shoe depends on numerous factors: the material from which the shoe is made, the surface of the ground and roads travelled over, the work performed and the conformation and action of the individual horse.

Horses wear out their shoes more quickly when working on macadamised and concrete roads, which provide a poor foothold and especially when they are wet. The pace at which a horse works has a marked effect on the length of wear of its shoes. The shoes of heavy draught horses working at a slow pace (about 2½ mph/4 kmph) have a longer life, both in respect of time and distance, than horses working at a trot (about 6 mph/10 kmph) because of the friction created by slipping and pulling up more sharply.

For driving horses the type of vehicle affects the wear of the shoes. A vehicle with freely moving shafts gives a horse more freedom when placing its feet, thereby reducing slipping, than a vehicle with rigid shafts.

Hind shoes wear more rapidly than front shoes and some horses will wear out their shoes twice as fast as others.

Horses which wear out their shoes faster than average may be fitted with slightly heavier shoes. Thicker shoes will reduce frog pressure, so when changing to a heavier shoe it is better to change from concave bar to flat bar or to increase the width of the web rather than fit a thicker shoe. Excessively heavy shoes will tire the horse causing it to drag its feet more, which will be counter-productive.

Uneven wear of a shoe is a different problem and the appropriate correction should be made after looking at the conformation, action and foot balance of the horse.

A horse with normal conformation and foot balance, soundness and action will wear its shoes evenly except:
1) at the toe, which is always more worn, usually to the outside, and
2) the outside branches of the hind shoes which usually wear more heavily than the inside branch.

When a shoe has worn evenly it indicates that the foot has been reduced to its correct proportions and the type of shoe is suitable.

Wear can be related to weight bearing while the foot is on the ground or to dragging of the shoe as the foot lands or as it leaves the ground (breakover).

Studs, projections or non-slip nails in a shoe will alter the pattern or wear.

The toe of a front shoe is commonly worn as a result of a horse pawing the ground. Because the leg that paws the ground is adducted to help the horse balance, it is the outside of the toe that is scraped on the ground. Heavy wear of the toe of a shoe is otherwise usually due to dragging of the shoe at breakover. There may be a number of causes. The toe of the foot is too long, the shoe has excessively high calkins, or the horse goes on its toes to alleviate pain, as is seen in cases of navicular and bone spavin disease. Correction is by rolling the toe of the shoe to resemble the worn surface of the old shoe.

Heavy wearing on one branch of a shoe is often a sign of uneven weight bearing caused by poor conformation or hoof imbalance. It is necessary to examine the leg for deviation to see whether the balance of the hoof is consistent with the conformation of the leg.

For example, take a horse which wears the outside branch of its front shoes heavily. It has a base narrow and toe-in posture. The hooves are wry, the insides being longer than the outsides. The wear is probably due to excess weight bearing on the lateral sides of the feet. The conformation of the leg is examined:
1) If there appears to be no limb deviations it is likely that the wear is due to hoof imbalance. Correction by trimming is indicated.
2) If the limb can be seen to deviate medially at the knee or at the fetlock then the wear is caused by the horse's conformation. It is not advisable to attempt correction, which puts strain on the joints and may cause lameness. All that can be done is to keep the feet balanced.

When the heels of a shoe are excessively worn it is generally due either to laminitis or low ringbone disease. Increasing wear in these cases should be attempted not by increasing the thickness of the heels of the shoe but rather by lowering the heels of the foot. If this does not suffice consideration will have to be given to fitting a bar shoe.

7.5 Removing a shoe

To remove a shoe, the clenches are first cut off or straightened with a buffer and then, using the pincers, the shoe is eased at the heels and along each branch until it is loose, when it is grasped at the toe and pulled backwards across the foot and off. If a horse dislikes hammering the clenches may be filed off with the rasp.

Care must be taken to ensure that the clenches are cut or straightened cleanly as a rough clench pulled through the wall causes unnecessary damage. The jaws of the pincers must be fully closed when levering the shoe or the inner jaw may press into the sole causing pain. Any nail stubs embedded in the wall must be removed by punching them out either with the buffer or with a new nail which has had

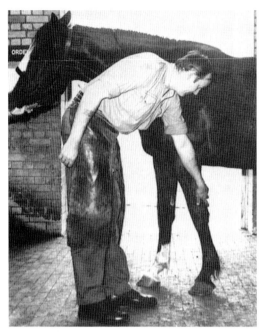

Fig. **7.24** *To pick up a left forefoot, stand close to the horse's shoulder, face to the rear, run the left hand firmly but unhurriedly down the back of the limb.*

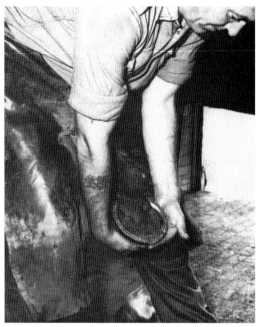

Fig. **7.26** *Take a step forward with the left leg, and at the same time bring the horse's foot under the knee and hold it in both hands.*

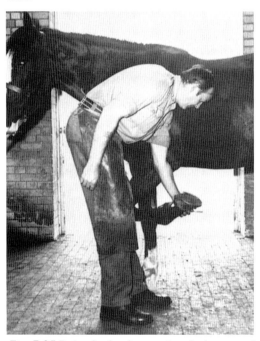

Fig. **7.25** *Raise the foot by grasping the leg around the pastern.*

Fig. **7.27** *Left foot correctly positioned. Note the position adopted by the farrier to secure the foot: knees slightly bent and brought together with the toes turned in.*

its point cut off. A nail striking a stub may buckle and prick the sensitive foot.

Front foot

The method of picking up a left front foot and positioning it is shown in Figs.7.24–7.27, and the method of removing a front shoe is illustrated in Figs.7.28–7.30.

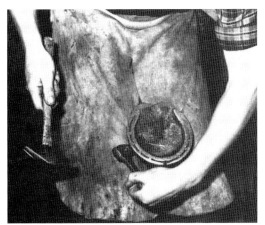

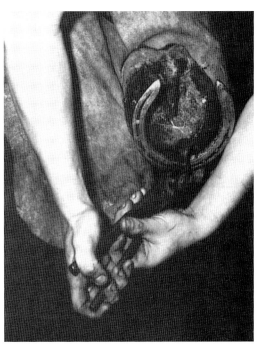

Fig. 7.28 The clenches are cut off or straightened with a buffer. The blade is held close against the wall to prevent cutting into it.

Fig. 7.30 The toe of the shoe is grasped with the pincers and removed by pulling it upwards, backwards and off across the foot.

Hind foot

The method of picking up a left hind foot and positioning it is shown in Figs.7.31–7.33.

The hind shoe is then removed using exactly the same method as described for a front shoe.

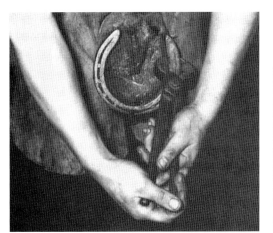

Fig. 7.29 The inside heel of a shoe is raised by closing the jaws of the pincers under it and prising downwards towards the toe. The outside heel is next eased in like manner. This manoeuvre is continued alternately, along each branch, until all the nails are partly withdrawn and the shoe loose.

Fig. 7.31 Stand close in to the horse's side, facing to the rear, and run the left hand firmly but unhurriedly across the quarters and down the back of the limb to just above the fetlock.

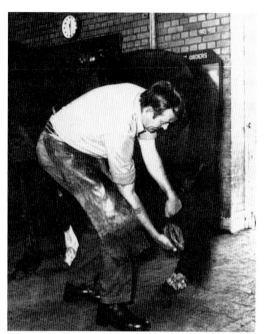

Fig. *7.32* Raise the leg by pulling it forwards and, immediately the foot is off the ground, take a step forward and support it in the right hand.

Fig. *7.33* Left hind foot correctly positioned. The farrier has taken a step forward with his left foot and placed the leg across his left thigh with the foot resting against his right knee.

Method of withdrawing nails individually
(Figs.7.34–7.37)

When it is necessary to remove each nail individually the clenches are cut off or straightened and the heels raised as described for removing

Fig. *7.34* Cutting off the clenches on the outside of the left hind foot. Note the position of the hand holding the buffer and the method of using the wrist to support the foot.

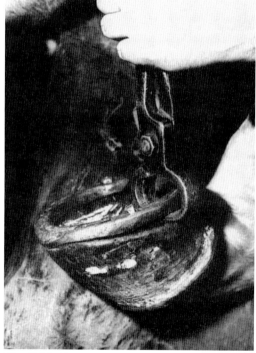

Fig. *7.35* The jaws of the pincers are closed under the heel of the shoe which is raised by pushing the handles downwards and towards the toe.

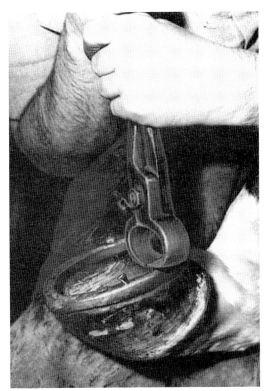

Fig. 7.36 The raised heel of the shoe is knocked back into position by striking it with the closed jaws of the pincers which results in the head of the nail being extruded.

Fig. 7.37 The head of the nail is grasped with the pincers and withdrawn.

a front or hind shoe. Then the raised heel is given a sharp tap down with the closed jaws of the pincers leaving the nail heads up. The nail heads can then be grasped with the pincers and withdrawn on each side alternately. When all the nails are withdrawn the shoe can be removed.

Alternatively if the shoe is fullered nail pullers can be used to withdraw the nails. Nail pullers are especially useful when removing a shoe from a horse with sore, flat or thin-soled feet as there is no need to lever the shoe up against the wall and sole.

7.6 Trimming the foot (Figs. 7.38–7.50)

The normal proportions of the unshod foot are maintained by wear under most circumstances. But once a shoe is fitted the hoof continues to grow and is protected from wear except at the heels where there is slight friction between the hoof wall and the shoe as a result of the normal expansion of the foot. As the foot grows it widens and may descend over the shoe at the

Fig. 7.38 Looking at the raised foot.

157

quarters and heels. It is the lowering of the heels, coupled with lengthening of the toe, which gradually alters the pastern foot axis and the normal balance of the shod foot (Fig. 8.1).

After removing the shoes and before proceeding to prepare the foot, its shape and proportions must be studied.

First, with the horse standing on a level surface the foot pastern axis is looked at from the side and the slope of the foot is compared with the slope of the pastern to see how much toe and how much heel need to be removed. The foot pastern axis is looked at from the front and then with the foot raised (Fig. 7.38) to see whether one side needs to be lowered more than the other. Any flares, cracks, curving inwards of the heels or other abnormalities should be noted. The outline of the ground surface is examined for shape and symmetry with the point of the frog used as indicating the centre. The condition of the frog is noted, whether there is any contraction of the heels and if the sole is convex, flat or dropped.

The old adage that 'The shoe should be made to fit the foot and not the foot the shoe' is only a half truth. They are complimentary, as the foot and shoe have to be fitted to each other. Indeed, to fit a shoe to a foot that has not been correctly prepared may be as injurious to the horse as fitting the foot to the shoe.

Stage 1: Attention to the frog and sole

For the frog to function properly it must be large and healthy, but not project beyond the

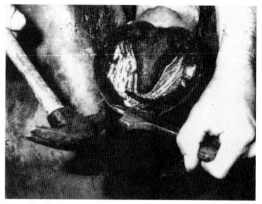

Fig. 7.40 Removing loose flakes of the sole.

bearing surface of the heels by more than the thickness of the shoe.

The frog should be trimmed (Fig. 7.39) to remove ragged or loose tags or any horn which has been undermined by thrush. It is easy to cause bleeding when trimming a frog which has been severely attacked by thrush, and although this is excusable it does mean that extra care is required. The frog may also be trimmed lightly to allow free use of the hoofpick in the grooves.

A normal healthy sole, because of its method of growth, is covered with flakes of horn. The sole protects the foot against injury. If the sole is to function effectively its protective thickness must be preserved. Excessive paring is a bad practice. Only flakes of the sole that have failed to shed should be removed (Fig. 7.40) except sometimes at the seat of corn: this is referred to as easing the seat of corn, which is done with a drawing knife, to keep the sole lower than the wall otherwise pressure from the heel of the shoe may cause corns to develop.

Stage 2: Trimming the wall

Careful use of the hoof cutters reduces rasping to a minimum. The excess horn is removed with half a cut at a time to leave a smooth surface (Fig. 7.41). It is usual to start at the toe. It is easy to cut too deeply at the heel quarter, as the wall is thin here and the sole dips, so care is needed or the hoof will be unlevel.

The wall should not be lowered below the

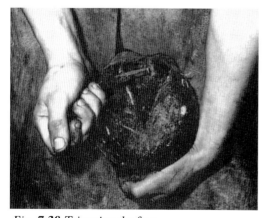

Fig. 7.39 Trimming the frog.

level of the sole, especially if a hot shoe is to

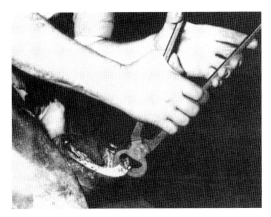

Fig. 7.41 Hoof cutters being used to lower the wall. Always start at the toe.

Fig. 7.43 Second step. The wall is rasped across the quarters and toe.

be taken to the foot, unless the sole is thick and there is a good reason, such as the need to balance the foot or to trim away damaged hoof wall. When the sole must be pared its thickness is tested continuously by pressing with the thumb so that the sensitive tissues are not approached too closely.

Stage 3: Rasping

Rasping is carried out in a continuous circular movement. A right-handed person holds the handle of the rasp in his right hand and places his left hand, palm down, over the other end. To dress a left hoof commence at the outside

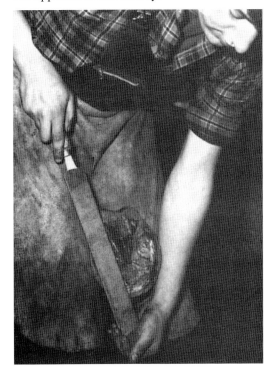

Fig. 7.42 First step. The outside wall is rasped from heel to toe.

Fig. 7.44 Third step. The inside wall is rasped from toe to heel. Note that the farrier has changed the position of his hands.

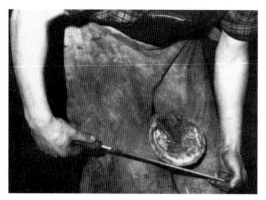

Fig. 7.45 Fourth step. The edge of the wall is lightly rasped round, using the file surface of the rasp, to remove its sharp edge which prevents the hoof from breaking or splitting.

heel and quarter. Then gradually work round to the opposite quarter. As the toe is passed it becomes necessary to change the position of the hands. A left-handed person reverses the method.

The preparation of a level bearing surface using a rasp is conveniently described in four steps (see Figs.7.42–7.45).

Faults in using a rasp
At all times the rasp must be held level. If not, more horn will be removed from some areas than others and result in an unlevel bearing surface (Figs.7.46–7.49).

When the foot surface is level and balanced the foot should be brought forward and the outside of the wall rasped to remove any flare

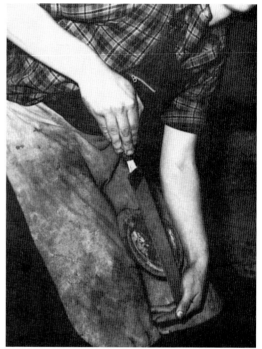

Fig. 7.47 Overlowering the wall at the toe by raising the handle of the rasp.

Fig. 7.48 Overlowering the outer quarter by dropping the handle of the rasp.

that exists. This ensures that the wall continues to grow down straight. No more rasping should be performed on the outside of the hoof than is necessary to remove flare.

When flared hoof wall bears weight it becomes pushed out further, tearing the laminae and putting more weight on to the rest of the wall leading to weak heels and a flat

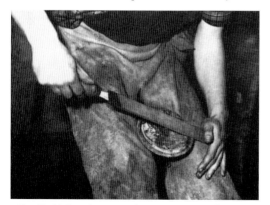

Fig. 7.46 Overlowering the inner quarter by raising the handle of the rasp.

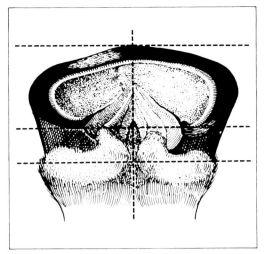

Fig. 7.49 Unlevel bearing surface. The toe and opposite heel have been overdressed.

foot. As much flare should be removed as is consistent with being able to fit and nail on a shoe. There is no objection to removing the entire thickness of the flaring wall at some point if deemed desirable.

Finally the file side of the rasp is run round the edge of the hoof to round it off which reduces the chance of it breaking when placed on the ground.

Some farriers check their work by measuring the distance from the coronet to the ground surface with a ruler and the angle at

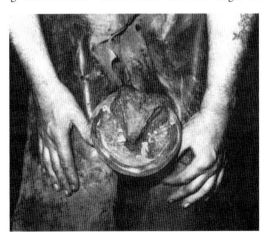

Fig. 7.50 A well-dressed foot – wall is level, bars, frog and sole lightly trimmed, and seat of corn lightly pared to prevent pressure from the shoe.

the toe with a hoof gauge. Use of these aids is time-consuming but they make the user objective and self-critical and result in better work.

A well-dressed foot is balanced, the bearing surface is level, frog and sole lightly trimmed, bars preserved and seat of corn lightly pared to prevent pressure from the shoe (Fig. 7.50).

7.7 Fitting the shoe

When a shoe is fitted its foot surface has to correspond with the bearing surface of the hoof (surface fitting) and its outer edge has to be adapted to the circumference of the wall (outline fitting).

An exact fit between foot and shoe ensures that the pressure of weight bearing is equally distributed over the whole of the hoof wall. Thus the shoe can be said to resemble very closely a continuation of the wall, an ideal arrangement to prevent wear of the hoof and reduce interference with normal function.

Surface fitting
Surface fitting involves adapting exactly the foot surface of the shoe to the bearing surface of the foot.

A horse with normal feet and action wears the toes of its shoes excessively and therefore it is basically correct to fit shoes with a rolled toe. Such shoes are economical regarding wear and in reducing concussion, but more difficult to make and fit. Therefore, for all practical purposes, an exact and satisfactory fit is obtained by simply fitting two level surfaces together.

Outline fitting
Outline fitting is the adaption of the shoe to the length and breadth of the hoof, with the outer border of the shoe adapted to the outline of the bearing surface.

Close fitting. The edge of the shoe is brought within the circumference of the wall and the projecting horn is rasped away until the wall is flush with the shoe. This gives the appearance of neatness but is a bad practice because valuable bearing surface is lost, less wall remains to secure the nails, it contributes to brittleness and the hoof soon overgrows the shoe.

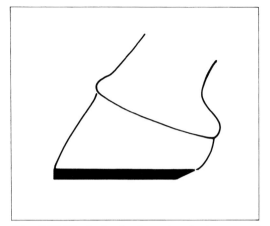

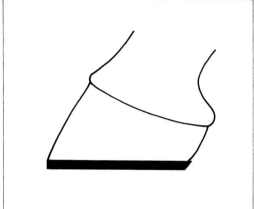

Fig. **7.51** *The heels of a front shoe for horses used for galloping should end just within the bearing surface and be sloped obliquely.*

Fig. **7.52** *The heels of a front shoe should extend slightly behind the bearing surface and be sloped at the same angle as the heels.*

Wide fitting. The shoe is fitted wide or full to the hoof so that the edge of the shoe projects beyond the circumference of the wall. It is a good idea to fit shoes wide to accommodate the increase in width of the hoof as it grows. The more sloping the sides of the hooves the wider the fit will need to be to accommodate this growth. Wide fitting involves the risk that the protruding edge will be stepped on and the shoe lost. Boxing off the protruding edge will reduce this risk but defeats the purpose since there is less of a level surface for the growing hoof to rest on. It is safest to fit shoes wide only from behind the widest part of the hoof and back to the heel.

In sloping feet, which will benefit most from wide fitting, the bulbs of the heels will be found to extend over the shoe at the heels and reduce the risk of it being stepped on. As the growing hoof is preserved by wide fitting the wall at the heel will become stronger, the hoof more upright and a less wide fit will be required at each shoeing.

It is customary for heavy horses to be fitted with shoes wide at the heels. In this case the projecting edge is boxed off. In addition, for show purposes, heavy horses are often fitted with bevelled shoes to make their feet appear larger.

Length of shoe. It is important that the heels of the shoe extend back to the end of the horn

to cover the wall and the bars so that the weight of the horse is spread over the whole hoof wall.

It is common practice to fit front shoes with the heels extending slightly beyond the extremity of the horn and to slope them to conform with the angle of the heels. For horses which work at fast paces it is customary to fit shoes with heels which extend to just within the termination of the horn and to slope them at a more acute angle. This is referred to as 'pencilled heels' (Fig. 7.51).

Heels too long. Front shoes with heels too long are liable to be trodden on by a hind foot and be pulled off, or may result in a fall. The horse may also catch the protruding heel in a wire fence and pull the shoe off. Also, long heels can injure the point of the elbow when the horse is lying down. In practice there is little danger in fitting heels 1/8 in. (3 mm) longer than the foot (Fig. 7.52): this is better than being too short, and with a sloping foot the heels can be fitted longer still.

Hot shoeing

Horn is a poor conductor of heat and therefore a hot shoe can be applied to the horse's hoof without causing pain or injuring the underlying sensitive foot. Obviously a hot shoe should not be held in contact with the foot any longer than necessary to decide on any alterations to the shoe or hoof to ensure a correct fit. If the method is abused by applying the shoe too hot or holding it in contact too long, then a burnt sensitive sole will result, especially if the horny sole is thin.

When a shoe is fitted hot it is applied at a dull red heat to the bearing surface. The clip or clips are allowed to mark the wall at the correct position and the shoe is shaped from these points. If the shoe does not fit exactly to the desired outline it is taken back to the anvil and altered. It is much easier to shape shoes hot than cold because the steel is softer. This procedure is followed until a perfect outline fit is obtained.

Both the hoof and the shoe are levelled as far as possible by eye so that the two surfaces fit together evenly. The horn is charred at the areas of contact thus revealing any irregularities between the two surfaces. If the bearing surface is unlevel the charred areas are taken down with a rasp or drawing knife to level it. Finally the hot shoe can be applied to the hoof without rocking and allowed to bed itself so that the surface fit is perfect. This should only require a moment and should not be abused by allowing an unlevel shoe to be burnt on to the hoof, or by allowing a level shoe to burn itself onto an unlevel hoof.

It has been said that the charring of the horn fibres reduces the absorption of moisture by the horn and that heat softens and expands the horn which makes driving the nails easier and secures them more firmly when the horn contracts. It is doubtful if these factors are significant.

The advantage of hot shoeing over cold shoeing is that it enables the shoe to be fitted more accurately.

Fitting a shoe hot
The method of fitting a shoe hot is shown in Figs.7.53–7.58.

Cold shoeing
All shoes have to be altered to obtain a perfect fit and when fitting a cold shoe it is possible only to alter it imprecisely. A perfect outline fit and a perfect surface fit are very difficult to achieve.

Without an exact surface fit uneven pressure results in a slight rocking of the shoe, which

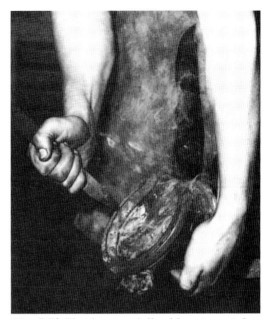

Fig. 7.53 The shoe at a dull red heat is carried on a pritchel to the foot. The toe clip is centred and the outline fit is studied starting from either side of the clip. The shoe is taken back to the anvil and altered as many times as it takes to get the desired outline fit.

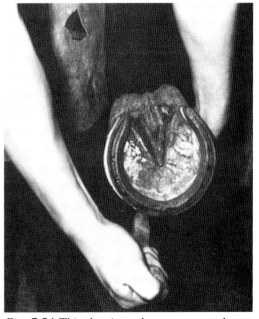

Fig. 7.54 This shoe is at the moment too close at the outside quarter and too wide at the inside heel.

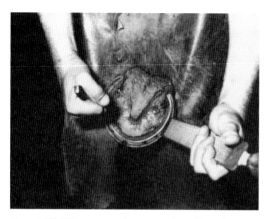

Fig. **7.55** *When a satisfactory outline fit is obtained a perfect surface fit is ensured. The shoe is levelled carefully on the anvil. The end of a rasp or the handle or blade of a drawing knife is used to press the hot shoe into position.*

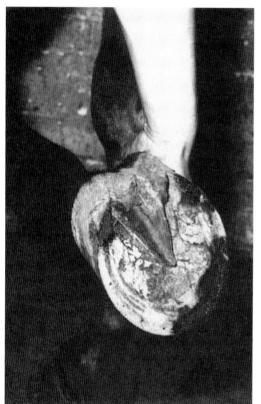

Fig. **7.56** *The horn is unevenly charred. This indicates that either the bearing surface of the foot or the foot surface of the shoe, or both, are not level and must be re-examined and levelled accordingly.*

Fig. **7.57** *The bearing surface of the foot is evenly charred. This indicates even contact between the foot and shoe. A thin rim of charred horn is removed with the drawing knife to relieve pressure on the sole.*

gradually raises the clenches and loosens the shoe.

Without a good outline fit the shoe will be difficult to nail on safely or securely, will be overgrown more quickly where it fits too close, or will be trodden off where it is too full.

Thus cold-fitted shoes are more liable to become loose than those fitted hot and it is more difficult to maintain the hoof in good condition.

If the heels of a cold-fitted shoe are too long it is difficult to rasp or file them shorter and the temptation is to lower the heels of the

Fig. **7.58** *If the sole at the seat of corn is up to the level of the wall it is eased slightly with the drawing knife to relieve pressure from the shoe.*

Fig. **7.60** *Opening a heel.*

Fig. **7.59** *Opening the toe.*

Fig. **7.61** *Closing the toe.*

Fig. **7.62** *Closing a heel.*

Fig. **7.64** *Levelling the shoe.*

Fig. **7.63** *Closing the toe.*

Fig. **7.65** *Holding a shoe to check whether its surfaces are level.*

hoof to lengthen the bearing surface, which unbalances the foot.

Methods of altering the shape of a cold shoe. Farriers develop their own individual methods for altering the shape of shoes cold. Figs.7.59–7.65 illustrate the basic principles of altering the outline of a cold shoe using an anvil.

7.8 Nailing on a shoe and finishing off (Figs.7.66–7.78)

A number of important points have to be taken into account when nailing on a shoe and unless due attention is paid to them, a well-made shoe, accurately fitted to a correctly prepared foot, will soon become loose.

No nail should be driven to enter or cross a crack. If the feet are broken or cracked the nail holes should be stamped so that the nails can be driven through sound horn.

The nails selected must be in proportion to the shoe and foot. It is bad practice to drive small nails high to obtain a good hold, as the clenches will be small and weak, or to use large nails which will split the horn.

The number of nails used to secure a shoe should be the minimum necessary but since nails of the right size and correctly placed cause little damage to the horn it is better to have one nail too many than one too few and risk losing a shoe. Three nails have been proven to be able to secure a shoe effectively. Four are a reasonable number for a small pony and six for most horses, though it is common practice to use seven nails with four in the outside branch and three in the inside branch. The presence of clips reduces the number of nails required, not because the clips hold the shoe to the hoof but because they reduce shearing forces on the nails. The better the fit of the shoe the fewer the nails that will be required.

Opinions differ as to whether the first nail to be driven should be at the toe or the heel. This is a matter of personal preference. Driving a toe nail first tends to move the shoe slightly backwards. This is an advantage if the shoe has clips and has been accurately fitted as it ensures that the clips rest firmly against the wall. If fitting a shoe without clips, it may be better to drive a heel nail first so that the shoe is accurately positioned.

The nail should enter the wall at or just outside the white zone to obtain a secure hold and be pitched to emerge about one third of the way up the wall. As the wall is thicker towards the toe it is customary to drive the nails at the toe somewhat higher. This is at the farrier's discretion, however. There is no reason why a nail should not be pitched higher or lower than this or into an old nail hole if it helps to retain the shoe effectively with the minimum of damage to the hoof.

Generally speaking a short and thick hold of the wall by a nail is better than driving it shallow and high. Ideally no more of the wall should be included within the grasp of the nail than is likely to be removed at the next shoeing, thus maintaining a constantly sound wall. This is not really practical when a horse is being shod every four to six weeks. The height that a nail can be driven depends on the condition of the wall, the number and position of the old nail holes and on the size and shape of the foot.

The farrier judges the direction the nail is taking by the resistance encountered and the sound made by the hammer. As the nail passes outward from the soft horn at the white zone to the hard horn of the middle layer of wall so the sound changes and resistance increases. A soft sound indicates that the nail is running in an old hole or crack or is still in the white zone and proceeding towards the sensitive foot.

Immediately each nail has been hammered home the protruding point is either twisted off using the claw of the shoeing hammer or cut off with pincers about ⅛ in. (3 mm) from the wall.

When all the nails have been driven they are each given a further couple of blows to ensure that they are well down in their holes in the shoe.

The nails are then 'drawn up'. The closed jaws of the pincers are placed under each stub of the cut-off nail and the nail is given a few sharp blows with the hammer. This draws the shank of the nail well up into the wall and at the same time turns the stub over to form a clench.

Nailing on the shoe

Fig. **7.66** *The shoe is held in the fitted position and the first nail, the inside heel nail, is driven.*

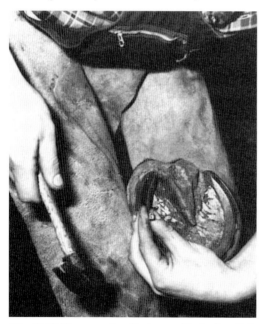

Fig. **7.67** *The second nail, the outside heel nail, is driven, and the remaining nails are then driven on each side alternately.*

Fig. **7.68** *Immediately each nail is hammered home the protruding point is twisted off using the claw of the hammer. Care must be taken to leave enough of the shank to form the clench.*

Fig. **7.69** *When the nails have been driven and the points wrung off, each nail head is given a couple of light blows to ensure it is driven deep into its hole. The closed jaws of the pincers are then pressed firmly upwards against the stubs and the nail heads given some more light blows to turn the stubs out at a right angle. This is called drawing up the clenches.*

Methods of holding the foot for clenching up

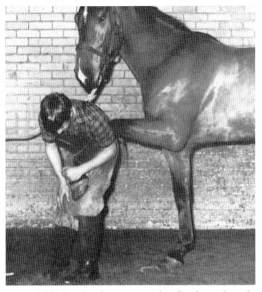

Fig. 7.70 To clench up one side of a front foot the farrier draws the leg forwards and rests the foot on and grips it with his thighs.

Fig. 7.72 To work on the outside of a hind foot the farrier draws the leg forward and with his back to the horse rests the foot on and grips it with his thighs.

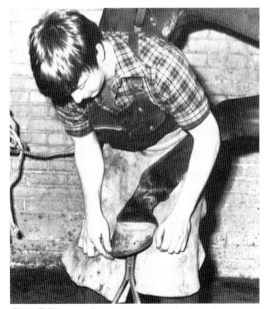

Fig. 7.71 An alternative method of positioning a front foot is to rest it on a tripod which takes the weight. The tripod is steadied with the farrier's feet on two of the feet of the tripod and the horse's hoof is gripped with the farrier's thighs as before.

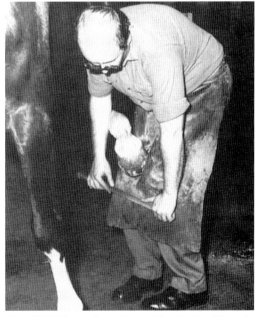

Fig. 7.73 To work on the inside of a hind foot the farrier faces the horse and rests the foot on and grips it with his thighs.

Clenching up and finishing off

Fig. 7.74 The split horn underlying the clench is smoothed off with the file edge of the rasp, care being taken not to cut a notch.

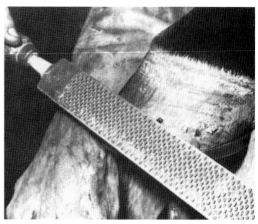

Fig. 7.75 The clench is shortened with the file side of the rasp until it is as long as it is wide. It is designed to hold the shank securely and not for stapling the shoe to the hoof.

Fig. 7.76 The clench is turned and bedded by tapping it with the hammer until it lies flat against the wall. At the same time the closed jaws of the pincers are pressed firmly upwards against the head of each nail in turn to prevent it being driven back.

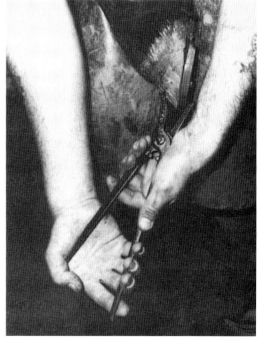

Fig. 7.77 An alternative method of turning the clenches is to use clenching tongs. Note the position of the farrier's hands. The left hand holds the clenching tongs firmly against the wall whilst with his right hand he closes the handles. Clenching tongs are particularly useful for young and nervous horses, and for horses with sensitive feet which they resent being hammered.

Fig. 7.79 A very carelessly driven nail which caused a nail bind. Not only was it driven with its straight side to the inside but also its point did not emerge to be twisted off and a clench formed.

Fig. 7.78 The clenches are smoothed off with the file side of the rasp, care being taken not to weaken them by excessive rasping, and the edge of the wall is under-rasped to give it a final finish.

7.9 Causes of lameness associated with shoeing

1) *Pricks* occur when the nail penetrates the sensitive foot. Usually, though not always, the horse will feel pain and snatch its foot away. When the nail is withdrawn there may be a smear of blood on the nail or blood may ooze from the hole.

Pricks are most likely to occur if the horse is restive or if the conditions are poor, e.g. bad light or rain, and particularly if coupled with a thin, broken or excessively rasped wall, shoe fitted close, coarse nail holes or the nail driven with the straight side to the inside (Fig. 7.79).

Lameness will usually disappear once the nail has been removed and in many cases there are no complications. However, sometimes in two or three days a sterile inflammation develops due to tissue damage and is accompanied by lameness, heat in the foot and an increased digital pulse and will clear up in a

few days. The horse will not usually be severely lame. Recovery will be hastened by hot poultices or foot baths.

If infection supervenes the lameness will be severe and will not improve until drainage of pus is established through the nail hole being opened up by the farrier or veterinary surgeon, combined with hot foot baths or poulticing. Antibiotics may be administered by a veterinary surgeon but establishing drainage is the crucial factor. In neglected cases the infection may work its way out at the coronet.

A prick is traditionally treated by pouring some antiseptic solution into the hole. In practice the solution does not penetrate very far as the hole closes up when the nail is withdrawn.

The horse's tetanus vaccination records should be checked and if not up to date a veterinary surgeon will be required to administer antitoxin.

2) *Nail binds* occur when a nail has been driven sufficiently close to the sensitive laminae to cause pressure which will result in inflammation and lameness after one to three days. Usually no infection is present and the horse will only be slightly lame at the walk. There will be heat in the foot and an increased digital pulse. Tapping the clench of the offending nail will cause pain. Once the nail is removed the lameness and heat should disappear within a few days. If infection develops the horse will

be very lame at the walk and the withdrawal of the nail will be accompanied by a discharge. In these cases the hole must be opened to provide drainage combined with hot foot baths and poulticing and antibiotics. Tetanus protection should be provided if the horse's vaccinations are not up to date.

3) *Sole pressure* occurs when the inside edge of the shoe presses on the sole. Flat or dropped soles can be relieved of excessive pressure by seating out the shoe. A shoe can be seated out either at a red heat with the round face of the hammer or (lightly) by running the edge of a rasp round the inside edge, which can satisfactorily be done cold.

Pressure is most likely to occur at the toe and is due either to the wall being lowered below the level of the sole, or to the foot surface of the shoe being prominent on its inner edge. The horse will usually become lame the day it is shod. Removing the shoe and seating it out slightly or easing the sole slightly with the hoof knife and replacing the shoe will provide instant relief.

Pressure on the sole at the seat of corn leads to corns which usually only develop if the shoes are left on too long.

4) *Overlowering the hoof.* If the wall of the hoof is lowered below the level of the sole and near to the sensitive tissues soreness may result even if the shoe does not press on the sole. This will usually develop within twenty-four hours and pass off within another day or two.

If a hot shoe is applied to an overlowered foot or if a hoof is overlowered by excessively burning on a hot shoe the sensitive tissues may be burnt which will cause a marked lameness. Serum will weep from the injured border of the sole, which will swell creating pressure from the shoe. The horse will be more comfortable with the shoe seated out and put back on rather than standing unshod which puts weight on the injured area. No nails should be driven near this area. A poultice should be applied daily or hot foot baths twice daily and the horse kept on a clean dry bed. Usually recovery is rapid.

5) *Changes in hoof balance.* If the balance of a hoof is altered markedly this may create lameness by altering the stresses caused by weight bearing throughout the limb. This is more likely to occur if a balanced hoof has been unbalanced but can also occur if a previously unbalanced hoof is corrected too much at one attempt.

6) *Changes in hoof length.* If hooves have been allowed to grow very long then the farrier is obliged to reduce them to their natural length in one trimming. There is little danger in so doing but it is advisable for the horse to be rested for a day or two so that it may become accustomed to the change. If ridden too soon the horse is liable to stumble and sprain the fetlock joint. If the fetlock joint is slightly sprained there will be moderate lameness and often puffiness around the fetlock, both of which will usually have disappeared by the following day. Cold water applications may hasten recovery.

7) *Coincidental lameness.* Horses may go lame at any time and for many reasons, most of which are unconnected with trimming and shoeing.

7.10 Causes of lost shoes

1) *Normal wear and tear.* A shoe can only stay on for a limited period even if it receives negligible wear.

The hoof wall at the heels will be worn away by friction against the shoe as the heels expand and contract with changes in weight bearing. This will cause the nails nearest the heels to become loose.

In normal horses whose hooves slope outwards on both sides the lengthening of the hoof through growth will result in a widening of the ground surface. The wall of the hoof which was resting on the shoe moves over it on either side and the shoe becomes loose.

These factors combine to loosen the shoe which finally comes off.

2) *Wear of the shoe.* As the shoe wears the heads of the nails are also worn away until there is nothing remaining to retain what is left of the shoe.

3) *Poor surface fit.* Uneven contact between the hoof and the shoe will cause the shoe to rock and loosen the clenches.

4) *Loose nails.* Nails become loose if they are not driven tightly into their holes in the shoe or are inadvertently loosened when being clenched, or too small a nail is selected and its head does not protrude above the shoe which makes tight clenching difficult.

5) *Badly fitting nails.* If the nail holes are badly formed then the nails may engage only at the tops of the holes. Once the tops of the nail heads are worn away the nails become loose. This is a fault in shoemaking and fitting.

6) *Poor nail placement.* Sufficient nails must be driven deeply into solid horn. This is more difficult to attain in cracked, brittle or broken feet where the positioning and pitch of the nail holes and the fitting of the shoe is crucial. The horn can become more broken without obtaining a secure hold for the shoe. Using nails which are too large can make this situation worse. Four well-placed nails are better than eight poorly placed nails. Well-fitting clips will support the nails by bracing the shoe against shearing forces.

7) *Buckling of the shoe.* Buckling can happen to any shoe if subjected to sufficient stress through the horse landing on uneven ground or kicking out at hard objects. A stone trapped between the shoe and sole can cause a flimsy shoe to buckle. The thinner the shoe the more likely it is to buckle.

8) *Spreading of the shoe.* Spreading happens as a result of forces occuring when the foot comes to the ground. The narrower the web of the shoe and the softer its material the more likely it is to spread. Spreading results in failure of outline fit, loosening of the nails and the protrusion of an edge liable to be stepped on.

9) *Shearing* of the shoe backwards or sideways from the hoof occurs due to excessive stress. It is more common in larger horses than in ponies. A toe clip helps to prevent a shoe being driven backwards but only quarter clips will resist a shoe being driven sideways.

10) *Treading.* Part of a shoe may protrude from under the hoof as a result of wide fitting, the absence of a piece of hoof wall, or spreading of the shoe. The horse may tread on the protruding inside branch of one of its own shoes or on the outside branch of the shoe of another horse. A horse with a wide hind leg action may tread on the outside of its own front shoe. Boxing off slightly the upper outside edge helps to prevent this and is a useful modification to all shoes. If there is a piece of hoof wall missing then boxing off is the simplest and safest procedure to adopt. Shoes should not normally be fitted wide except from behind the widest part of the hoof sufficient to allow for hoof growth for a reasonable period. Preserving the hoof at the heels and quarters by preventing them overgrowing the shoe must take priority over the slight risk of losing the shoe.

11) *Over-reaching and catching the heels.* When the heels of front shoes extend behind the heels of the foot the toe of the hind shoe can catch them. This is likely to happen when a horse loses some degree of co-ordination due to tiredness or uneven or slippery ground. It is more likely to happen when jumping. The more upright the hoof the more likely is even a small projection of the front heels to be caught as it stands out more from the hoof. A projecting heel can also be caught by a strand of wire if the horse puts its foot through a fence. Horses have also been known to deliberately pull off shoes by scraping the heels against a solid object such as a railway sleeper or a wooden gate.

12) *Mud.* Deep mud of the kind that is common during the British winter may provide enough suction to remove a shoe, especially if fitted full and long, in which case the hoof will not fill the hole made by the shoe. A shoe which is loose is always liable to be sucked off in mud, as are broad webbed and seated-out shoes.

13) *Pads.* Pads between the shoe and the hoof

become compressed on weight bearing thus loosening the clenches. Alternate loosening and tightening of the clenches is likely to cause them to rise. Soft pads also allow some rocking of the shoe with the same effect on the clenches.

14) *Shoes not bearing on solid horn.* A brittle, thin-walled, cracked or soft hoof wall may disintegrate or collapse under the horse's weight thus loosening the shoe. Often a hoof may appear perfect but the deeper layers of the wall may contain cracks, or be disintegrating as a result of moist debris having been trapped between the shoe and the sole.

7.11 Examining a newly shod horse

Foot on the ground (Fig. 7.80)
(i) Clenches are even, flat and broad. Nails not driven into cracks. Nails pitched higher at the toe than at the heels.
(ii) Both front and hind feet should be pairs, be the same size and shape and with the same pastern foot axis.
(iii) No rasping of the wall, except to remove flare. A little rasping always occurs below the clenches when they are rasped smooth.
(iv) No dumping of the wall, especially of the toe of the front feet to conceal a badly fitting shoe (Fig. 7.81).
(v) Clips low and broad and the toe clip centred.
(vi) Shoe fits the outline of the foot. Heels of correct length.

Foot lifted off the ground (Fig. 7.82)
(i) Nails driven home and the heads fit their holes, protruding slightly.
(ii) Heels not opened up.

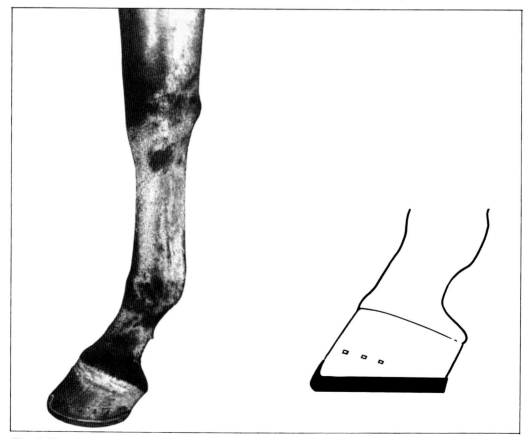

Fig. 7.80 Foot on the ground.

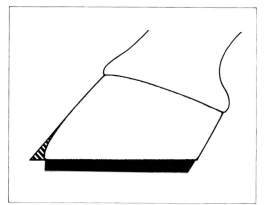

Fig. **7.81** *Dumping. The shoe is fitted close across the toe and the overhanging wall is rasped away to make the foot fit the shoe and to disguise an excessively sloping foot.*

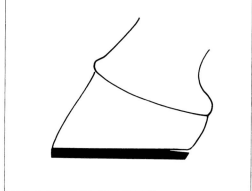

Fig. **7.83** *Sprung heel.*

(iii) Toe clip centred and in line with the point of the frog.

(iv) The sole has been eased at the seat of corn.

(v) No daylight between the foot and the shoe, which would indicate an unevenness of either the bearing surface of the foot or the foot surface of the shoe. A sprung heel (Fig. 7.83) is a gap between the heel of the shoe and the hoof and at times has been recommended with the idea of relieving weight from the heels of the hoof and allowing expansion. Abnormal pressures are created and the practice is not recommended.

(vi) Shoe fits the foot and the heels do not interfere with the function of the frog.

(vii) The shoe is properly finished off.

Finally the horse should be walked and trotted up to reassess its gait.

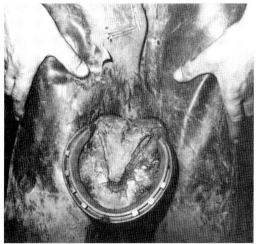

Fig. **7.82** *Foot lifted off the ground.*

CHAPTER 8

CARE OF THE FEET

8.1 The shod horse

Although shoes are necessary for continuous work on roads to prevent the hoof being worn away by friction they are detrimental because they interfere with the normal function of the foot.

In the care of horses' feet a number of general factors have to be taken into account, such as whether the horse is stabled in a loose box or stall, the type of bedding used and the amount and type of work.

Hygiene
Stable hygiene is most important. Horn cells are dissolved by alkalis, and the ammonia present in decomposing urine and manure softens the horn and predisposes to thrush.

For feet to be kept in a healthy state they require to be picked out at least twice daily, morning and evening, and each time the horse returns from work. Extra care must be taken to keep the space between the shoe and the sole, especially if the shoe is seated out, and the grooves of the frog free of all dirt and grit.

Shoeing
Shoes require to be removed every four to six weeks, the feet trimmed to balance them and at the same time loose flakes of the frog and sole are removed. By regular shoeing, before the hoof grows excessively long or the shoes

(a)

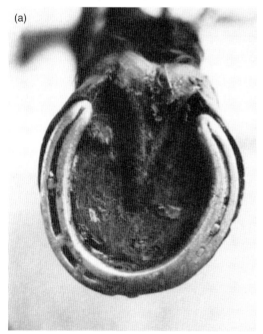

(b)

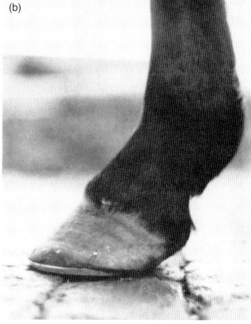

Fig. 8.1 (a) Shoe left on far too long. The hoof has grown wider than the shoe which comes to rest on the sole causing pressure and bruising, especially at the seat of corn.

(b) Side view. The hoof is too long. The shoe no longer supports the hoof wall at the quarters and heels and the hoof is unbalanced, being unnaturally sloping.

become loose, the feet are maintained in the best possible condition (Fig. 8.1 a-c).

Moisture

For healthy function of the foot the moisture content of the hoof must be maintained. The normal water content of the hoof ranges from approximately 25% in the wall to 33% in the sole and 40% in the frog. The horn tubules contain fluid which either comes from the papillae of the corium or is absorbed from the outer surface of the hoof. Constant evaporation from the outer surface is replaced from these two sources. If evaporation is excessive then the hoof becomes dry, brittle and cracks. On the other hand if evaporation is checked the hoof becomes too soft.

When horses are stabled for long periods and during dry weather the hoof is unable to make good the moisture lost by evaporation. If the feet are washed daily sufficient moisture will be absorbed to make good this loss. A soft brush should be used so as not to remove the periople. The hair above the coronet which

protects the growing periople should not be trimmed. A considerable amount of water is absorbed by the sole and the frog and very hard hooves rapidly become supple following cold water foot baths.

Hoof oil

The advantages of applying impervious materials, such as hoof oil or ointments, merit careful consideration. There is no evidence that they stimulate growth. Their action is to control the delicate balance between evaporation and absorption of moisture by the hoof.

Under ordinary conditions the continuous application of a waterproof material to the hoof prevents evaporation and the hoof becomes soft and crumbly. Conversely, if dry and brittle hooves are soaked in water to replenish their moisture content this can be followed by an application of hoof oil to help retain it.

Hoof growth

The hoof wall grows evenly all around the coronet at the rate of about $^5/_{16}$ in. (8 mm) per month, taking on average to grow from the coronet to the ground surface about twelve months at the toe and about six months at the heels (Fig. 8.2).

The rate at which the hoof wall grows varies with individual horses. It grows faster in

(c)

(c) Rrshoving restores the correct hoof length and balance.

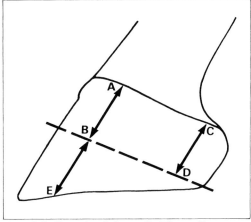

Fig. 8.2 Growth of the wall. The wall grows at the same rate around the coronet A-C. Therefore the horn along the line B-D is the same age but the horn at the toe E is older than the horn at the heels D.

younger horses and in foals often grows as much as ½ in. (12 mm) per month. Hoof growth is also faster in horses at work and can be accelerated by applying a counter irritant to the coronet such as a liniment or blister. With age the rate of hoof growth decreases and also is slower when a horse is confined to a stable and during the winter months when it averages only ¼ in. (6 mm) per month. Dietary supplements are unlikely to have any effect upon the growth rate of the hoof wall except in cases of malnutrition.

The sole and the frog are replaced every two months.

Summary

The hooves of shod horses can be kept healthy by picking out their feet regularly, providing dry standings and bedding, washing as necessary and the judicious application of oil to maintain the moisture content of the horn within its normal limits, combined with regular shoeing.

Thrush (Fig. 8.3)

This is a disease of the frog which is characterised by an unpleasant odour and a dark-coloured discharge from the central and sometimes the medial and lateral grooves, associated with the disintegration of the horn and in neglected cases small pockets of infection. It does not cause lameness except in neglected cases when the underlying sensitive foot becomes exposed. Thrush leads to the development of a small atrophied frog which can in turn lead to contraction of the foot.

The cause of thrush is not known, but is invariably associated with poor stable management and lack of exercise. Stalls and loose boxes not regularly mucked out, wet standings, failure to pick out or wash the feet and irregular shoeing favour its development.

It is a preventable disease and in the first instance attention must be directed to improving stable management and general hygiene. Clean, dry loose boxes and standings, regular use of the hoof pick and regular shoeing are all called for.

Shoeing means that the hoof wall is trimmed, promoting frog pressure, but taking care not to unbalance the foot by overlowering the heels. The frog can also be lightly trimmed to remove ragged portions and expose the grooves.

Local treatment comprises paring away all diseased and loose horn and keeping the grooves of the frog clean and dry. In slight cases an astringent powder, such as a mixture of one part powdered copper sulphate to two parts boric acid powder, should be instilled every time the hooves are picked out. A 1% formalin solution is an effective remedy which can be applied once daily but rubber gloves and eye protectors should be worn when applying it. In severe cases when infection is present the grooves should be treated with either sulphalinamide powder or an antibiotic spray and then packed with cotton wool and Stockholm tar every two to five days to keep out the wet and dirt.

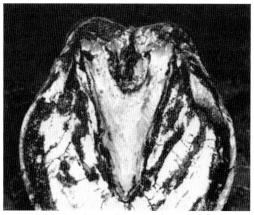

Fig. 8.3 Thrush in the central groove has eaten away the horn of the frog.

8.2 The unshod horse

It is customary to turn out all types of working horses for a few months during the summer. This not only gives them a rest and improves their general condition, but allows their shoes to be removed which gives the hooves a chance to grow without being damaged by nails.

Trimming

Without the protection of a shoe the hoof is worn away by friction and the rate of wear depends on the quality of the horn and the state of the ground. Whether the horse is out at grass or confined to a yard, its feet require attention every four to six weeks. Normal growth is not always controlled by friction, and in many cases the toe requires to be shortened and the heels lowered to balance the foot. The flare should be removed from the outside of the wall, especially at the quarters, and the edge of the wall rounded off with a rasp to prevent it from splitting or pieces breaking away. To prevent excessive wear and the horse becoming foot sore a little more of the wall should be left than when dressing the foot to fit a shoe.

During the dry season in hot climates horses are worked on unmetalled roads without hind shoes and mules are not shod. In these conditions it is most important to carry out routine inspections. The edges of the walls must be kept rounded off to prevent them from splitting, the feet kept balanced and the animals examined at the trot to make sure they are not becoming footsore. If there is a spell of wet weather or the animals have to be worked on metalled roads the hooves are rapidly worn down and shoeing becomes necessary.

Tips (Fig. 8.4)

These are short or half shoes which protect the wall around the toe and back to the quarters from wear while permitting the heels and frog to contact the ground naturally (Fig. 8.5). They are sometimes fitted to front feet when horses are turned out to grass, but they have their disadvantages. They are not easy to fit,

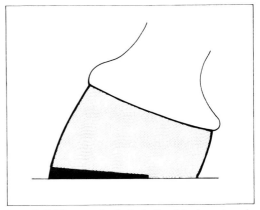

*Fig. **8.5** The standard tip is fitted by lowering the front half of the foot so that when the tip is fitted the ground surface of the tip and the unprotected heels are level.*

frequently become loose and have to be removed at regular intervals so that the growth of the wall at the toe can be reduced.

Tips require to be fitted full to prevent the growth of the wall from spreading over them and splitting, and are retained with four or five nails.

8.3 Young stock

When foals are given free exercise ordinary wear may be sufficient to keep their hooves within normal proportions, but if they do not get sufficient exercise their hooves soon become overgrown. If the toes are too long a sloping fetlock develops which upsets the balance of the foot, puts strain on the flexor tendons and predisposes to stumbling. But more frequent, and more important, is the development of high heels. This results in loss of frog pressure, contracted and weak heels which curl inwards, often followed by a twisted or deformed foot.

Foals should be examined and their feet kept trimmed from one month of age and then at monthly intervals, or every one or two weeks if a problem exists that requires correction. The foal should be examined by being walked on a level surface towards and away from the farrier so that the conformation of the limbs, and the action and the placement of the feet can be noted. In addition to observing the foal

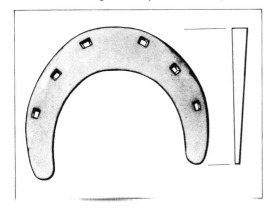

*Fig. **8.4** A standard tip.*

from a distance it is helpful in assessing limb deviation or rotation, to stand close to the foal's shoulder and look down the limb. After trimming the feet the examination should be repeated to assess the effect of any changes that have been made on the foal's action and foot placement.

Yearlings should be given adequate exercise on hard ground, especially if they are reared under cover because the hoof will grow too long, especially the toe, the heels will curl inwards and the foot become unbalanced. It is essential that the feet of yearlings are attended to at regular intervals of four to six weeks to correct any unevenness of wear and to balance the feet.

Angular limb deformities

Defects of conformation are all too frequent and it is essential they are recognised and dealt with as soon as possible. Deviations of the limb are usually caused by uneven growth at the growth plates. Lateral angulation of the distal limb is known as a *valgus* deformity. Medial angulation is known as a *varus* deformity.

Deviation at the knee (carpus) usually originates from the growth plate at the distal radius. This growth plate does not close until two years of age but the rapid period of growth is during the first eight months of life.

Front legs which deviate laterally from the carpus (carpus valgus) wear the hoof on the medial side excessively and therefore are corrected by lowering the lateral side of the hoof.

Front legs which deviate medially from the carpus (carpus varus) are corrected by lowering the medial side of the hoof.

Care must be taken that correction aimed at the knee is not too severe and causes the fetlock to become deviated in the opposite direction.

Deviation at the hock (tarsus) usually originates from the growth plate at the distal tibia. This growth plate does not close until two years of age but the rapid period of growth is during the first six months of life.

Foals which have *bow legs* (tarsus varus) wear the hoof on the lateral side excessively and therefore are corrected by lowering the medial side of the hoof.

Foals with *cow hocks* (tarsus valgus) are corrected by lowering the lateral side of the hoof.

The majority of foals with deviation at the knee or hock, including extreme cases, generally respond to corrective trimming. But if a gradual improvement is not achieved by corrective trimming then veterinary advice should be sought without delay as surgical procedures can be carried out with success provided the growth plate has not closed.

Deviation at the fetlock usually originates from the growth plate at the distal end of the metacarpal and metatarsal bones. These growth plates close at about twelve months of age with most rapid growth during the first three months of life. Toes turning in or out as a result of limb deviation at the fetlock need to be corrected early.

Toes turning in from the fetlock (fetlock varus) are corrected by lowering the medial side of the hoof and toes turning out from the fetlock (fetlock valgus) by lowering the lateral side of the hoof.

The longer attempts at correction of the fetlock are delayed after three months of age the less successful they will be, the effect being instead on the knee or hock resulting in a deviation in the opposite direction. Early correction is most important.

In all cases of corrective trimming, care must be taken not to lower excessively the appropriate side of the hoof in the hope of obtaining a quicker and better correction as this will only result in abnormal and excessive strains on the fetlock and pastern joints, which may cause the onset of degenerative joint disease.

Rotation of a limb can exist, about the long axis, causing a toe in or toe out conformation without any angular deviation being present. Commonly this occurs at the knee and also sometimes at the fetlock. Corrective trimming has little effect on rotation.

Contraction of the flexor tendons

A common and important problem is contraction of the flexor tendons. This occurs mostly during the summer of the first year and during the spring and summer of the second year of life, when the foal and yearlings are going through their most rapid periods of growth. It is very much a problem associated with over-feeding and rapid growth, when the foal's metacarpal and metatarsal bones increase in length faster than the flexor tendons which results in a relative contraction of the tendons in relation to the bones.

Whatever line of treatment is adopted the first priority is to slow down the rate of growth by reducing the food intake. In the case of the suckling foal this means feeding the mare less to reduce her milk yield, and in weaned foals to feeding only hay with a calcium supplement but no concentrate.

Superficial digital flexor tendon contraction results in the fetlock knuckling forward but the hoof stays flat on the ground. This condition is most frequently seen in yearlings.

The farrier can only assist in these cases by keeping the hoof trimmed and balanced normally.

If the condition does not show any improve-ment or deteriorates then veterinary advice should be sought as surgical intervention may prove beneficial.

Deep digital flexor tendon contraction results in the distal interphalangeal joint becoming flexed and the foal has difficulty in keeping its heels on the ground. In extreme cases they can end up walking on the dorsal surface of the wall.

The farrier has an important role to play. By keeping the heels lowered and encouraging the foal to take plenty of exercise, the tendons are kept under constant tension which prevents

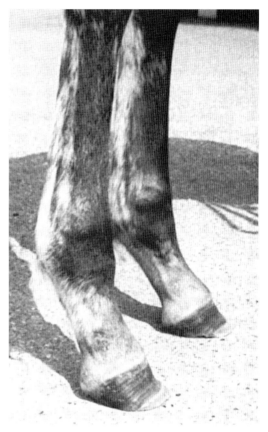

Fig. 8.7 Boxy foot of foal showing concavity of the front of the hoof.

their progressive and permanent shortening. In the majority of cases these simple measures result in a gradual correction of the defect and a return to normality in four to six weeks. These foals wear the toe excessively which can lead to splitting of the wall or infection in the white zone which needs to be checked by the farrier. A simple tip or an ordinary shoe may help to protect the toe.

If the condition does not respond to keeping the heels lowered a shoe with an extended toe piece may help (Fig. 8.6), but there are disadvantages. The shoes become loose at the heels, they restrict growth of the foot leaving it smaller in size and the extended toe piece causes abnormal pressures which result in a concavity of the front of the wall.

Some cases are characterised by the devel-opment of a narrow, upright or 'boxy' foot

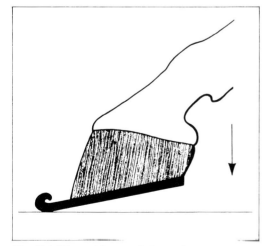

Fig. 8.6 Shoe with extended toe piece.

which is generally accompanied by a slight concavity of the front of the wall (Fig. 8.7). Extension of the distal interphalangeal joint is restricted and a radiograph of the foot reveals rotation of the distal phalanx. These cases seldom respond to corrective trimming.

When contraction of the flexor tendons does not respond to keeping the heels lowered or continues to deteriorate veterinary advice should be sought as soon as possible because surgical treatment is successful.

8.4 The donkey

Donkeys require the same foot care as horses. Unfortunately their feet are often neglected. Their hooves should be kept trimmed at regular intervals not exceeding two months.

CHAPTER 9

PREVENTION OF SLIPPING

The methods employed to give horses a secure foothold have included special shoes, calkin and wedge heels, toe pieces, studs, non-slip nails and a variety of pads.

Different methods are indicated for jumping horses in soft going, for roadwork and for icy conditions. For slippery going and for ice, projections are needed. For better grip on the roads, plugs or non-slip nails are best as they will not unbalance the feet.

Shoes with a toe piece and calkin for draught horses, and with a wedge heel and calkin for riding horses have stood the test of time as the most satisfactory methods of providing a secure foothold. But these shoes take time and skill to forge and, therefore, more simple and economical methods are required. These requirements have been met by the introduction of a wide range of horse-shoe studs, plugs and non-slip nails. These studs have been designed to meet the requirements of all types of horses and conditions of work and in addition to providing a good grip they reduce the wear of the shoes.

9.1 Horseshoe studs

Studs are available in a range of sizes to suit ponies, hacks and harness horses and of different shapes to meet the special require-ments of various sports such as show jumping and other events.

The standard studs (Fig. 9.1) for routine non-slip purposes are low and broad, which allow the frog to function normally and are tapered so that once fitted they remain perma-nently in the shoe. It is common practice to insert one stud in each heel (Fig. 9.2).

The durability of these studs greatly increases the life of the shoe and, under normal conditions, they can be expected to last for a minimum of 350 miles (560 km) for hacking and hunting and 250 miles (400 km) for light draught work. As these studs wear down they continue to retain their non-slip properties because of a central core of tungsten carbide which wears down much more slowly than the surrounding mild steel and persists as a projection (Fig. 9.3).

If it is considered that the standard stud raises the heels of the shoe excessively, then the plug-type stud is used (Fig. 9.4). These plugs are countersunk into the shoe until level with the ground surface. As the surrounding metal wears down the tungsten carbide core remains to provide a good grip and prevent slipping (Fig. 9.5).

As an alternative to inserting a stud or plug the tungsten carbide pins which make up the cores of these studs can be obtained and

(a)

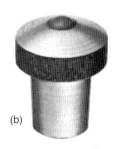
(b)

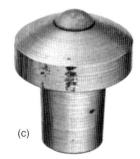
(c)

Fig 9.1 Standard tapered studs. Type (a) for small ponies and lightweight hunters; type (b) for hacks, hunters and light harness horses; type (c) for heavy draught horses.

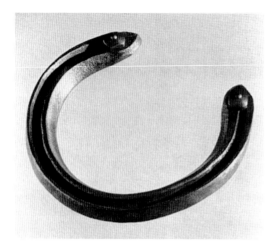

Fig. 9.2 A concave fullered hunter shoe with a standard type stud fitted in each heel.

Fig. 9.3 A well-worn shoe fitted with standard type studs. As the studs wear down the tungsten carbide core persists as a projection and prevents slipping.

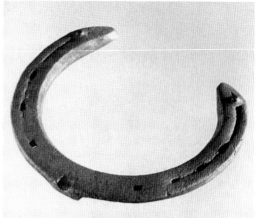

Fig. 9.5 A well-worn shoe fitted with plug type studs. As the heel of the shoe wears down the tungsten carbide core persists to provide a good grip and to prevent slipping.

inserted directly into the shoe, in a smaller hole than would otherwise be necessary.

For sporting activities such as show jumping and horse trials in particular, which require studs to be exchanged quickly to meet the changes of pace and ground conditions, the screw-in stud is used (Fig. 9.6).

Another non-slip device is the non-slip nail (Fig. 9.7). This is an ordinary horseshoe nail with a central core of tungsten carbide in the head. When used the nail must be driven until it is flush with the shoe otherwise the nail head will wear away too quickly and the tungsten core lost prematurely. These nails are currently available in sizes E3 to E8 and one

Fig. 9.4 Standard plug type studs which are countersunk into the shoe level with the ground surface. They combine the advantage of flat shoeing and prevent slipping.

(a)   (b)

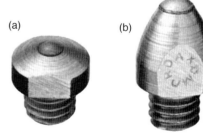

Fig. 9.6 Standard screw-in type studs: (a) suitable for hacks and hunters; (b) suitable for jumping and eventing.

Fig. **9.7** *Non-slip horseshoe nail.*

Fig. **9.8** *A hole is started at a yellow heat from the foot surface of the shoe on the face of the anvil. This pushes metal into the fullering, giving a complete collar around the hole.*

nail inserted in each shoe, usually at the outside heel, is generally sufficient.

The method of punching a hole to take a standard-type stud is conveniently described in five steps, shown in Figs 9.8– 9.12

The method of making and tapping a hole to take a screw-in type stud, is illustrated in Figs 9.13–9.15.

9.2 Horseshoe borium

This is the trade name for tungsten carbide crystals packed into a tube of mild steel. The tube melts and the steel acts as a bond enabling the crystals to be deposited on a shoe. This produces a rough surface which prevents slipping and at the same time reduces the wear of the shoe.

As the bonding steel wears away the particles of tungsten carbide left exposed must be large enough to remain prominent and provide a good grip. To meet this requirement a screen size of 8 to 10 (¼ in.) is required. If smaller particles are used their hardness satisfactorily reduces the wear of the shoe but the surface is too smooth and the non slip properties are lost.

Fig. **9.9** *The hole is completed by punching from the ground surface of the shoe, the first blows being on the face of the anvil and the final blows being over the hardie hole. The branch is levelled.*

185

Fig. **9.10** *The hole is enlarged to size with a drift, the same shape and size as the shank of the stud.*

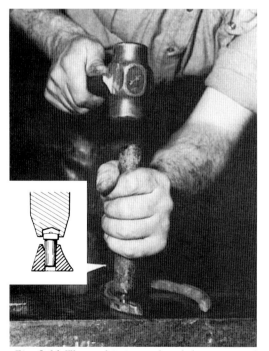

Fig. **9.11** *The stud is inserted and driven in with a special tool, made to fit its shape.*

Fig. **9.12** *The stud inserted, and driven home in the outside heel of a hind shoe.*

Fig. **9.13** *A hole is either drilled or punched from the ground surface of the shoe.*

Applying horseshoe borium. Rods of horseshoe borium are supplied in 14 in. (35 cm) lengths and with a grain size from ⅛ in. (3 mm) to ⅜ in. (10 mm) in diameter. The ¼ in. (6 mm) size is most suitable. Shoes must be fitted and cleaned before the borium is applied.

(i) The area of the shoe to which borium is to be applied is heated, either with an oxy-acety-lene torch (Fig. 9.16) or in the forge fire, until

Fig. 9.14 A hole is punched as in Figs 9.8–9.9 and the shoe is quenched. The shoe is held in a vice and the hole is tapped to cut the threads.

Fig. 9.16 Applying horseshoe borium.

The amount of borium required to treat a shoe depends on the purpose for which the horse is required. Horses used across country, for example, will only require a spot on each heel to prevent slipping. Horses which do a lot of road work will require a liberal covering of the toe and heels (Fig. 9.20) not only to provide a good foothold but also to prevent wear. In these cases the outer edge of the shoe at the toe, between the first two nail holes and from the heel nail holes to the end of the shoe, are treated to a height of about ¼ in. (6 mm). It is important that all deposits of horseshoe borium are of equal thickness so as to preserve the balance of the shoe.

Fig. 9.15 Hole tapped and screw-in stud being inserted. This is normally done by the owner as and when required. When the shoe is nailed on the farrier plugs the hole with cotton wool to keep out the dirt.

it is at white heat and the surface begins to melt (Fig. 9.17).

(ii) The end of the borium rod is preheated, applied to the molten metal of the shoe and the tungsten carbide crystals puddled over the surface of the shoe until the desired area is covered (Fig. 9.18).

(iii) Finally, the treated area is heated with the flame to melt and flatten the bonding metal and leave the crystals exposed (Fig. 9.19).

(iv) The treated shoe is left to cool slowly. If it is quenched and cooled quickly it becomes very brittle and easily chips and flakes if altered cold.

Fig. 9.17 Branch of shoe heated in the forge fire to a white heat and held on the face of the anvil, for applying the horseshoe borium.

187

Fig. 9.18 The end of the borium rod is preheated, applied to the molten metal of the shoe and the tungsten carbide crystals are puddled over the surface.

Fig. 9.20 Shoe treated with horseshoe borium at the toe, between the first two nail holes, and at the heels, from the heel nail holes to the end of the branch.

Fig. 9.19 The treated area is finally heated with the oxy-acetylene torch to melt and flatten the bonding metal, and to leave the crystals of tungsten carbide exposed.

Composite rods are tungsten carbide bonded with nickel-silver, easily applied in a gas forge using flux coated brazing rod.

Shoes treated with borium provide a better grip and last longer than a standard plain shoe (Fig. 9.21), but this advantage leads, all too often, to shoes being left on for too long. The longer life of the shoe results in a gradual increase in the size of the nail holes, which makes the use of larger nails necessary. This can lead to split hooves and loose shoes. In time the normal movements of the heels wear a groove which produces an uneven foot surface that is difficult to correct. Horseshoe borium is expensive and shoes once fitted are difficult to shape and level.

In spite of these disadvantages horseshoe borium can be valuable in providing a secure foothold, preventing wear and prolonging the life of the shoe.

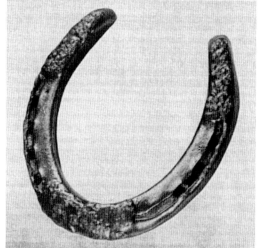

Fig. 9.21 This shoe has been refitted several times over a period of five months. Wear has been minimal and sufficient horseshoe borium remains to provide a good grip.

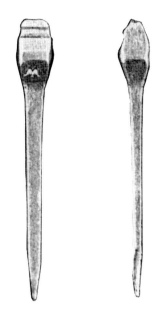

Fig. 9.22 Frost nail.

a lot of road work because it necessitates the shoes being replaced before the branches are worn out. Various methods are used to combat this problem. A rod of stainless steel or tungsten carbide welded into the toe is very effective, but an application of borium or a plug inserted on either side of the toe is equally good and also improves the foothold. Rolling the toe of the shoe, using a plain rather than a fullered shoe or using a wider webbed shoe can also be helpful in prolonging wear.

9.3 Frost nails (Fig. 9.22)

Originally designed as a temporary measure to prevent working horses slipping on icy roads, frost nails have a large wedge-shaped head. Nowadays it is neither necessary nor safe to take pleasure horses on icy roads. Frost nails are sometimes used as a simple alternative to studs to provide grip at shows, being inserted into an existing nail hole at the outside heel and driven and clenched in the normal way. Frost nails are available in sizes E4, E5 and E6.

Horses with a normal action invariably wear the toes of their shoes excessively. This can become a real problem when horses are doing

CHAPTER 10

PADS AND MODERN MATERIALS

A pad may be described as a sheet of leather, rubber, plastic, metal or some other material which is placed between the foot and the shoe and held securely with nails to protect the foot, reduce concussion, or alter foot balance.

All pads have disadvantages. They make nailing on of the shoe more difficult, and they make the shoe less secure on the hoof. Pads which cover the frog encourage thrush.

Synthetic materials such as plastics are available that have great potential in hoof care.

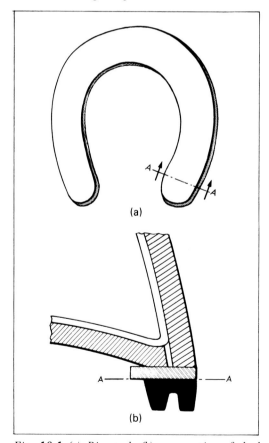

Fig. 10.1 (a) Rim pad; (b) cross-section of shod foot with rim pad.

10.1 Pads for protection

Pads can be a useful protection for thin and bruised soles and for punctured and diseased feet. Leather is traditionally used but is rather soft and rapidly worn. Hard plastic pads or a thin sheet of aluminium alloy may be used depending on availability and personal preference.

10.2 Pads to reduce concussion

There are several types of synthetic pads designed to reduce concussion, all of which can be referred to as hoof cushions:

(a) Rim pads. Leather used to be fitted in a ring between the foot and the shoe with the idea of reducing concussion. This had no significant effect. Plastic rim pads are currently available for the same purpose but it is doubtful if they are any better than leather ones (Fig. 10.1 a-b).

(b) Full pads. These pads are fitted between the hoof and the shoe and cover the whole of the sole and frog (Fig. 10.2). They may be leather or a hard or soft plastic.

Unfortunately the thicker and softer the pad the more likely it is that the shoe will be lost. The cavity between a full pad and the sole will tend to accumulate dirt and should be packed with tow (a coarse hemp or flax fibre) and Stockholm tar to obliterate the space.

(c) Liquid solutions can be used to fill the cavity between a full pad and the sole which will set to a firm rubber consistency (Fig. 10.3). Proprietary preparations such as silicone rubber, which is sold widely as a general-purpose sealant, can be used.

A small amount of concussion may be absorbed using these methods but most of the concussion on a hoof still passes through the shoe to the hoof wall and via the laminae to the distal phalanx and the upper leg.

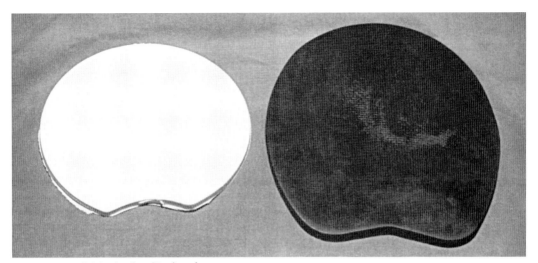

Fig. 10.2 Full 'shock-absorbing' pads.

(d) The Strömsholm hoof cushion (Fig. 10.4) is held by a thin outer rim which fits between the shoe and the hoof. The thicker inner part of the pad has a porous core and rests on the sole. It should be slightly recessed from the ground surface of the shoe so that the initial impact goes onto the shoe and the wall of the hoof (Fig. 10.5). On uneven ground a proportion of weight and concussion is likely to be taken by the pad and has the effect of increasing the amount of weight borne by the outer edge of the sole. This may benefit a horse with weak walls by creating a distribution

Fig. 10.4 Strömsholm hoof cushion.

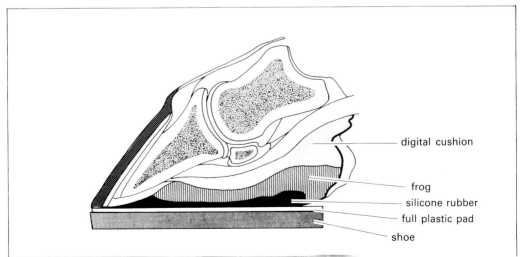

— digital cushion

— frog

— silicone rubber

— full plastic pad

— shoe

Fig. 10.3 Rubber solution injected under a pad.

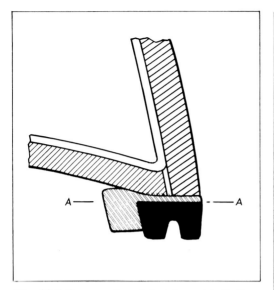

Fig. 10.5 Cross-section of shod foot with Ströms-holm hoof cushion.

of weight between wall and sole closer to that of the unshod horse. If the inner part of the pad is fitted too proudly it contacts the ground before the shoe and bruising of the sole results. Another disadvantage is that grit may accumulate under the pad.

A normal healthy hoof requires no protection against concussion and pads should not be used by horse owners as a substitute for regular good shoeing to improve the condition of the hoof.

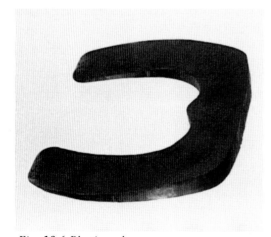

Fig. 10.6 Plastic wedge.

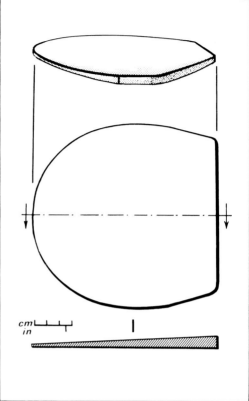

Fig. 10.7 Full wedge pad.

10.3 Pads to alter hoof balance

Plastic wedges in the form of a 'U' (Fig. 10.6) are used to raise the heels of a foot. Plastic wedges in the form of full pads (Fig. 10.7) can be used to raise any part of the hoof depending on how they are fitted (Fig. 10.8). Plastic wedges also help to absorb concussion but ordinary flat pads should be used for this purpose unless the foot is unbalanced and a wedge is indicated.

Normal flat pads, either full or rim pads, also alter foot balance by increasing the length of the shod foot. This effect is not significant unless very thick pads are fitted to gaited horses for showing, such as Morgans and Hackneys, with the intention of increasing flexion of the limb (Fig. 10.9). When fitting pads for this purpose the shoe must have coarse nail holes and be fitted full, so that the pad can continue the slope of the hoof wall.

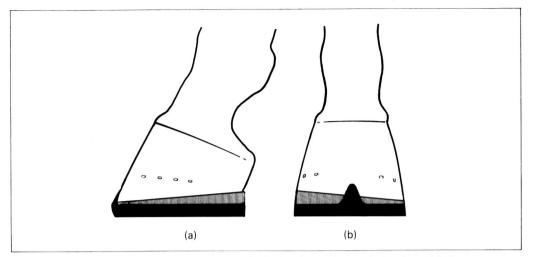

Fig. 10.8 Use of a full wedge pad (a) to raise the heels; (b) to alter medial to lateral balance.

Longer and larger nails than normal will be required and the horse must be exercised with great caution as the pads and shoes will easily be cast. Clips must be very long in order to rest on the hoof wall above the pad.

Applying a pad
1. Fit the shoe ready for nailing on.
2. Place the pad on the shoe and cut notches for the clips with a drawing knife. Rivet the shoe and pad lightly together by driving two nails and cutting off their shanks flush with the pad with pincers. Trim the pad around the shoe leaving the pad a little full.
3. If a full pad is being applied pack the sole and grooves of the frog with tow or cotton wool and either Stockholm tar, Vaseline or hoof dressing to keep out dirt and moisture.
4. Nail on the shoe. Once the first two nails are driven, the two rivetting nails can be removed with pincers or nail pullers.
5. When finishing off the clenches the excess pad material is rasped away so that the pad is flush with the shoe.

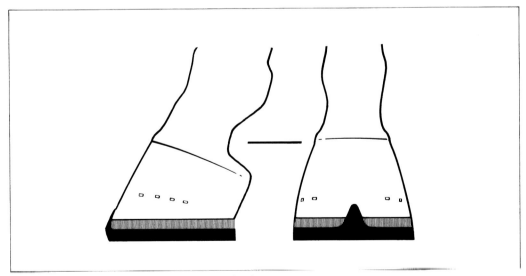

Fig. 10.9 Use of a full flat pad to lengthen the foot.

10.4 Modern materials

Plastics

Plastic solutions can be used for a variety of purposes. In particular they have potential as a prosthetic replacement where there is severe loss of hoof wall. In general the potential of modern plastics in shoeing has not been fully explored, perhaps because a skilled farrier can successfully adapt and nail on a shoe in the majority of cases.

Hard-setting plastics such as plastic wood and car-body filler can be used as fillers for hoof defects either for cosmetic purposes or to keep out dirt and moisture. Plastics can also be used as a weight-bearing replacement for damaged hoof wall and will support a shoe and perhaps take nails or resist wear in an unshod foot. For these purposes it is best to use a proprietary acrylic-based hoof repair compound such as Technovit, a rapid-curing resin on a methyl methacrylate basis (made by Kulzer and Co., Freidrichsdorf). No plastics adhere to horn satisfactorily unless it is thoroughly cleaned and prepared by removing loose horn and dirt. For best results then apply ether to remove fats. When filling a defect it is always best to undercut the edges so that even if adhesion is lost the plastic will not fall out. Wire sutures can also be used to reinforce and support the plastic. Heat is generated as some plastics set and if they are applied close to sensitive tissues they must either be applied in layers or else allowed to set under cold running water.

Fibreglass

Fibreglass and resin will not adhere to horn. It can be used to make a patch for repair of cracks, which can be secured with screws to the hoof wall. Self-tapping sheet metal screws are best, preferably with hexagonal heads so that they can be inserted using a socket drive rather than a screwdriver. The points must be cut off and they must be inserted to the depth of pre-drilled holes in the hoof wall so as not to impinge on the sensitive laminae.

Miscellaneous

Hot glue will adhere both to horn and to steel if the surfaces are thoroughly cleaned and pre-warmed. It is sold in solid sticks and is normally applied with an electric gun which heats and melts the glue which then solidifies as it cools. A hot-air blower may be needed to pre-warm the hoof to aid adhesion of the glue. Care must be taken not to apply heat too closely to the sensitive foot.

Adhesives may also have applications for filling and stabilising hoof defects and cracks.

CHAPTER 11

SPECIAL HORSESHOES

Farriers are frequently called upon to make special shoes to prevent injuries, to improve defective feet and to alleviate lameness.

11.1 Injuries caused by the shoe

Treads

A tread is the name given to an injury of the coronet caused by a shoe. It is generally caused by the shoe of the opposite foot when the horse is turning or, when horses are working in pairs, by one horse treading on its fellow.

Another cause is itchy legs. This is due to the parasite *Chorioptes equi* which causes the horse continually to stamp its feet and often rub one leg with the shoe of the opposite foot with resulting injuries to the coronet.

Treads occur most frequently when horses are shod with a calkin on the inside heel, or if the outer edge of the inside branch of a shoe is prominent or sharp.

A tread can range from a simple bruise to an open wound. All treads are serious and veterinary advice should be sought because not only is a deep wound of the coronet followed by a false quarter but also, if infection supervenes, it may result in necrosis of the cartilage and the development of a quittor.

Rasping away some horn below an injury to the coronet serves no useful purpose, it weakens the hoof and does not assist healing.

Capped elbow

A capped elbow is the name given to any swelling at the point of the elbow. In most cases it is an acquired bursa due to slight but repeated injury from contact with the ground.

A horse adopts two positions when lying down. He is either flat on his side with head and limbs extended, or sitting up obliquely on his chest. In this latter position the knees and hocks are flexed and all four feet come together under the body. If the horse is sitting

on the right side of his chest the right front foot is placed close to the sternum with the elbow in contact with the ground. The right hind leg is resting on the ground with the foot close to the abdomen. The left front foot lies near the elbow but the elbow does not come into contact with the heel of the shoe as is commonly assumed. The left hind leg lies with the point of the hock resting on the ground and the foot directed forwards.

A capped elbow is rarely due to it coming into contact with the heels of the shoe, unless they are very long and especially if with calkins, but rather by coming into contact with the ground. This is exacerbated by hard and uneven stable floors coupled with insufficient bedding. It is also seen in horses which, having extended their front legs prior to getting up, have the habit of resting on the points of their elbows.

Shoeing. Firstly it is essential to determine the cause of the injury by observing the horse lying down. If it is due to the heel of the shoe striking the point of the elbow, and provided the heels of the shoe are not too long in which case they need to be reduced to a normal length, this can be alleviated by fitting a shoe with the inner heel shortened and fitted close. Short and close fitting is likely to weaken the medial wall of the hoof and thus be detrimental in the long term to the balance of the foot, and may lead to corns. The point of the elbow can be protected without recourse to altering the shoe by simply putting on a sausage boot around the pastern when the horse is stabled.

Shoe for capped elbow (Fig. 11.1). This shoe has a short inner heel. The heel is hot rasped off obliquely and rounded to resemble the back of the bowl of a spoon.

Threequarter shoe (Fig. 11.2). This shoe has up

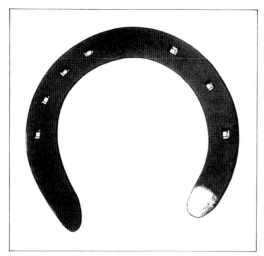

Fig. **11.1** *Shoe for capped elbow made from flat bar.*

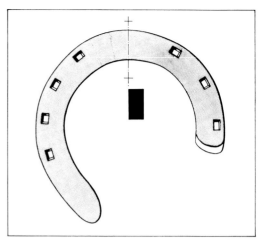

Fig. **11.2** *Threequarter shoe made from flat bar. An ordinary shoe which has up to a half of one branch cut off.*

to a half of one branch, usually the inner, cut off and the end sloped and filed smooth. As this shoe has no heel to strike the elbow it is often used in the treatment of capped elbow but has little to recommend it for this or any other purpose. The shoe reduces the area of bearing surface, permits downward movement of the wall at the heel and the end of the shortened branch produces an abnormal pressure point.

11.2 Injuries caused by abnormalities of gait

These injuries are frequently referred to as interferences. A leg is struck by the shoe of another foot causing a bruise or wound. It may be due to working an unfit, immature or tired horse. It may be due to faulty dressing of the feet or shoeing; such cases are dealt with by careful attention to balancing the feet and fitting the shoes. It may be due to poor conformation and action; such cases can be alleviated only by corrective shoeing.

Before a horse is shod to prevent interferences the cause must be sought and identified. The conformation of the horse's limbs and pastern foot axis must be examined and its action observed at all paces. Each horse has to be considered individually in order to select the most suitable shoe as all horses with the

same abnormality of gait do not necessarily require the same shoe or to be shod in the same manner. Protective boots are useful in many cases.

Brushing

Brushing is the term used to describe an injury caused by the horse striking the inside of one leg, generally in the region of the fetlock, with the shoe of the opposite foot.

Brushing is particularly common in young, unfit and tired horses. Cases due to unbalanced hooves or shoes are easily dealt with as obvious faults. On the other hand when brushing results from a defect of conformation the actual cause of the injury has to be identified before the most suitable corrective shoe can be fitted.

It is not always easy to decide which part of the shoe is responsible for the injury because the leg may be struck by either the toe, quarter or heel of the shoe. This can be detected by chalking or greasing the hoof wall or the shoe and noting where it is rubbed off and at what pace.

The action taken to prevent brushing has to be related to the cause, the frequency and the severity of the injury. Many cases of slight brushing can be overcome by simply fitting a flat and lighter shoe. The hoof should be balanced in accordance with the horse's conformation: for instance a horse with toe-in conformation should be allowed to retain its naturally wry hoof, slightly longer and more sloping on the inside. If these simple measures do not prevail then fit the inner branch of the shoe close, and round off the overhanging wall.

Shoeing. A variety of shoes are recommended to prevent brushing injuries. Each shoe has its special merit which has to be related to the cause in each individual case.

Knocked-up shoe (Fig. 11.3). The inner branch is narrow with the outer edge rounded off. It is fitted close and the projecting wall is rounded off. The branch is blind except for one or two nail holes at the toe. The outer branch is fitted to the outline of the wall, has three or four nail holes and sometimes a quarter clip.

A knocked-up shoe is recommended to prevent brushing injuries caused by the toe or mid-quarter of the shoe.

Feather-edged shoe (Fig. 11.4). This is an exaggerated type of knocked-up shoe. The inner branch is blind and as the name implies is

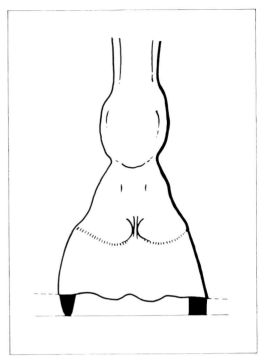

Fig. 11.4 Feather-edged shoe.

very narrow and higher than the outer. It was claimed that this shoe by raising the inside of the foot throws it outwards from its normal line of flight and thereby prevents brushing.

In practice the shoe encourages both a toe-in and base-narrow posture. Moorcroft in 1800 showed that by altering the thickness of the branches of a shoe the action of a horse is modified in a definite manner. Firstly (i) he trotted a horse, with shoes of even thickness, that had never brushed, in soft ground and measured the distances between the imprints of the outer edges of the front shoes. This was 9½ ins (24 cm). He repeated the experiment (ii) with the shoes thicker on the inner quarter, when the distance between the outer edges of the shoes were regularly reduced to 8½ ins (21.5 cm), and (iii) where the outer quarter of the shoes was thicker the distance was regularly increased to 11 ins (28 cm). These experiments indicate that the theory behind raising the medial side of the foot to throw it outwards and thereby prevent brushing is erroneous and probably accounts for the disappointing results attributed to this shoe.

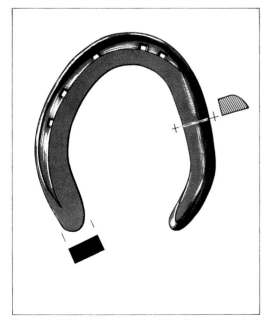

Fig. 11.3 Knocked-up shoe. The inner branch is narrow with the outer edge rounded off.

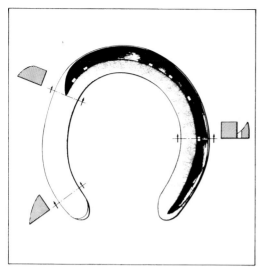

Fig. 11.5 Knocked-down shoe.

Speedy-cutting shoe (Fig. 11.6). This shoe is recommended for horses which brush at speed. The inner branch is made straight from toe to quarter with the outer edge rounded off. The branch is secured with one or two heel nails. After fitting the shoe the projecting wall is rounded off level with the straight edge.

There are a number of inherent disadvantages associated with fitting anti-brushing shoes. These include the difficulty of securing a blind branch, the close fitting of the inner branch which may result in pressure on the sole, and reduction of the bearing surface which can lead to uneven distribution of weight. Against these disadvantages must be weighed the advantages of the shoes preventing or alleviating the injuries, and keeping the horse in work. Furthermore with careful attention to dressing the foot and forging the shoe, the loss of bearing surface is minimal, a level bearing and good ground surface can be maintained and with good nailing shoes can be adequately secured. But it cannot be over-emphasised that the correct pattern of shoe has to be selected to meet the defects of conformation and gait for each individual case.

Knocked-down shoe (Fig. 11.5). Both branches are the same width and the edge of the inner branch where it strikes the opposite leg is knocked down and rounded off. The shoe is usually fitted with a toe and outside quarter clip and sometimes with one or two nails at the heel of the inner branch to prevent it from lifting and to keep the shoe in place. A knocked-down shoe is recommended for horses with a toe-out conformation which brush with the heel of the shoe.

Speedy-cutting

Speedy-cutting has no exact definition. It is a general term applied to interference occurring at speed and generally in the knee or hock region. It is an injury which most commonly occurs on the inside of a front leg, in the region of the knee and is caused by the inner branch of the shoe of the opposite front foot. Such a case is a form of brushing. It is more liable to occur in horses that are base narrow, have turned-out toes and large flat feet, and tends to happen when the horse is leading with the wrong leg or changing legs. Sometimes the medial side of the front leg is struck by the lateral side of the hind foot on the same side. In trotters the toe of the front foot sometimes hits the dorsal surface of the pastern of the hind leg on the same side: this is also called speedy-cutting and is a form of scalping.

Forging

Forging is due to faulty action and occurs at the walk or trot when the horse strikes the

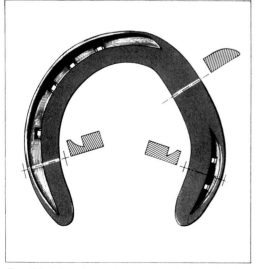

Fig. 11.6 Speedy-cutting shoe made from flat bar.

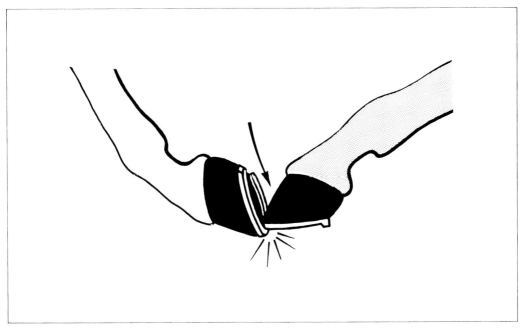

Fig. 11.7 Forging. The inside of the toe of a front shoe is struck with the toe of the corresponding hind shoe.

front shoe with the hind shoe on the same side (Fig. 11.7). The part of the front shoe struck is the inner edge around the toe. The part of the hind shoe that strikes is the outer edge at the toe. Forging is an annoyance due to the noise made and a danger when the shoe is struck as it may be pulled off or bring the horse down.

Forging is met with in young horses and in horses that are tired or out of condition. In these cases it gradually disappears as the horse improves in condition and gets fit. It is particularly common in short-bodied and long-legged horses, horses that go wide behind and especially if their hooves are long.

Shoeing. The actual contact between the shoes takes place when the hind foot is reaching the end of its flight and as the front foot leaves the ground. Therefore, to prevent forging attention has to be given to fitting a shoe to hasten the breakover of the front feet and to delay the breakover of the hind feet.

Many cases of forging can be prevented by fitting a concave shoe in front and hastening the breakover by rolling the toe and slightly

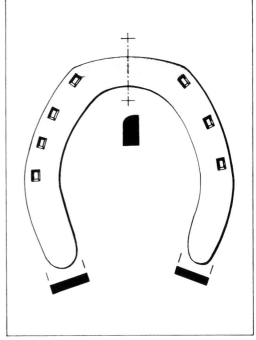

Fig. 11.8 Dub-toed shoe. The toe is squared and rolled and the heels are about half the thickness of the shoe at the toe.

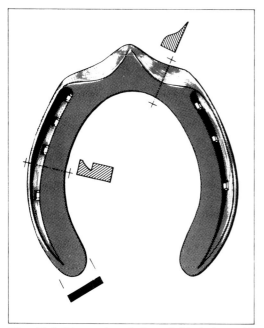

Fig. **11.9** *Diamond-toed shoe. A hind shoe with the ground surface, on both sides of the shoe, sloped downwards and backwards.*

raising the heels. The hind feet should be lowered slightly at the heels. If this does not prove satisfactory a dub-toed shoe may be fitted to the hind feet (Fig. 11.8). The shoe should be set well back and the protruding wall rounded off. To delay breakover the heels should be lowered and the branches fitted a little long so as to trail when the foot comes to the ground and act as a brake.

Diamond-toed shoe (Fig. 11.9). This shoe is only suitable for horses which forge by carrying a hind foot outside a front foot. It is a hind shoe with the ground surface, on both sides of the toe, sloped downwards and backwards. It is only necessary to modify the inside of the toe but both sides are dealt with to balance the shoe. The heels are about ⅛ in. (3 mm) thinner than the toe and the shoe is fitted with quarter clips.

When this shoe is used the outside branch of the front shoe should be fitted close at the heels and in some cases it may be necessary to hasten breakover by rolling the toe and raising the heels.

Fig. **11.10** *Over-reaching. A front leg is overtaken and struck by the inner edge of the hind shoe, usually on the bulb of the heel. Sometimes the heel of the shoe may be struck and the shoe pulled off.*

A diamond-toed shoe should not be used to combat simple forging as the point may strike and bruise the sole of the front foot.

Over-reaching

An over-reach is the name given to an injury which occurs between the back of the knee and the bulbs of the heels. It is caused by the inner edge of the ground surface of a hind shoe striking the front leg, usually when the horse is moving at a fast pace, and the front leg is not sufficiently extended or the hind leg is over extended (Fig. 11.10). As the hind leg moves backwards the inner edge of the shoe catches the back of the front leg and either bruises or cuts the skin, when it hangs downwards as a triangular flap. If the injury occurs above the fetlock joint it is called a 'high over-reach', and if at the back or side of the heels, the most common site, a 'low over-reach'. If any of these areas is hit by the toe or outer edge of the shoe the injury is called a 'strike'.

Horses with a short body and long hind legs are considered to be most prone to over-reaches. These injuries occur most frequently at the gallop, although they are sometimes met with in trotters, and when a horse jumps onto rising ground.

Modern over-reach boots are so simple and effective for low over-reaching that in most cases special shoeing is not necessary.

Shoeing. To prevent over-reaches the horse must be shod to hasten the breakover of the front feet and delay the breakover of the hind feet. The front heels should be raised and the hind heels lowered in moderation, without markedly breaking the hoof pastern axis. This can be achieved by trimming or by shoeing or both.

Front shoes should have a rolled toe and raised heels and the heels may be a little short to prevent them being caught by a hind shoe.

The heels of the hind shoes should be about half the thickness of the shoe at the toe to delay breakover and a little long so as to trail when the foot comes to the ground and act as a brake. In addition, to assist prevention further and reduce the severity of the injury the toe of the shoe should be set well back with the overlapping horn rounded off, and

Fig. 11.11 Shoe for over-reaching. The inner border at the toe is well concaved and the heels are about half the thickness of the shoe at the toe.

with the inner border of the toe of the shoe concave (Fig. 11.11).

Stumbling

Stumbling is due either to the horse catching its toe or digging it into the ground. It occurs when a horse is tired or goes on its toe due to lameness, when the hooves are too long or are unbalanced, or after shoeing when hooves which were excessively long have been shortened and the horse has not been given a day or two to become accustomed to the change.

Shoeing. To prevent stumbling the toe must be prevented from coming into premature contact with the ground. This is attained by rasping the toe short, leaving the heels long and fitting a shoe with a rolled toe and slightly raised heels to speed up breakover.

A good indication of the extent to which the toe will require to be shortened and the toe of the shoe turned up to prevent stumbling, and for the horse to travel safely, can be gained by studying the worn shoe.

Scalping

Scalping is the injury caused when the toe of a front foot hits the dorsal surface of the hind leg of the same side, anywhere from the coronet to the hock. It is mainly a problem of trotters. Scalping in the pastern area is also called speedy-cutting. Scalping in the cannon area is known as shin hitting and in the hock area is known as hock hitting. Prevention is by speeding the breakover of the front foot and slowing the breakover of the hind foot.

Cross-firing

Cross-firing is when the medial side of a hind foot hits the medial side of the fore leg or foot on the opposite side. It is mainly a problem of pacers.

11.3 Shoeing defective feet

Flat feet

Care must be taken to differentiate flat feet which are acquired as the result of disease such as chronic laminitis from those which are congenital and due to conformation.

Shoeing. Pressure on the sole can be alleviated by fitting a seated-out shoe. The sole should not be pared to increase its concavity as this reduces protection to the underlying sensitive foot. Horses with flat feet often have weak walls with flaring quarters and heels curving

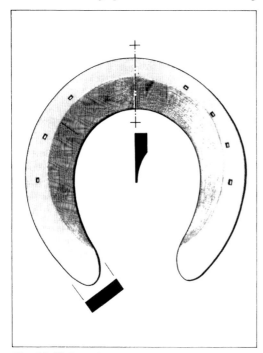

Fig. 11.12 Seated-out shoe. The seating is carried back to the nail holes and around the shoe except at the heels.

forwards. Improving the state of the wall will elevate the sole making it less vulnerable to bruising or to pressure from the shoe.

Seated-out shoe (Fig. 11.12). This is a most satisfactory shoe for flat feet as it relieves pressure on the sole towards its outer border. It should have a wide web with the inner edge of the foot surface seated. The seating can be carried back to the nail holes if necessary and extend around the shoe except at the heels which are left flat to allow normal weight bearing.

A disadvantage of seated-out shoes is that the suction created in heavy going may result in them being pulled off.

Flat bar is easier to seat out than concave bar though it is perfectly possible to achieve a modest degree of seating out in a concave shoe.

Upright feet

Upright feet in adult horses do not require any special shoes. Care must be taken that the hooves are balanced and a correct pastern foot axis maintained. An unnaturally upright foot will be corrected by proper trimming. A naturally upright foot should not be altered.

Unnaturally wry feet

An unnaturally wry foot is due to neglect (Fig. 11.13 a-b). It cannot be accounted for only by the horse's conformation. Attention to dressing the foot and to shoeing will result in a gradual return to a normal shape.

If the ground surface of a hoof is not kept level or wears unevenly there is an uneven distribution of the body weight which results in the wall being deflected. Excessive length of one side of the wall results in it flaring out while the other side wears more heavily, becoming upright or sloping inwards.

An unnaturally wry foot is corrected by gradually lowering, at two-to three-week intervals, the part of the wall which is too long until a level and balanced ground surface is obtained. When this is done the weight over the hoof is correctly distributed.

Shoeing. A standard shoe is fitted but made to conform to the adjudged normal outline of the foot and not to that of the wry foot.

On the side of the foot where the wall turns in the shoe is fitted wide, to conform with the adjudged normal outline of the bearing surface, and its sharp outer edge is boxed off. On the side of the foot where the wall flares out the shoe is fitted as close as possible, consistent with being able to drive the nails safely, and the overhanging wall is rasped off flush with the shoe (Fig. 11.14).

In severe cases a bar shoe may be used to transfer some of the weight from the upright side to the frog and to the sloping side of the hoof. A gap may be left between the upright quarter and heel and the shoe.

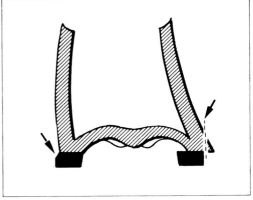

Fig. **11.14** *Fitting a shoe to an unnaturally wry foot. The shoe is fitted wide on the upright side and the other side of the wall is trimmed as short as possible, the shoe fitted close and the flare rasped away.*

Weak and unnaturally low heels

Unnaturally low heels are caused either by excessive trimming or by excessive wear of the hoof wall if the shoes are left on too long. The cure is to preserve the horn at the heels by fitting the shoes wide and reshoeing regularly.

Weak heels curve forwards and the weight is borne on the outside of the wall. Weak heels are usually also low heels.

Shoeing. Weak heels cannot be corrected until weight bearing is reduced. Weight can be transferred to the quarters by careful fitting of an ordinary shoe. It may be necessary to remove some flare at the quarters to encourage the wall to grow down straight. It is not until strong straight quarters are established that weight can be relieved from the heels.

Wide fitting is essential to prevent further damage due to the wall overgrowing the shoe, and for the same reason the shoes should not be left for more than five weeks at the most without being refitted. In some cases, especially in larger horses, shoeing every three weeks will be required. An egg bar shoe (Fig. 11.15) allows wide fitting of the shoe and eliminates the pointed projections of each heel making the shoe less liable to be pulled off.

A shoe with raised heels or a plastic wedge may be used to produce an immediate improvement in the hoof pastern axis but this

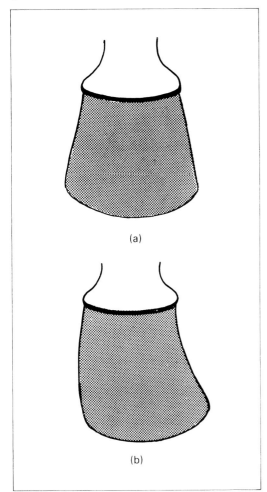

(a)

(b)

Fig. **11.13** *(a) Normal foot. (b) Unnaturally wry foot. Excess wear of one side of the wall results in it turning in while the longer wall flares outwards.*

Fig. 11.15 Egg bar shoe.

increases the weight on the back of the foot and may delay any natural strengthening of the heels. An alternative method is to fit a bar shoe to relieve some of the weight bearing on the heels by transferring it to the frog.

Contracted feet

A contracted foot is smaller than normal being narrower at the quarters and heels, has an excessively concave sole and an atrophied frog. The commonest causes are prolonged disuse of the limb due to lameness, and thrush. Methods of shoeing can also contribute, for example calkins reduce frog pressure.

The method of treatment employed to treat a contracted foot will depend on the cause. If it is associated with disease or injury which responds to treatment then as normal function of the limb returns so gradually the foot will regain its normal shape. On the other hand if it is associated with an incurable condition there is no useful purpose in trying to effect expansion.

Conditions due to faulty preparation of the foot or shoeing improve immediately these errors are corrected. For example, curing thrush, lowering calkins to obtain frog pressure or turning out the horse unshod to allow the foot to take weight and function normally. In addition grooving the heels to obtain expansion is helpful in some cases.

Grooving the wall (Fig. 11.16). A number of techniques are employed to obtain expansion at the heels. The following method is both simple and effective. The foot is brought forward and positioned either on the farrier's leg or on a tripod. Using a drawing knife, three or four parallel grooves are cut at intervals of ¾ in. (2 cm) from the coronet to the ground surface. The grooves are placed on both the medial and lateral heel, extend almost down to the white zone and each is ⅕ in. (5 mm) in width. If the wall is very hard it can be softened by cold water foot baths, one hour daily for two to three days, or by poulticing the foot.

Shoeing. Many ingenious designs of shoes have been used to treat contracted feet. They range from shoes with the foot surface sloped outwards to exert counter pressure, to shoes hinged at the toe and mechanical devices designed to force the heels of the shoes apart. The majority have been based on a misunderstanding of the anatomy and function of the foot which has led to unsound arguments in their support and few have met with any lasting success.

Slipper shoe. The foot surface of this shoe is sloped outwards which allows the wall to expand under the pressure of weight bearing.

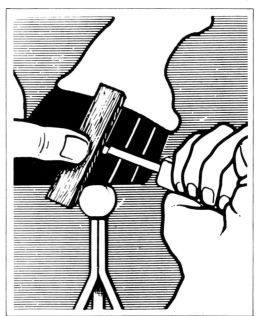

Fig. 11.16 Method of grooving the wall.

The slope must not be excessive and is confined to the heels. If the outer edge of the foot surface is more than ⅛ in. (3 mm) lower than the inner edge it puts excessive strain on the white zone which leads to separation of the wall from the sole. For this reason this shoe fell into disfavour but with due attention to the slope the shoe is useful in the treatment of slight cases of contraction.

11.4 Surgical shoes

Surgical shoes are designed to assist in the treatment of diseases and injuries of the limb and foot by providing protection and relieving pressure.

Corns

A corn is a bruise of the sole in the angle between the wall and the bar, the 'seat of corn'. Corns occur most frequently in front feet, the medial side being more often affected, and are especially common in horses with flat feet and low heels. They are rarely seen in hind feet or in unshod feet.

A corn is caused by pressure. It may be due to a stone under the heel of the shoe, leaving the shoes on too long so that the heels come to press on the seat of corn, or faults in shoeing such as fitting the heels too close or too short and narrow or not easing the seat of corn. Concussion will make corns worse, and upright pasterns and roadwork result in excessive concussion.

Clinical features. In the acute stages a corn is recognised by lameness, abnormal heat and pain on percussion and compression of the affected heel. Corns are classified as *dry* when no inflammatory exudate is present. In these cases, if the overlying horn is pared, the corn is recognised by a deep red discoloration due to an escape of blood from injured blood vessels into the newly formed horn. It should be appreciated that the deeper the discoloration the more recent the bruising because the stained horn cells will only reach the surface of the sole at the normal growth rate. A severe bruise results in an infiltration of serum into the horn, a *moist corn*, which is seen when the overlying horn is pared. If infection super-

venes, a *suppurating* corn, then veterinary advice should be sought.

Treatment. This comprises removing the cause, controlling the inflammation and relieving pressure. In the majority of cases all that is required is to ease the seat of corn and fit an ordinary shoe, making sure that the shoe rests evenly on the wall and the bar, and fitted wide to allow room for growth and expansion. There is no merit in trying to cut out all the discoloured horn.

Shoeing. A shoe is required which will protect and relieve pressure on the seat of corn enabling the horse to continue in work. A *three-quarter shoe* is often recommended for treating corns but it is not suitable as it provides no protection and has other disadvantages, creating an abnormal pressure point and providing inadequate support for the hoof wall. A *bar shoe* which takes pressure off the heels by transferring it to the frog is useful for bilateral cases. A horse with corns usually has low heels and therefore measures which will improve the heels will reduce the incidence of corns.

Threequarter bar shoe (Fig. 11.17). This shoe has from 1 in–1½ ins (2.5 cm – 4 cm) missing

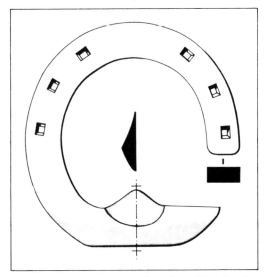

Fig 11.17 Threequarter bar shoe. The shoe has 1½–2 ins (2.5–4 cm) missing at one heel.

Fig. **11.18** *Shoe with 'set' heel made from flat bar.*

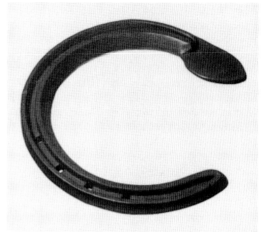

Fig. **11.20** *Set-heeled shoe made from concave full-ered bar.*

Fig. **11.19** *Setting the heel of a shoe.*

from one heel. The bar rests on one heel, the base of the frog and the bar of the opposite heel. It is used for treating single corns as it has the advantage of supporting the heels whilst relieving the seat of corn of pressure but has the disadvantage that the corn is left unprotected.

Set heeled shoe (Figs 11.18–11.20). The ground surface of one heel of this shoe is lowered (set down) about ¼ in. (6 mm) and so makes no contact on hard level ground. The foot surface of the shoe makes normal contact with the foot

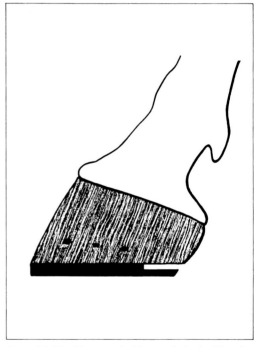

Fig. **11.21** *Shoe with 'dropped' heel. The foot surface of the heel is lowered by about ⅛ in. (3 mm).*

and the heel is spread out a little. This is a good shoe for treating corns as it protects and relieves pressure over the area and, because the foot surface of the shoe is wider and longer, overgrowth by the hoof of the shoe is delayed.

The reduced ground-bearing surface of the shoe is a technical disadvantage but in practice is of little significance.

Shoe with dropped heels (Fig. 11.21). This is the opposite to a set heeled shoe. The foot surface of the heel of the shoe is lowered about ⅛ in. (3 mm) and so makes no contact with the hoof.

Although this shoe relieves a corn of pressure it is not satisfactory. It does not provide protection because the recess soon accumulates dirt and grit, and as the heel of the hoof is not weight bearing an abnormal pressure point is present.

False quarter (Fig. 11.22)

A false quarter is a permanent defect of the wall. It is due to an injury of the coronary corium which results in the production of abnormal horn.

Clinical features. A false quarter appears as a depression in the wall which extends, in the direction of the horn fibres, from the coronet to the ground surface of the hoof. The defect may have irregular margins which sometimes overlap. False quarters persist throughout life with no adverse effects unless they become infected.

Treatment. No treatment is required unless the false quarter becomes infected, when a veterinary surgeon should be consulted. Any excess of horn on either side should be rasped down to maintain a smooth surface.

Shoeing. No special shoe is required. Fit the shoe best suited to the horse. The horn in and adjacent to the defect will not be strong enough to take nails and so the nail holes must be placed accordingly.

Keratoma

A keratoma is a horn tumour which develops on the inner aspect of the wall and sometimes in the sole.

Clinical features. The tumour is composed of hard glistening horn, generally cylindrical in shape, ranging from ¼ in. (6 mm) to 1½ ins (4 cm) in diameter and extending varying distances up the wall from the bearing surface towards the coronet. It is first detected at the bearing surface where it appears as a mass of hard horn, between the wall and the sole, which deflects the white zone inwards. As the tumour increases in size lameness may gradually develop. An X-ray of the distal phalanx at this stage will reveal a groove caused by pressure from the keratoma (Fig 11.23).

Treatment. In the early stages the extremity of the tumour is pared to relieve pressure by the shoe. This measure is only palliative and does not check the growth of the tumour, which may eventually have to be removed surgically

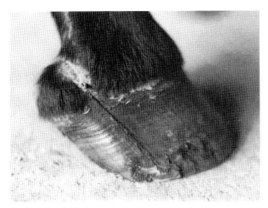

Fig. 11.22 False quarter.

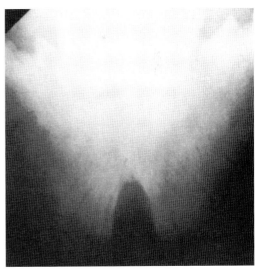

Fig 11.23 Radiograph of a distal phalanx showing the groove caused by the pressure of a keratoma.

by a veterinarian. This involves stripping that portion of the wall on which the tumour is growing.

Shoeing. A shoe with plenty of cover is called for to protect the tumour from weight bearing. Alternatively pressure can be relieved by easing the underlying foot surface of the shoe by ⅛ in. (3 mm). No nails should be driven near the tumour.

Laminitis

This disease is an aseptic inflammation of the sensitive laminae. Usually both front feet or all the feet are affected but it can develop in one foot only as a result of increased weight bearing following an injury to the opposite leg. Rarely laminitis is seen to develop in the hind feet before there are any symptoms in the front feet. A number of other causes are recognised which include errors in diet, such as over-feeding, overwork and concussion, and infections such as metritis following foaling.

Acute laminitis. The feet are hot and painful with a pronounced digital pulse. The horse is reluctant to move and adopts a stance to relieve weight on its affected feet. It lifts its feet quickly with each stride and puts the heels to the ground first.

The inflammation of the sensitive laminae is accompanied by marked exudation of serum and weakening of the laminae, which tear due to the horse's weight. This tearing of the laminae usually commences at the toe and is followed by rotation of the distal phalanx with its solar border pressing on the sole which becomes flat or convex, when it is commonly referred to as a 'dropped sole'. A depression can also be felt at the front of the coronet. If very severe the sole will be perforated (Fig. 11.24). Abscesses often develop as a complication.

If very severe all the laminae tear and the distal phalanx does not rotate but sinks within the hoof. The only indication that this is happening may be a depression which can be felt all round the coronet. The hoof may subsequently be shed completely.

Treatment and shoeing. Shoeing cannot influence the acute stages of the disease. Pressure on the sole from the ground may be painful to the horse so it is usually better to leave its shoes on. A deep soft bed will also make the horse more comfortable.

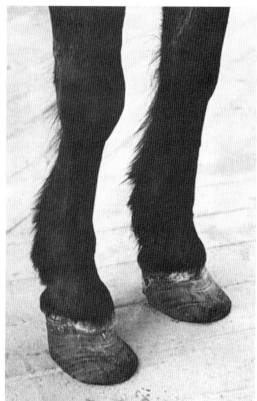

Fig. 11.24 Sagittal section of a foot affected by severe acute laminitis. The distal phalanx has rotated and perforated the sole.

Fig. 11.25 Chronic laminitis showing rings of horn.

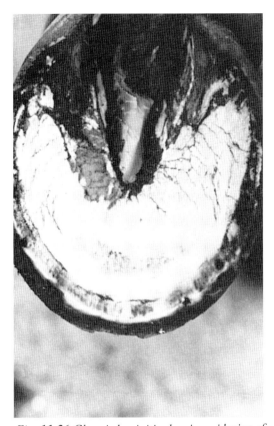

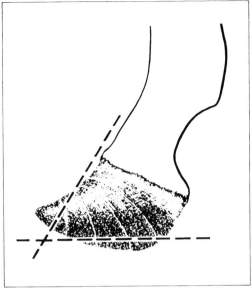

Fig. 11.27 Trimming for chronic laminitis.

Fig. 11.26 Chronic laminitis showing widening of the white zone at the toe and bruising of the sole.

Chronic laminitis is a sequel to the acute form and is characterised by changes in the form of the foot. The wall at the heels is longer than normal and the wall at the toe is concave in profile. The hoof wall is characterised by laminitic rings which differ from the normal growth rings in that they are widely spaced at the heels but close together at the toe (Fig. 11.25). The sole is flat or dropped due to pressure from the solar border of the distal phalanx and frequently has blood staining in front of the point of the frog, where in severe cases it may be perforated. The white zone at the toe is widened due to the tearing of the laminae, and may be blood stained (Fig. 11.26). The space between the wall and the sensitive laminae, which are protected by a thin layer of horn, contains a mass of degenerated horn and laminal tissue. The horse walks on its heels and in a stiff and shuffling manner.

Treatment. The foot should be trimmed to reduce weight on the hoof wall at the toe thereby relieving pain, reducing further separation of the wall at the toe from the distal phalanx, and encouraging new wall to grow down close to and parallel with its dorsal surface.

This is attained by trimming the lower part of the wall at the toe back to the white zone, and to preserve as much clearance as possible between the sole and the ground it is important not to lower the ground surface at the toe quarters. The heel quarters and the heels should be lowered to tip the distal phalanx backwards to assume a more normal angle with the ground (Fig. 11.27). The lowering should be done gradually to allow the heels to come to the ground without putting excessive tension on the tendon of the deep digital flexor muscle and causing discomfort. The trimmed foot will now have a very square shape, being straight across the toe with straighter than normal quarters, which makes the horse more comfortable. The ground surface will not be completely level but will roll upwards in front of the point of the frog (Fig. 11.28 a-g).

If the hoof is trimmed properly and regularly the new hoof wall will grow down in a normal relationship with the distal phalanx and in time

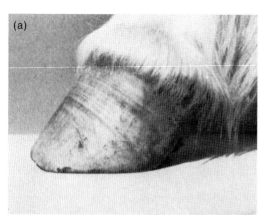

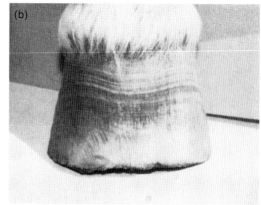

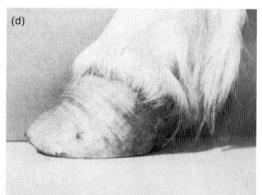

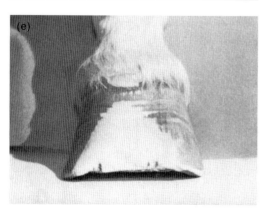

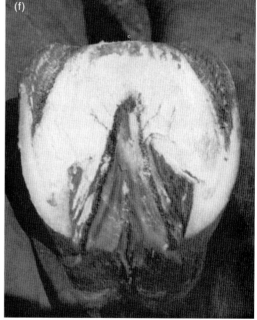

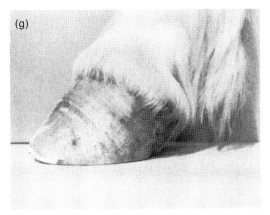

(g)

Fig. **11.28** *Trimming for chronic laminitis; (a) before trimming, side view; (b) front view; (c) the wall is lowered from the level of the point of the frog to the heels; (d) side view; (e) the lower part of the wall at the toe is rasped back to the white zone; (f) ground surface; (g) side view.*

the shape of the foot will improve and in many cases will return to normal.

Shoeing. Shoeing is directed towards protecting the dropped sole from pressure and improving the horse's gait.

An *ordinary shoe* in many cases is quite satisfactory provided it is shaped to fit the foot, does not press on the sole and has a clip at each quarter instead of a toe clip as the lower wall has been removed at the toe. If the sole is severely dropped the shoe will need to be *seated out*. Flat bar is often better for a severely dropped sole as it is easier to seat out than concave fullered stock. A wide-webbed shoe may be used to give cover or a thick shoe may be used to give elevation to the sole. Either way bruising will be reduced but a thin shoe cannot be seated deeply and a shoe both thick and wide will be heavy unless a light material such as aluminium alloy is used. In practice the seating-out process will give increased cover and ¾ in. x ½ in. (20 mm x 12 mm) flat steel bar is ideal for the average foot. A *rolled toe* or a *set toe* is useful in easing breakover and in fitting the shoe to the shape of the trimmed foot.

A *rim pad* may be used to give increased elevation to the sole as a simple alternative or addition to seating out of the shoe. A *full pad*

may be used to protect the sole from bruising on uneven or stony ground.

A *bar shoe* has been used for chronic laminitis. The bar does not press on the frog. It offers only one advantage and that is in prolonging the wear of the heels of the shoe. However, if the heels of a horse with chronic laminitis are wearing excessively this is a sign that the heels of the hoof have not sufficiently trimmed.

An *open-toed bar shoe* is basically an ordinary shoe put on back to front so that the branches are joined at the heels instead of at the toe. This has the advantage that the shoe does not project at the toe where the hoof wall at the toe has been removed, and is relatively simple to make and fit. The bar should not interfere with the function of the frog and should either come behind it or rest lightly on it.

A *heart bar shoe* (Fig. 11.29) has a bar fashioned to press just behind the point of the frog with the aim of mechanically opposing rotation of the distal phalanx but is incapable of doing so effectively. By transferring a small proportion of weight bearing from the wall to

Fig. **11.29** *Heart bar shoe made from flat bar.*

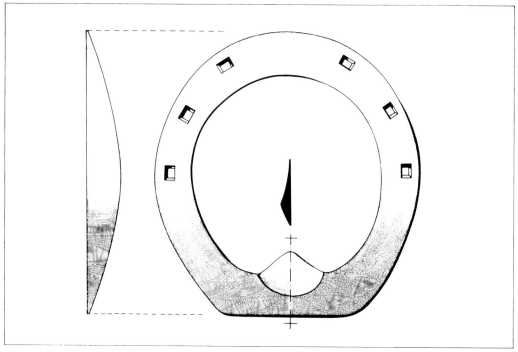

Fig. 11.30 Rocker-bar shoe.

the frog the forces responsible for tearing the laminae are reduced, but excessive pressure from the bar will damage the sensitive tissues underlying the horny frog, causing pain and can result in infection.

A *rocker bar shoe* (Fig. 11.30) is twice the thickness of a standard shoe at the quarters and gradually gets thinner towards the toe and heels. It is seated out, and may have a rolled toe. A horse with chronic laminitis lands on its heels and then rolls its foot over on to its toe. The rocker bar shoe thus reduces concussion and assists the action of the foot but is suitable only for horses working at a slow pace.

Navicular disease

Navicular disease is the name given to a pathological lesion of the distal sesamoid (navicular bone) which is characterised by erosion of the fibro-cartilage on its tendon surface with destruction of underlying bone (Fig. 11.31) and associated with a chronic bursitis of the navicular bursa and inflammation of the deep digital flexor tendon due to friction with the roughened surface of the bone.

Clinical features. The disease affects the front foot, rarely a hind foot, and may be unilateral or bilateral. It is commonest in hunters and hacks, rare in ponies and often affects horses in the prime of life, between seven and nine years of age. The disease is gradual in onset

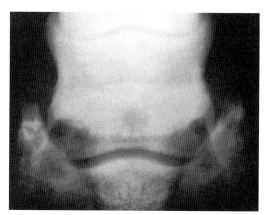

Fig. 11.31 Radiograph of a classical case of navicular disease. The dark shadow at the centre of the bone indicates rarefaction and cavitation of the underlying bone.

and with the passage of time lameness increases accompanied by alterations in the shape of the foot, which becomes 'boxy', that is contracted, high at the heels with an atrophied frog and a very concave sole. These changes are the effect of the disease and should not be confused with the cause.

Shoeing. The disease is incurable, but in the early stages pain and stumbling can be alleviated and the usefulness of the horse prolonged by attention to shoeing. Lameness is intensified by frog pressure and so the horse goes on his toes and keeps his heels raised. To accommodate this action fitting a shoe with a rolled toe and raised heels is helpful (Fig. 11.32).

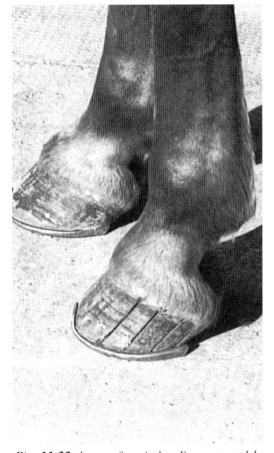

Fig. 11.32 A case of navicular disease treated by grooving the heels and fitting a rolled toe shoe with raised heels.

Sandcrack

A sandcrack is a fissure of the wall which commences at the coronet, extends a variable distance down the hoof, and can be at the toe, quarters or heels or in the bars. A *complete sandcrack* extends from the coronet to the ground surface and an *incomplete sandcrack* extends only part of the way. A *simple sandcrack* does not extend to the sensitive structures or cause lameness whereas a *complicated sandcrack* involves the sensitive structures, causes lameness, may appear suddenly with blood escaping from the crack and may become infected. Old sandcracks have prominent edges which often overlap.

Sandcracks are associated with wry hooves; where weight is taken unevenly. Sandcracks are more frequently seen in dry brittle hooves. They tend to occur at the toe in upright feet and at the quarters in flat feet. Cracks can result from tension at the coronet. Toe cracks were more common in the hind feet of heavy draught horses, presumably due to starting heavy loads when violent dorsal flexion of the distal interphalangeal joint results in the middle phalanx forcibly pressing against the coronet causing the horn to split.

The two sides of a crack will never grow together. A crack will disappear only when it has grown out and been replaced by a new growth of horn. The normal movements of the hoof tend to lengthen and deepen cracks – often cracks can be seen to widen when the foot is raised and close when the foot takes weight.

Treatment. Treatment of a *simple sandcrack* is directed to limiting movement between the sides of the crack by isolating the affected part of the hoof wall. This can be done by cutting two grooves. If the crack is incomplete they should be cut in the form of a V from the coronet to the extremity of the crack (Fig.11.33a). If it is complete then two parallel grooves are cut, one on each side of the crack from the coronet to the ground surface (Fig.11.33b).

The grooves must be about $\frac{1}{5}$ in. (5mm) wide and cut to the depth of the white zone. The ground surface at the extremity of a complete crack is eased to prevent any pressure from the shoe at this point.

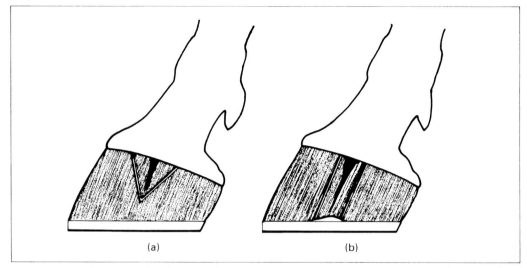

Fig. 11.33 (a) Simple sandcrack, incomplete. Two grooves are cut from the coronet in the form of a V to meet at the lower limit of the crack. (b) Simple sandcrack, complete. Two parallel grooves are cut, one on each side of the crack, from the coronet to the bearing surface.

Complicated sandcracks extend through the entire thickness of the wall down to the sensitive laminae and require their edges to be held together by some mechanical method to obtain immobilisation. This can be attained by either driving a horseshoe nail across the crack or applying sandcrack clips. Both methods are more satisfactory for treating toe sandcracks than quarter sandcracks where the horn has a flatter surface and is thinner.

Immobilising the edges of a complicated sandcrack using a horseshoe nail.

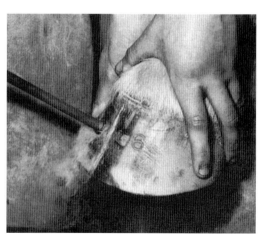

Fig. 11.35 After paring the edges of the sandcrack a special tool, heated to a dull red heat, is used to fashion a bed for the nail on each side of the sandcrack. If only one nail is to be used the beds are fashioned just above the centre of the sandcrack with the inner edge of the bed about a ¹/₄ in. (6 mm) from the edge of the sandcrack. If two nails are used then the proximal nail is inserted ¹/₂ in. (12 mm) below the coronet and the other nail ³/₄ in. (20 mm) below it.

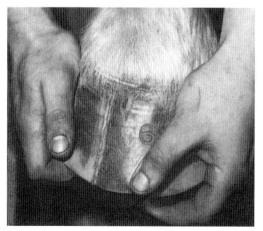

Fig. 11.34 A typical complicated sandcrack extending from the coronet to the bearing surface of the wall.

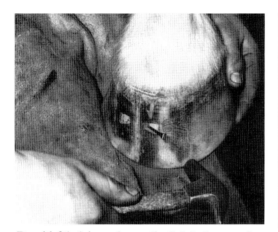

Fig. 11.36 A horseshoe nail, slightly bent on flat, is driven across the sandcrack.

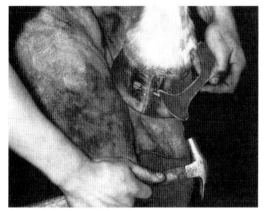

Fig. 11.37 The nail is driven home using the point of a buffer as a punch.

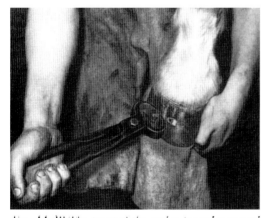

Fig. 11.38 The point of the nail is turned over and cut off with pincers.

Fig. 11.39 The end of the nail is turned over and tapped into position whilst the head of the nail is retained in position with the end of a handle of the pincers.

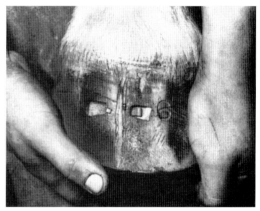

Fig. 11.40 Procedure completed, the edges of a complicated sandcrack immobilised with a horseshoe nail.

Sandcrack clips are easier to apply. A small groove is either cut or burnt on opposing sides of the crack, into which the clip is placed and compressed with pincers which forces the edges of the crack together and immobilises them (Fig. 11.41).

Both these methods bring the edges of the crack together but in complicated and wide cracks may result in pinching of the sensitive structures. This can be prevented by converting the crack into a recessed groove, some ½ in. (12 mm) wide, to the depth of the thickness of the wall and filling it with plastic.

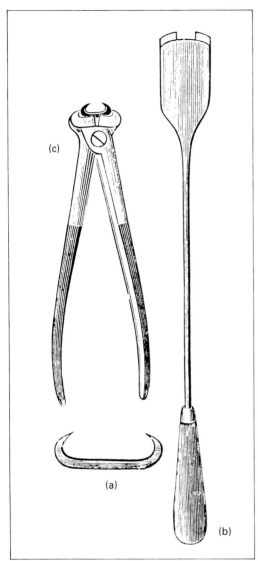

Fig. **11.41** *Sandcrack: (a) clips; (b) firing iron; (c) pincers.*

The soundness of new horn growth is encouraged by thinning the hoof wall with a rasp below the coronet so that any remaining movement between the sides of the crack is not transmitted to the top of the crack at the coronet.

Shoeing. This should be directed to preparing a level bearing surface and fitting a shoe which does not put pressure on the crack or tend to force the crack apart. It is customary to either ease the bearing surface or seat out the shoe under the crack. If the crack is incomplete ensure that the easing or seating out are located in direct line with the crack.

In most cases all that is required for a toe sandcrack is an ordinary shoe with a clip on either side of the crack and flat heels because if they are raised the weight is thrown forwards which forces the edges apart.

For quarter sandcracks, because downwards movement of the heels forces the crack open, the heels must be absolutely flat with no suggestion of a sprung heel.

For draught horses a bar shoe is popular with ½ in. (12 mm) cut out immediately under the sandcrack. The gap prevents any direct pressure on the crack and pressure on the heels can be relieved by lowering them and ensuring weight is taken by the frog.

Bar sandcracks. The bars are in the most yielding part of the hoof, and cracks open and shut with weight bearing causing severe pain. To obtain a growth of sound horn the borders of the crack should be removed, the heels lowered and a bar shoe fitted to relieve pressure by the heel of the shoe.

False sandcrack (Fig. 11.42). A false sandcrack is a simple crack which commences at the ground surface and extends a variable distance up the hoof. It is most liable to occur in dry and brittle hooves, and especially if the shoe

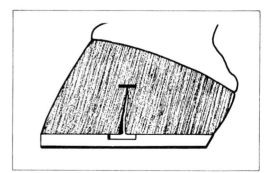

Fig. **11.42** *False sandcrack. A horizontal groove is cut across the apex to prevent it extending and the base is relieved of pressure either by easing the foot surface of the shoe or the bearing surface of the wall.*

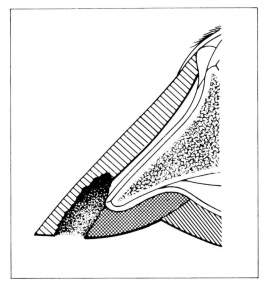

Fig. **11.43** *A seedy toe is a cavity between the horny and sensitive laminae, filled with a mealy type of horn.*

has been left on too long or has been fitted too close, and in consequence the wall protrudes over the edge of the shoe.

All that is required in these cases to prevent the crack from extending is to cut a horizontal groove across the top, ½ in. – ¾ in. (10 mm–20 mm) in length and down to the depth of the crack, and relieve pressure on its extremity by either easing the bearing surface of the wall or the foot surface of the shoe.

Seedy toe

A seedy toe results from the separation of the horny and sensitive laminae at the toe to form a cavity which opens at the white zone and is filled with a crumbling and mealy type of horn (Fig. 11.43). The cause has not been established except where it is a result of laminitis or white zone infection (gravel). A similar condition can occur not just at the toe but anywhere in the white zone.

Clinical features. In simple cases the cavity only affects the lower portion of the wall but in severe cases may extend up to the coronet. Lameness is not present unless there is infection or an accumulation of dirt and grit pressing on the sensitive laminae.

Treatment. In simple cases this consists of scooping out the degenerate horn and packing the cavity with cotton wool and Stockholm tar. In more extensive cases the wall over the whole of the cavity has to be removed. The cavity can be filled with plastic or packed with cotton wool and Stockholm tar retained with either a large clip or a thin metal plate and screws.

Shoeing. Fit an ordinary shoe with a wide web to protect the bearing surface and to retain the dressing. A large clip may also be used to help retain the dressing. If it is considered necessary to take the weight off the area then ease the foot surface of the shoe over that area. In extensive cases it may be necessary to provide extra protection over the ground surface and help retain the dressing by fitting a full pad under the shoe.

Sidebone

Sidebone disease is an ossification of the cartilages of the distal phalanx (Fig. 11.44). It is very common in draught horses and the lateral cartilage of the front foot is most frequently affected.

The actual cause of sidebone is not clear. It is recognised as hereditary, and a direct blow and concussion are accepted causes. There is a natural tendency for cartilage contiguous with bone to become ossified and this may account for many cases.

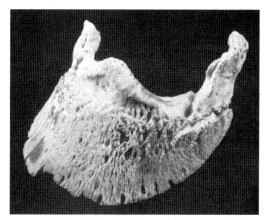

Fig. **11.44** *Sidebone disease. Ossification commences at the attachment of the cartilage to the palmar process of the distal phalanx and gradually extends to involve the whole of the cartilage.*

Clinical features. As the cartilage ossifies it gradually loses its elasticity, becomes more rigid and sometimes assumes an enormous size. These changes can often be felt just above the coronet. In these cases the branch of the shoe on the affected side wears progressively thinner from the quarter to the heel.

Treatment. Unless lameness is present no treatment is indicated. Lameness when present is due to compression between the ossifying cartilage and the non-yielding wall, especially when complicated by a contracted foot. Relief may be obtained by grooving the wall at the heels which, by allowing expansion, reduces pressure and pain (Fig. 11.16).

Shoeing. In a unilateral case the branch of the shoe on the affected side is fitted full so that the outer edge corresponds with the outline of the overhanging coronet. To encourage expansion, nails should not be driven as near to the heels as is customary. The traditional shoe is one which corresponds to the worn shoe (Fig. 11.45).

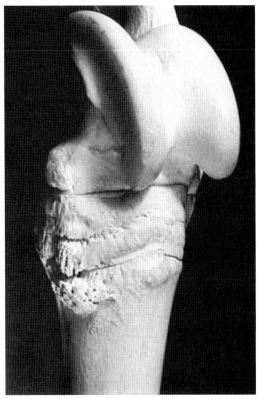

*Fig. **11.46** Bone spavin disease. A bone spavin is a degenerative joint disease which involves the medial aspect of the intertarsal and tarso-metatarsal joints.*

Horses with bilateral sidebone wear the toe of the shoe and their action is improved by fitting a rolled toe. Raising the heels may also help.

Bone spavin

Bone spavin disease is a degenerative joint disease involving the medial aspects of the intertarsal and tarso-metatarsal joints, and is characterised by new bone formation at the joint margins (Fig. 11.46).

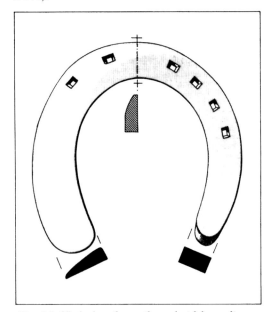

*Fig. **11.45** A shoe for unilateral sidebone disease. The branch on the affected side is thinned down and gradually increased in width from the toe to the heel and is blind except for the two nail holes at the toe.*

Clinical features. The most significant local sign is a distortion of the outline of the medial and lower hock by new bone formation (Fig. 11.47). The lameness is distinguished by imperfect flexion of the hock and is due to the pain caused by compression. In consequence the horse drags its toe which results in excessive wear of the shoe at the toe.

Shoeing. To overcome the horse dragging its toe and to facilitate its action, the toe of the hoof is shortened and a shoe fitted with a rolled toe. The heels are raised, preferably by trimming the toe and allowing the heels to grow longer, or alternatively by fitting a shoe with raised heels. As calkins are designed to catch in the ground it is recommended they are replaced by sloping wedge heels (Fig. 11.48). These measures certainly improve the horse's action but increase the tendency to the development of contraction of the flexor tendons.

Sprained joint

A sprained joint occurs when a joint, as a result of an accident, passes beyond its normal range of movement and tears the joint capsule and ligaments. Healing is by the laying down of fibrous tissue and is followed by a reduction in the normal range of joint movement.

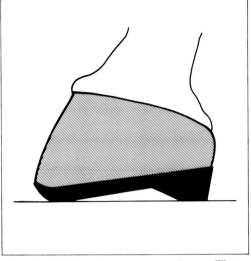

Fig. 11.48 Shoe for bone spavin disease. The toe of the foot is shortened and a shoe is fitted with a rolled toe and sloping wedge heels which do not catch and allow the foot to slide.

The fetlock joint is most commonly affected and is characterised by enlargement and restriction of normal movements, particularly flexion, that leads to stumbling. In these cases the horse's action varies considerably. Some wear only the toe of the shoe while others wear both the toe and the heel. The new shoe should be made to conform with the wear of the old shoe, which always requires the toe to be rolled and in some cases has to be combined with lowering the heels.

Curb

A curb is a sprain of the plantar ligament and is seen as a well-defined swelling at the plantar aspect of the hock (Fig. 11.49), and is not to be confused with a 'false curb', which is merely a large or prominent head of the fourth metatarsal bone.

Curb is most frequently seen in riding horses and is caused either as a result of hyperflexion of the hock when a horse is pulled up sharply and thrown back on its hocks, or whilst jumping when violent efforts are made to extend the hock.

To relieve tension on the plantar ligament the horse stands with its heels raised, and goes markedly on its toe.

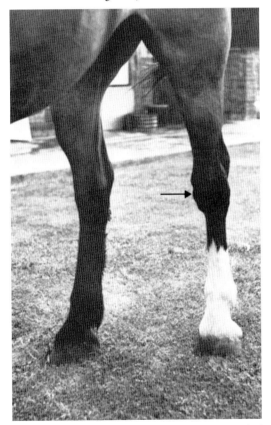

Fig. 11.47 Bony enlargement on the lower medial side of the hock caused by bone spavin.

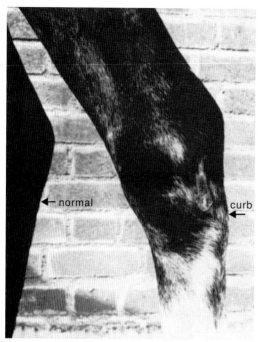

Fig. **11.49** *A curb is a sprain of the plantar ligament.*

Shoeing. To relieve tension on the plantar ligament the horse should have the heels raised, preferably by leaving them long when trimming the hoof, or by fitting a shoe with raised heels. Calkins are not advisable as they cause too much resistance and therefore a shoe with sloping wedge heels that do not catch and allow the foot to slide is recommended.

Splints

A splint is an exostosis which develops on or near a second or fourth metacarpal or metatarsal bone. Splints most frequently develop in young horses, up to six years of age, doing fast work on hard surfaces. Splints are classified according to their size, position and shape. A small, well-developed exostosis is simply termed a splint; if it encroaches on the knee joint it is called a knee splint. A number of splints along the edge of the bone is termed a chain splint (Fig. 11.50).

The cause of a splint is concussion which results in a sprain of the interosseous ligament and a tearing of the adjacent periosteum. The second metacarpal bone is more commonly

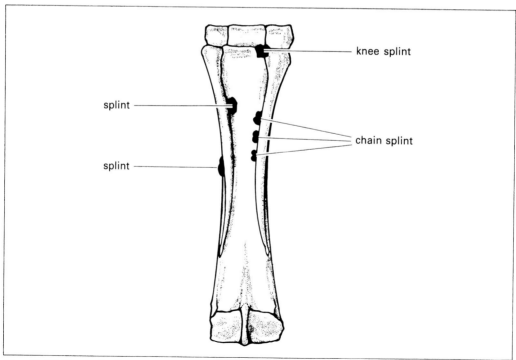

Fig. **11.50** *Types of splint.*

affected and this may be accounted for by direct weight bearing between it and the second carpal bone, whereas on the lateral aspect the fourth carpal bone articulates with both the third and fourth metacarpal bones.

Clinical features. The local signs are pain and swelling. The degree of lameness is directly related to concussion. Lameness increases with exercise, is more severe on hard ground and a horse which walks almost sound will be very lame at the trot. Once the inflammatory symptoms have subsided and the splint is no longer active the horse will go sound provided the splint does not interfere with the action of the knee, the suspensory ligament or the flexor tendons.

Shoeing. Treatment is based on limiting concussion which can be achieved by complete rest in a loose box. A variety of shoes both with and without pads have been used to reduce concussion and thereby relieve splint lameness. The results have been disappointing. All that can be done, or indeed is required, is to ensure an even distribution of concussion by a level bearing surface and a well-fitted shoe.

In severe cases a pad to reduce concussion, and a rolled toe shoe with raised heels to assist breakover, may be helpful.

Tendon strain
The term 'tendon strain' implies a strain of the superficial and/or deep digital flexor tendons of the front legs. Most cases involve only the superficial digital flexor tendon in the mid-cannon area. It is generally due to muscle fatigue during fast work or towards the end of a race, which results in the tendon fibres being torn, and is accompanied by heat, pain and swelling.

Shoeing. Raising the heel reduces tension in the deep digital flexor tendon and accessory ligament but has no significant effect on the superficial digital flexor tendon and suspensory ligament since their attachments are above the distal interphalangeal joint.

When appropriate the heels may be raised with a Patten shoe (Fig. 6.174) The height of the heels will vary from 1 in. (25 mm) to 3 ins

(75 mm) depending on the severity of the injury and the type of horse. Strained tendons heal by fibrosis which is accompanied by contraction. Therefore, as healing progresses the height of the heels must gradually be reduced, otherwise contraction of the tendon will result with the horse unable to put its heels to the ground. It is doubtful if a Patten shoe has a place in the treatment of strained tendons. Pressure bandaging or a plaster cast provide the necessary support. As pain is relieved and healing takes place the horse takes increasing weight on the limb, which prevents excessive contraction and shortening of the strained tendon.

Ruptured tendon
When the deep digital flexor tendon is ruptured in a front leg the fetlock sinks and the toe turns up. If the suspensory ligament is also ruptured then the fetlock and pastern rest on the ground. In a hind leg weight bearing is less and these signs may not be so obvious.

Shoeing. To assist healing, the ends of the ruptured tendon must be retained in close apposition and this can be assisted whether or not the tendon is sutured by supporting the

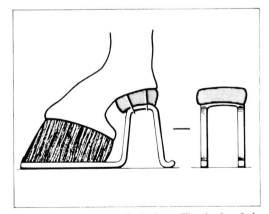

*Fig. **11.51** Swan-necked shoe. The heels of the shoe are continued upwards to the height of the palmar surface of the normal fetlock, and bent at right angles for 2 ins (5 cm). The branches are then continued downwards and backwards to the ground level of the shoe. The top of the two branches is joined by a bar, which is padded, to form a platform on which the fetlock rests.*

fetlock with a swan-necked shoe (Fig. 11.51).

This is a most useful shoe which has a very definite place in the treatment of rupture of the tendon of the deep digital flexor and suspensory ligament.

It is surprising how quickly horses adapt to this shoe and how soon they move around freely, but they should not be bedded on straw as they can easily get tangled up, fall and injure themselves.

When the superficial digital flexor tendon only is ruptured there is slight sinking of the fetlock and the foot remains flat on the ground. No special shoeing is generally required.

HOOF CARE FOR CATTLE, SHEEP AND GOATS

Farriers are frequently asked to trim the hooves of the house cow or of the pet goat or sheep at stables. This can satisfactorily be carried out by the farrier with the tools used for horses. These animals commonly suffer foot lameness due to neglect which would be prevented if their hooves were regularly attended. Cows, goats and sheep have two hooves or claws on each leg. Similar principles apply as for horses' hooves in that excess growth is removed while leaving enough wall for the animal to walk on and enough sole for protection. The two claws should be trimmed to the same length.

To assist farriers who may be reluctant to undertake this work it is hoped this series of photographs will help them to learn the appropriate methods of restraint and enable them to work with ease and confidence.

Cattle

It is essential to have an attendant with a halter or headcollar at the head, and where possible to have an assistant to hold up the leg so that the farrier can work independently.

Front leg

Fig. 1. Front leg lifted and held by hand.

Fig. 2. Front leg being held up with a rope noose around the pastern, pulled up over the withers and held by the assistant. Note the use of a sack to protect the withers.

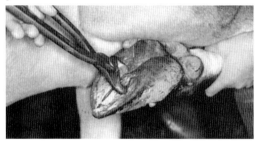

Fig. 3. Trimming excess growth of hoof wall with hoof cutters.

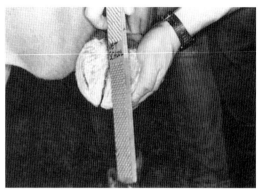

Fig. 4. Levelling claws with farrier's rasp.

Fig. 5. Completed foot.

Hind leg

Fig. 6. Hind leg being lifted by hand. This position is satisfactory but may be resented by the cow.

Fig. 7. Lifting and restraining a hind leg using a padded pole and two assistants. A good method if the cow is unco-operative.

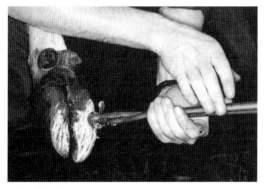

Fig. 8. Trimming the hoof wall with hoof cutters.

Fig. 9. Lightly paring the sole with a drawing knife.

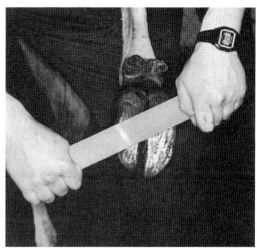

Fig. 10. Rasping claws level.

Sheep

Fig. 11. Positioning and holding a sheep prior to turning it over and sitting it up.

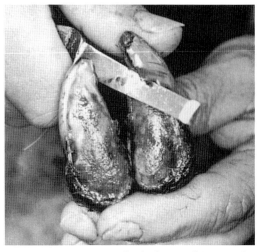

Fig. 14. Overgrown wall which turned in over the sole, being removed with a drawing knife.

Fig. 12. Sheep positioned ready for trimming both front and hind feet. Ensure the sheep is well on its back and pulled in close to the operator.

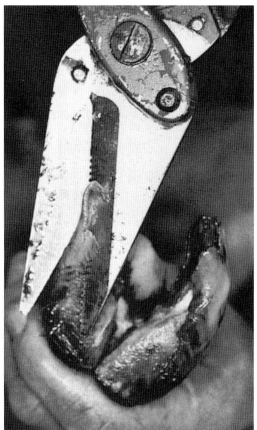

Fig. 15. Alternative method using foot trimming shears.

Fig. 13. An untrimmed foot with overgrown walls.

Fig. **16.** *One claw completed, the other requires the hoof wall at the toe to be shortened.*

Goats

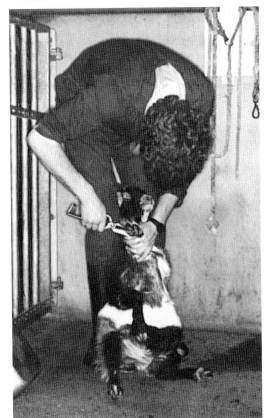

Fig. **17.** *Method of positioning a goat, as for a sheep, provided it does not have prominent horns.*

Fig. **18.** *Goats with horns can be safely restrained standing in a corner and pushed against the wall.*

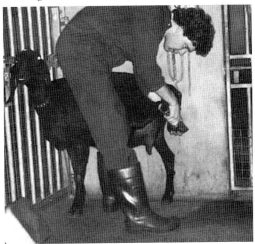

Fig. **19.** *When trimming hind feet, goats stand better if the foot is lifted without extending the leg too far backwards.*

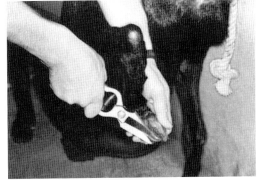

Fig. **20** *Trimming a hind foot with trimming shears.*

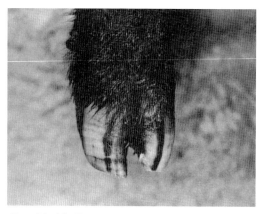

Figs 21–22. Foot completed.

WEIGHTS AND MEASURES

Weight

1 gram = 1000 milligrams = 0.0353 ounce
1 kilogram = 1000 grams = 2.2046 pounds
1 tonne = 1000 kilograms = 0.9842 ton

1 ounce = 28.35 grams
1 pound = 16 ounces = 0.4536 kilogram
1 stone = 14 pounds = 6.35 kilograms
1 ton = 2240 pounds = 1.016 tonnes

Temperature conversion

$$°C = {}^{5}/_{9}(°F - 32)$$

$$°F = {}^{9}/_{5}°C + 32$$

Length

1 millimetre = 1000 micrometres = 0.0394 inch
1 centimetre = 10 millimetres = 0.3937 inch
1 metre = 100 centimetres = 1.0936 yards
1 kilometre = 1000 metres = 0.6214 mile

1 inch = 2.54 centimetres
1 foot = 12 inches = 30.48 centimetres
1 yard = 36 inches = 0.9144 metre
1 mile = 1760 yards = 1.6093 kilometres

GLOSSARY

ABAXIAL – not situated in the axis of the body, away from the centre line

ABDUCT – draw away from a centre or median line

ABSCESS – a collection of pus

ACUTE – sharp, having severe symptoms persisting for a short time

ADDUCT – draw toward a centre or median line

ADHESION – abnormal joining of parts to each other

AFFERENT – conducting towards a centre

ALLOY – a mixture of metals

ANASTOMOSIS – a communication between two tubular organs or a connection between two normally distinct organs

ANATOMY – the science dealing with the form and structure of living organisms

ANKYLOSIS – abnormal immobility and consolidation of a joint

ANNEAL – to soften metal by controlled heating and cooling

ANTERIOR – situated towards the front, opposite of posterior

ANTISEPTIC – a substance which inhibits the growth of micro-organisms

APONEUROSIS – sheet-like tendon attaching or investing muscles

ARTERY – a vessel in which oxygenated blood flows away from the heart

ARTICULATION – the place of union or junction between two or more bones, a joint

ATROPHY – decrease in size of a normally developed organ, or tissue; wasting

AXIS – straight line through a centre, centre line of the body or any part of it

BASILAR – pertaining to the base

BASILAR PROCESS – old name for the upper part of the palmar process of the distal phalanx

BEARING SURFACE, FOOT – surface in contact with the ground or shoe

BEARING SURFACE, SHOE – surface in contact with the foot

BILATERAL – having or pertaining to two sides

BLIND, BRANCH OF SHOE – having no nail holes

BORIUM – trade name for tungsten carbide, a very hard material in a mild steel flux

BREAKOVER – point in the stride at which the foot leaves the ground

BROKEN-IN – of foot, when medial aspect of the wall is lower than the lateral side

BROKEN-OUT – of foot, when the lateral aspect of the wall is lower than the medial side

BURSA – a sac containing synovia interposed at points of pressure between a tendon and bone or between tendons

BURSITIS – inflammation of a bursa

CALKIN – square projection on the ground surface of the heel of a horseshoe

CANCELLOUS BONE – the lattice-like structure in bone

CANNON BONE – third metacarpal or metatarsal bone

CAPILLARY – hair-like extremity of an artery or vein

CARBOHYDRATE – an organic compound of carbon and water

CARPUS – the bones in the forelimb between the radius and metacarpal bones; in the horse, the knee joint

CARTILAGE – white elastic substance attached to the articular surface of a bone

CAUDAL – pertaining to the posterior or distal ends, nearest the tail

CHAMFERED – sloped or bevelled off

CHECK LIGAMENT – accessory ligament of the deep digital flexor tendon

CHRONIC – persisting for a long time, the opposite of acute

CLENCH – stub of shank of horseshoe nail that is bent over where it emerges from the hoof

CLIP – a small projection anywhere along the outside edge of the foot surface of a horseshoe

COFFIN BONE – distal phalanx, third phalanx, os pedis

COLLATERAL – being by the side, subsidiary

CONDYLE – rounded eminence at articular end of a bone

CONGENITAL – present at and existing from the time of birth

CONTUSION – injury to tissues which does not lacerate the surface; a bruise

CORIUM – fibrous inner layer of skin which is well supplied with blood vessels and nerves and contains the hair roots, sebacious and sweat glands

CORONET – prominent junction between the skin and the hoof

CRANIAL – pertaining to the cranium, surface of limb or organ towards the head

CREASE – groove on the ground surface of a shoe in which the nail holes are located; fullering

CRUCIATE – shaped like a cross

CYST – an abnormal cavity containing fluid or semi-solid material

DEGENERATION – alteration to a lower or to a less healthy state

DIAPHYSIS – the shaft of a long bone between the epiphyses

DIARTHROSIS – a synovial joint

DIFFUSION – a state or process of being widely spread

DIGIT – toe, portion of limb below the fetlock joint

DISHING – winging-in, foot moves forwards, inwards and then outwards in a circular movement

DISINFECTANT – a substance which destroys disease-producing bacteria

DISTAL – farthest from a point of reference, as from a centre, median line

DORSAL – directed toward or situated on the back of the body or the front of a limb, opposite to a ventral, in a limb opposite to palmar (fore limb) and plantar (hind limb)

DUMPED – hoof rasped away at toe to make a shoe fit

EFFERENT – conducting or progressing away from a centre

EMBRYO – an animal in an early stage of development

ENDOSTIUM – the lining membrane of a hollow bone

EPIDERMIS – the outermost, non-vascular layer of the skin

EPIPHYIS – portion of a bone which in early life is distinct from the shaft, the ends of a long bone

EPITHELIUM – the cellular layer lining the alimentary tract, the outer layer of mucous membranes and the skin

EXOSTOSIS – a new growth of bone protruding from the outer surface of a bone

EXTENSION – an increase in the angle of a joint, straightening a flexed limb

EXTENSOR PEDIS – common digital extensor

EXTENSOR SUFFRAGINIS – lateral digital extensor

FASCIA – a band or sheet of tissue investing or connecting muscles

FIRST PHALANX – proximal phalanx, os suffraginis, long pastern bone

FLEXION – the act of bending, a decrease in the angle of a joint

FLEXOR PEDIS PERFORANS – deep digital flexor tendon

FLEXOR PEDIS PERFORATUS – superficial digital flexor tendon

FOOT – hoof and all the structures contained therein

FOOT POUND – the amount of energy necessary to raise one pound of mass a distance of one foot

FOOT SURFACE – surface of shoe in contact with the hoof, bearing surface of the shoe

FORAMEN – an opening in various tissues of the body for the passage of other structures such as blood vessels and nerves

GANGRENE – death of tissue, associated with loss of blood supply, followed by invasion of bacteria and putrefaction

GELATINE – a transparent substance forming a jelly in water derived from skin and bones

GROUND SURFACE – surface of horseshoe in contact with the ground

HYPEREXTENSION – excessive extension

HYPERFLEXION – excessive flexion

HYPERTROPHY – increase in volume of a tissue

or organ produced entirely by enlargement of existing cells

INFERIOR – below or lower

INFLAMMATION – a protective tissue response to injury or destruction of the cells characterised by heat, pain, swelling, and loss of function

INORGANIC – not having the organ or instrument of life, not having organic structure, such as metals, rocks etc.

INTER- – word element, between

INTRA- – word element, inside of, within

KERATIN – a scleroprotein in hooves and horn

KERATINISATION – formation of microscopic fibrils of keratin

LAMINA – a thin, flat plate or layer

LAMINITIS – inflammation of the sensitive laminae of the horse's foot

LARGE METACARPAL – third metacarpal, cannon bone of fore limb

LARGE METATARSAL – third metatarsal, cannon bone of hind limb

LATERAL – pertaining to or situated at the side

LEG – lower extremity of limb distal to knee or hock joint

LESION – site of structural or functional change in body tissues produced by disease or injury

LIMB – leg and all the component parts which join it to the body

LONG PASTERN – proximal phalanx, first phalanx (P1), os suffraginis

LYMPHATICS – vessels containing lymph

MALIGNANT – progressing in virulence

MANUS – hand

MARROW – soft organic material filling the cavities of bones

MEDIAL – pertaining to or situated towards the midline

MEDULLA – the middle, applied to the marrow cavity of bones

METAPHYSIS – the wider part at the end of the shaft of a long bone, adjacent to the epiphysis

MUCOUS MEMBRANE – membrane covered with epithelium which secretes mucus, and lines canals and cavities

NECROSIS – death of a cell as the result of disease or injury

OEDEMA – an abnormal accumulation of fluid in inter-cellular spaces of the body

OLECRANON – bony projection of the ulna at the elbow

ORGANIC – pertaining to or having organs, pertaining to carbon compounds present in all living matter

OS CORONAE – middle phalanx, second phalanx (P2), short pastern

OS PEDIS – distal phalanx, third phalanx (P3), coffin bone

OSSIFICATION – formation of or conversion into bone

OS SUFFRAGINIS – proximal phalanx, first phalanx (P1), long pastern

OSTEOARTHRITIS – hypertrophic degenerative joint disease

OSTEOBLAST – an immature bone-producing cell

PADDLING – winging-out, foot moves forwards, outwards and then inwards in a circular movement

PALPATION – feeling with the fingers or hand to sense the physical characteristics of tissues or organs

PAPILLA – a small projection or elevation, nipple-shaped

PARIETAL – pertaining to the wall of cavity or organ of the body

PATELLA – a short bone which articulates with the distal end of the femur to form the femoro-patellar articulation of the stifle joint; the knee-cap of man

PATHOLOGY – the scientific study of the alterations produced in disease

PECTORAL – pertaining to the chest

PERIARTICULAR – situated around a joint

PERICHONDRIUM – the membrane covering the surface of cartilage

PERIOSTEUM – a specialised connective tissue covering bones and having bone-forming properties

PES – foot, the terminal organ of the limb, any foot-like part

PHALANX – any bone of a digit or toe

PHYSIOLOGY – the science of dealing with the

function of various parts and organs of living organisms

PHYSIS – segment of bone concerned mainly with growth

PLANTAR – pertaining to the back of a hind limb, opposite to dorsal

PLEXUS – network of blood vessels or nerves

POSTERIOR – directed towards or situated at the back, opposite of anterior

PRE- – used as a prefix, before

PROPHYLACTIC – tending to prevent disease

PROTEIN – an organic compound containing carbon, hydrogen, oxygen, nitrogen and usually sulphur and phosphorus

PROXIMAL – nearest to a point of reference, as to a centre or median line, or to the point of attachment or origin

PUS – a thick fluid composed of living and dead white blood cells with partially liquified necrotic tissue debris

PYRAMIDAL PROCESS – extensor process of distal phalanx

QUITTOR – discharge at the coronet due to necrosis of the cartilage of the foot

RAMIFY – to branch, to diverge in different directions

RAREFACTION – condition of being or becoming less dense

REFLEX – directed backwards, an automatic response to a given stimulus

RETROSSAL PROCESS – old name for the lower part of the palmar process of the distal phalanx

RHOMBOID – shaped like a kite

SEATING OUT – sloping the inner foot surface of a shoe

SECOND PHALANX – middle phalanx, short pastern, os coronae

SEMILUNAR – shaped like a half-moon

SESAMOID – shaped like a sesame seed, nodular

SHAFT – the mass of a simple elongate structure, as a long bone, between the extremities

SHORT PASTERN – middle phalanx, second phalanx, os coronae

SINUS – an abnormal channel permitting the escape of pus

SMALL METACARPAL – splint bone, second and fourth metacarpal bone

SMALL METATARSAL – splint bone, second and fourth metatarsal bones

SPICULE – a small sharp needle-shaped body

SPLINT BONE – second or fourth metacarpal or metatarsal bone

SUBCUTANEOUS – beneath the skin

SUPERFICIAL – situated on or near the surface

SUPERIOR – above or upper

SYNOVIA – a transparent, sticky fluid secreted by synovial membranes and found in joint cavities, bursae and tendon sheaths

TARSUS – the bones of the hind limb between the tibia and the metatarsal bones, in the horse the hock joint

TENDONITIS – inflammation of a tendon

TENOSYNOVITIS – inflammation of a tendon sheath

THIRD PHALANX – distal phalanx, pedal bone, coffin bone

TRANSVERSE – extending from side to side, situated at right angles to the long axis

TRAUMATIC – pertaining to external force which damages an organism

TUBEROSITY – an elevation or protuberance

UNILATERAL – arranged on or turned to one side only

VEIN – a vessel in which blood flows towards the heart, carrying blood that has given up most of its oxygen

VENTRAL – directed towards or situated on the belly surface, opposite of dorsal

VOLAR – pertaining to sole or palm, posterior surface of a horse's leg, palmar or plantar

WHITE LINE – white zone, junction between the sole and wall of the hoof

WING OF DISTAL PHALANX – palmar process of distal phalanx

BIBLIOGRAPHY

ADAMS, O.R., *Lameness in Horses*, 3rd edition, Lea and Febiger, Philadelphia (1974).

The Blacksmith's Craft, The Council for Small Industries in Rural Areas, Salisbury, Wiltshire (1983).

BLUNDEVIL*, Thomas, *The Fower Chiefyst offices belonyng to Horsemanshippe*, Wyllyam Seres, London (1565).

BOURGELAT, Claude, *Essai theorique et pratique sur la ferrure*, 3rd edition, Huzard, Paris (1813).

BRIDGES*, Jeremiah, *No Foot, no horse: an essay on the anatomy of the foot of that noble and useful animal a horse*, J. Brindlay and R. Baldwin, London (1752).

BURTT, E. H., *An analysis of physical, physiological and optical aspects of avian colouration with emphasis on wood warblers*, Ornithological monograph no 38, The American Ornithologists Union, Washington, DC, (1986).

BUTLER, D. *The Principles of horseshoeing*, Doug Butler, Maryville, MO 64468 (1985).

CANFIELD, D. M., *Elements of Farrier Science*, 2nd edition, Enderes Tool Company, Albert Lea, Minnesota 56007 (1968).

CLARK, Bracy, *A series of original experiments of the foot of the living horse, exhibiting the changes produced by shoeing, and the causes of the apparent mystery of this art*, B. Clark (1809).

CLARK, James, *Observations on the shoeing of horses: together with a new inquiry into the causes of diseases in the feet of horses*, 3rd edition, William Creech, Edinburgh; T. Cadell and T. Longman, London (1782).

COLEMAN, Edward, *Observations on the structure, economy and diseases of the foot of the horse, and on the principles and practice of shoeing*, Edward Coleman, London (1798–1802).

DOLLAR, J. A. W. and WHEATLEY, A., *A handbook of horseshoeing with introductory chapters on the anatomy and physiology of the horse's foot*, David Douglas, Edinburgh (1898).

FIASCHI*, Caesar, *Traite de la maniere de bien emboucher, manier, et ferrer les chevaux*, Dedie au Roi Henry II, C. Perrier, Paris (1564).

FITZWYGRAM, Lieut. Col. F., *Notes on Shoeing Horses*, 2nd edition, Smith, Elder and Company, London (1863).

FITZWYGRAM, Lieut. Gen. Sir Frederick, *Horses and Stables*, 5th edition, Longmans, Green & Company, London (1903).

FLEMING, George, *Horse-shoes and horse-shoeing*, Chapman and Hall, London (1869).

FLEMING, George, *Practical Horse-shoeing*, 3rd edition, Chapman and Hall, London (1878).

FRANDSON et al, 'Effect of slope of equine hoof on concussion and phalangeal angulation', *American Farriers Journal*, September (1983).

FRETZ, P. B., 'Angular Limb Deformities in Foals', (1980), Veterinary Clinics of North America Large Animal Practice, Symposium on Equine Lameness 125–150.

GAMGEE, Joseph, *A Treatise on Horse-shoeing and Lameness*, Longmans, Green & Company, London (1871).

GOODWIN, Joseph, *A new system of shoeing horses: with an account of the various modes practiced by different nations*, Longman, Hurst, Rus, Orme and Brown, London (1820).

HEINZE, C. D. and LEWIS, R. E., 'Bone Growth in the Horse (Shetland Pony) Determined by Orthopedic Markers', (1968), Proc. Am. Assoc. Equine Prctnr. 312–225.

HOLMES, C. M., *The Principles and Practice of Horse-shoeing*, The Farrier's Journal Publishing Company, Leeds (1949).

HUNTING, William, *The Art of Horse-shoeing*, 4th edition, revised and edited by A. B. Mattinson, Baillière, Tindall & Cox, London (1922)

KELLY, P. J., *Pathways of Transport in Bone*, Handbook of Physiology – The Cardiovascular System, III, chapter 12.

LAFOSSE, Etienne Guillaume, *Observations et decouvertes faites sur des chevaux, avec une nouvelle pratique sur la ferrure*, Hochereau le jeune, Paris (1754).

LEACH, D. H., 'The Structure and Function of Equine Hoof Wall', Ph.D. Thesis, University of Saskatoon (1980).

LEACH, D. H., 'Biochemical considerations in raising and lowering the heel', *Proc AAEP* (1983).

LEACH, D. H. and OLIPHANT, L. W., 'Annular gap junctions of the equine hoof wall', *Acta anat*, 116 (1983).

LEACH, D. H. and OLIPHANT, L. W., 'Ultrastructure of the Equine Hoof Wall Secondary Epidermal Lamellae', (1983), *Amer. J. Vet. Res.* 44 (8) 1561–1570.

LEACH, D. H. and ZOERB, 'Mechanical properties of hoof wall', *Am.J.Vet.Res.*, 44, 11 (1983).

LUNGWITZ, A., 'The Changes in the Form of the Horse's Hoof under the Action of the Body-weight', *J. Comp. Path.*, Vol. IV, No. 3, p.191 (1891).

LUNGWITZ, A. and ADAMS, J. W., *A Textbook of Horseshoeing for Horseshoers and Veterinarians*, 11th edition, 1913. Reprinted Oregon State University Press (1966).

MACQUEEN, J., *Fleming's Practical Horse-shoeing*, 11th edition, Baillière, Tindall & Cox, London (1921).

MEGNIN, J. P., *De l'origine de la ferrure du cheval*, P. Asselin, Paris (1865).

MILES, William, *A Plain Treatise on Horse-shoeing*, Longman, Brown, Green Longmans & Roberts, London (1858).

MILLER, W. C. and ROBERTSON, E. D. S., *Practical Animal Husbandry*, 5th edition, Oliver and Boyd, Edinburgh (1947).

MISHRA, P. C., *Extrinsic and intrinsic veins of the equine hoof wall*, M.Sc, thesis, Univ. of Saskatoon (1982).

MISHRA, P. C., 'Extrinsic and extrinsic veins of the equine hoof wall', J. Anat. 136 543 – 560 (1983).

MISHRA, P. C., 'Electron microscopic study of the veins of the dermal lamellae of the equine hoof wall', *Equine Vet. J* 15, (1), 14 – 21 (1983).

MIYAKI *et al*, 'Measurement of the water contents of the hoof wall, sole and frog in horses', Exp Rep Equine Hlth Lab, 11, 15 – 20 (1974).

MOORCROFT, W., *Cursory account of the various methods of shoeing horses, hitherto practised, with incidental observations*, W. Moorcroft, London (1800).

MOYER, W., 'Corrective Shoeing', Veterinary Clinics of North America, *Large Animal Practice*, Vol 2, No 1, pp3 – 24, (May 1980).

MYERS, V. S. and EMMERSON, M. A., 'The Age and Manner of Epiphyseal Closure in the Forelegs of Two Arab Foals', (1966), *J.Am. vet. Radiol. Soc.* 7. 39–47.

NICKEL, Richard, *et al*, *The Locomotor System of the Domestic Mammals*, translated by Walter G. Siller and William M. Shokoe, Vol. 1, Verlag Paul Parey, Berlin and Hamburg (1986).

Nomina Anatomica Veterinaria, 3rd edition, The International Committee on Veterinary Gross Anatomical Nomenclature under the financial responsibility of the World Association of Veterinary Anatomists, Ithica, New York (1983).

OSMER, William, *A treatise on the diseases and lameness of horses, in which is laid down a proper method of shoeing*, London (1759).

REEKS, H., Caulton, *Diseases of the horse's foot*, Baillière, Tindall & Cox, London (1906).

ROOT, W. S., *The Flow of Blood Through Bones and Joints, Handbook of Physiology* – SECTION 2: Circulation, Vol. II, Ch. 47, 1651 – 1665.

RUINI*, Carlo, *Dell'anatomia e dell'infermita del cavallo*, Heredi di G. Roffi, Bologna (1598).

SIMONS, M. A. P., 'The Future of Farriery', *Veterinary Record*, 98, 4 (1976).

SISSON, S. and GROSSMAN, J. D., *The Anatomy of the Domestic Animals*, 5th edition, W. B. Saunders, Philadelphia (1975).

SMITH, F., *A Manual of Veterinary Physiology*, 3rd edition, Baillière, Tindall and Cox, London (1907).

SMITH, Maj. Gen. Sir Frederick, *A History of the Royal Army Veterinary Corps 1796–1919*, Baillière, Tindall & Cox, London (1927).

SNAPE*, Andrew, *The anatomy of the horse*, T. Flesher, London (1683).

SOLLEYSEL, Jacques Labessie, de, *The complete horseman or perfect farrier*, translated into English by Sir William Hope, 2nd edition, R. Bonwicke, T. Goodwin, London (1706).

SPRINGHALL, J. A., *Elements of horseshoeing*,

University of Queensland Press, Brisbane (1964).

STUMP, J.E., 'Anatomy of the Normal Equine Foot, Including Microscopic Features of the Laminar Region', *J.A.V.M.A.* Vol. 151, No. 12, p.1588 (1987).

TOUSSAINT RAVEN, E., *Cattle Footcare*, Farming Press (1985).

VATOVEC, S., 'A contribution to the problem of relative tension in the flexor tendons of the phalanges and the interosseous tendon on the forelimb of the horse with regard to orthopaedic shoeing', Veterinarski arkiv, Zagreb, knjiya XXIII (1952).

WALKER, R. E., Bulletin of the Veterinary History Society, No. 1 (1972).

WISEMAN, R. F., *The Complete Horseshoeing Guide*, 2nd edition, University of Oklahoma Press (1974).

YOUATT*, William, *The Horse*, Baldwin and Cradock, London (1846).

(*as quoted by Fleming in *Horse-shoes and horse-shoeing*.)

INDEX